Public Finance in
Small Open Economies

Public Finance in Small Open Economies

The Caribbean Experience

Michael Howard

Westport, Connecticut
London

HJ
865
.H68
1992.

Library of Congress Cataloging-in-Publication Data

Howard, Michael.
  Public finance in small open economies : the Caribbean experience
  Michael Howard.
    p.   cm.
  Includes bibliographical references and index.
  ISBN 0-275-94205-8 (alk. paper)
    1. Finance, Public—Caribbean, English-speaking.   I. Title.
HJ865.H68   1992
  336.729—dc20   92-9805

British Library Cataloguing in Publication Data is available.

Library of Congress Catalog Card Number: 92-9805
ISBN: 0-275-94205-8

First published in 1992

Praeger Publishers, 88 Post Road West, Westport, CT 06881
An imprint of Greenwood Publishing Group, Inc.

Printed in the United States of America

∞™

The paper used in this book complies with the
Permanent Paper Standard issued by the National
Information Standards Organization (Z39.48-1984).

10 9 8 7 6 5 4 3 2 1

Copyright Acknowledgments

The author gratefully acknowledges the permission of *Social and Economic Studies* to reproduce sections of his "Public Sector Financing in Jamaica, Barbados and Trinidad and
Tobago—1974-1984," first published in *Social and Economic Studies*, Vol. 38, No. 3, 1989,
pages 121-131 and 140-145.

The author also acknowledges with thanks the permission of the International Bureau of Fiscal
Documentation to reproduce portions of his article, "Barbados: Income Tax Reform: An
Analysis of Two Budgets in 1986," first published in *Bulletin for International Fiscal Documentation*, Vol. 41, April 1987, pages 152 and 155. Contacting address is International Bureau
of Fiscal Documentation, P.O. Box 20237, 1000 HE Amsterdam, The Netherlands.

To June, Cherita and Steve

CONTENTS

TABLES

PREFACE

This study deals with fiscal issues in the English-speaking Caribbean. The first objective of the book is to provide a comprehensive and interpretative treatment of public finance in small countries. The work therefore analyzes and surveys the Caribbean literature on public sector development, and also presents my own interpretation and discusses my research in the field. The second objective is to provide an empirically oriented textbook for students of public finance in developing countries.

The thesis of the first part of this work is that rapid growth in the size of government has been a major proximate cause of fiscal and balance of payments problems in these countries. Chapters 2 through 6 examine this view. Chapter 2 looks at fiscal disequilibrium, and the role of excessive government expenditure in generating huge fiscal and balance of payments deficits in Jamaica, Guyana, and Barbados. This is followed by a more in-depth analysis of public expenditure growth in Chapter 3. Chapters 4 through 6 deal with public enterprises, defensive stabilization policies, and external debt.

Chapters 7 through 10 identify the structural and policy factors determining other fiscal problems in the Caribbean. Chapter 7 deals with the highly unequal income distribution and its structural causes, while Chapters 8 and 9 look at the evolution of the tax systems and tax reform. Chapter 10 is devoted to budgeting and development planning. Chapter 11 examines fiscal trends in the countries of the Organization of Eastern Caribbean States (OECS), comprising Antigua, Dominica, Grenada, Montserrat, St. Kitts and Nevis, St. Lucia, and St. Vincent.

I am grateful to a number of persons who supplied material for this book. These include Penelope Forde and Terrence Farrell of the Central Bank of

Trinidad and Tobago, and Joan Gibran of the Caribbean Development Bank. Over the years Karl Theodore of the Department of Economics, UWI, St. Augustine, Trinidad, has discussed with me some of the issues raised in this book.

I am highly indebted to Jacqueline Deane, who typed almost all of the manuscript. Jackie typed speedily and accurately and endured my requests for frequent changes in the various drafts. Jennifer Hurley also typed a part of the final draft.

I would also like to thank Donna Sisnett and the staff of Caribbean Contact for typesetting this work. I acknowledge with thanks the financial assistance of the Cave Hill Campus research fund. Finally, my wife June provided the moral support necessary for the completion of this task.

Public Finance in
Small Open Economies

THE ROLE OF GOVERNMENT IN SMALL DEVELOPING COUNTRIES

The purpose of this book is to analyze the fiscal problems which arise in the pursuit of economic development in small nations. The book's focus is close to the analysis of Richard Goode (1984), who recognizes the importance of the development objective. Many traditional public finance texts are not concerned with fiscal issues in developing countries. The contribution of this work resides in its interpretation of Caribbean fiscal problems, utilizing empirical evidence drawn primarily from the Caribbean territories of Jamaica, Barbados, Guyana, and Trinidad and Tobago. Chapter 11 discusses the public finances of the countries of the Organization of Eastern Caribbean States (OECS).

My investigation of fiscal issues in these small economies begins with an examination of the role of government in free market systems. The next section discusses the traditional, neoclassical approach to the role of government, based on the thesis that market failure justifies government intervention. Neoclassical analysis is concerned principally with static efficiency in the allocation of resources. Although the neoclassical approach has shed some light on the problems of resource allocation in market economies, this paradigm has some limitations when applied to the process of public sector decision making in small, developing countries.

This chapter also discusses the development role of government. Although the pursuit of economic efficiency is a legitimate goal of public policy in any modern economy, social justice is an overriding concern of governments in poor countries. The roles of poverty, human resource underdevelopment, foreign exchange depletion, and high levels of unemployment in the calculus of public sector decision making in poor countries are much more important than in highly industrialized economies. Further, the constraints on the effectiveness of fiscal policy are larger than in the developed countries. Such constraints include problems of small country size, which limit the resource base of these economies. The high degree of openness of small states increases their vulnerability to balance of payments problems.

My discussion of the development role of government paves the way for an examination of deficit financing in Chapter 2. Heavy deficit financing in the Caribbean is a post-colonial phenomenon and has increased since the establishment of central banks in the 1960s. Caribbean governments regard deficit financing as an instrument of economic development. However, the method of financing the fiscal deficit has posed problems for some governments. Financing by foreign borrowing has led to external debt repayment problems, while financing by borrowing from the central bank has adversely affected the balance of payments of some Caribbean economies. The excessive use of the central bank's overdraft facility, sometimes known as "printing money," was the policy adopted by Jamaica, Guyana, and Barbados in the context of the decline in the export sectors of these economies.

MARKET FAILURE AND GOVERNMENT INTERVENTION

The neoclassical approach has acquired a high level of acceptability in public finance theory. Neoclassical writers focus on the concepts of Pareto optimality and market failure. Certain marginal conditions must be satisfied in a market economy if the system is to guarantee optimal resource allocation. A Pareto optimum is defined as an allocation of resources such that no individual can be made better off without some other individual being made worse off. The necessary conditions for such an optimum are efficiency in consumption, efficiency in production, and optimal allocation of output. The rules which guarantee these efficiency conditions are as follows:

1. The marginal rate of substitution (MRS) between goods x and y must be the same for the consumers of both goods.
2. The marginal rate of substitution between two factors of production, say, capital (K) and labor (L), must be the same in the production of goods x and y.
3. The marginal rate of transformation (MRT) for any two goods x and y along the production possibility curve must be the same as the marginal rate of substitution between the two goods.

The Pareto optimal conditions work under highly restrictive assumptions. The utility function of the consumer, as well as the production function of the firm, are assumed to be free of externalities. Consumers are price takers, and market prices are known with certainty. Consumers maximize utility, and their utility functions have strictly diminishing marginal rates of substitution. The state of technology is given, and the factors of production have positive marginal products. Under perfect competition, price equals marginal cost and the Pareto optimal conditions are satisfied.

Most public finance texts have identified a number of qualifications and criticisms of these marginal conditions, since they work under static assumptions. External effects create divergences between private and social costs and returns, and therefore between private and social MRSs and MRTs. In the real world, risk and uncertainty with regard to technology and tastes imply that the market mechanism will not yield an efficient allocation of resources (see, for example, Boadway and Wildasin 1984).

Market failure is said to exist when the Pareto optimality conditions break down. Several factors lead to market failure, including imperfect competition, public goods and externalities, and income distribution (see Davis and Meyer 1983). Under imperfect competition, the producer no longer maximizes profit at the point where price equals marginal cost. The monopolist, faced with a downward-sloping demand curve for his product, will produce at the point where his marginal revenue equals marginal cost and price is greater than marginal cost. In decreasing cost industries, such as natural monopolies, the latter condition holds, but the government has to intervene by setting a price which would be acceptable to consumers. If marginal cost pricing is used in a public enterprise, a loss is incurred which has to be financed either through taxation or price discrimination. However, public utility economics is a specialized area and should not detain us here. Other practical considerations affect the pricing of public utilities in the real world. These considerations reflect the need for a "good rate" structure, which should be equitable and provide a stable cash flow to the firm, as well as achieve some efficiency in resource allocation.

The existence of public goods implies that a political process must replace the market mechanism in the provision of these goods. This is so because public goods are subject to the nonexclusion principle. That is, it is not possible to exclude individuals from the consumption of such goods. Further, public goods have the characteristic of nonrivalry in consumption. This means that the same output of the public good is enjoyed by multiple individuals simultaneously. However, some people prefer not to contribute to the cost of the public good or service but still benefit from its consumption; this is known as the free rider problem. Because of the difficulty of forcing individuals to reveal their preferences for public goods, compulsory taxation is normally required to cope with this problem.

Neoclassical theory in the 1950s and 1960s was concerned with the characteristics of the polar case of the pure public good. Paul Samuelson's (1954) major finding was that the Pareto optimality conditions for private goods do not hold for public goods. Samuelson derived efficiency conditions in the two-good case, where one of the two goods is a public good. Samuelson's early work has been criticized as not having any application to the real world. His model assumes the existence of a central planner who knows the prices consumers are willing to pay for public goods. In the real world this is not possible unless the group of individuals is very small.

The concept of a pure public good is not very operational, and perhaps its strongest application is defense. Most goods provided by the public sector exhibit partial rivalry in consumption. These include congested goods such as highways, public swimming pools, and so forth. Furthermore, the fact that a good has some of the characteristics of a public good does not mean that it must be produced by the public sector: a public good can be provided by the private sector. In this respect, the idea of a merit good or a merit want, a term used by Richard Musgrave (1959), may be a more operational concept than the notion of a pure public good. According to Musgrave, merit wants are subject to the exclusion principle. However, these goods are considered so meritorious that they are provided by the government's budget above what is provided by the private sector and sold to private consumers. These wants include education up to the tertiary level, health care, housing, and transport. In some countries the private sector is active in the provision of services, such as sanitation, and other goods which have been traditionally regarded as public goods.

The modern debate on privatization has led to some rethinking about the nature of public goods provision. Privatization is discussed further in Chapter 4 where the view advanced is that heavy provision of public goods by the public sector in small developing countries implies rising recurrent expenditure and declining foreign reserves. In the context of the large budget deficits faced by these countries, as well as the financial indebtedness of many state-owned enterprises, privatization may be considered as a means of relieving the public sector of the burden of providing certain goods and services.

Externalities also cause market failure. Externalities exist whenever the decision of an economic unit benefits or worsens the utility or production of another without being priced. Therefore, externalities cannot be dealt with by the market mechanism. Governments are interested in projects generating a high level of external benefits. However, in the case of external diseconomies such as pollution, the state is forced to intervene to protect the welfare of individuals. The difficulty of controlling external diseconomies can be traced to lack of property rights or difficulty in enforcing them (Boadway and Wildasin 1984: 60, 61). Edward Mishan (1971) has outlined a number of methods for correcting spillovers or external diseconomies. These include various types of tax/subsidy solutions. The government can tax the producer to reduce damages by charging a rate that equals the marginal damage done by the spillover. In cases where property rights can be assigned, the agent responsible for the spillover can be legally ordered to pay compensation to the party affected by the spillover. However, most methods, including subsidization and charges, can incur high costs of enforcement.

Pareto optimality says nothing about the prevailing distribution of income. If the distribution is highly unequal, individuals can place political pressure on government to alter the prevailing distribution. Governments may use the budget to redistribute income by altering tax structures, increasing transfer payments or reallocating expenditures. More radical measures, like land reform, are adopted in some countries.

When market failure causes private resource allocation to be Pareto inefficient, the traditional role of government is to intervene to correct distortions in the market; Musgrave (1959) defines this as the allocative role of government. Failure of the market to lead to a fair distribution of income provides another rationale for government intervention; Musgrave describes this as the distributive role of government. If the market is plagued by cyclical instability, unemployment, and inflation, government must intervene to stabilize the economy; Musgrave refers to this as the stabilization role of government.

Allocation, distribution, and stabilization are legitimate objectives of governments in free market economies. Although Musgrave analysed these objectives as if they existed in watertight compartments, there is considerable overlap between them. Stabilization policies, such as devaluations and credit restrictions, can worsen the income distribution. Allocation policies can also achieve distributional goals by increasing employment levels. Walter Heller (1967) has suggested that for developing countries these goals should be pursued according to the specific conditions the countries face. This can be done by utilizing a stage-of-development approach to fiscal policy. In the early stages, priority should be given to allocation in order to deepen social overhead capital, but as the economy becomes more exposed to external shocks, price inflations, and divergences between social and private costs and benefits, stabilization and distribution should be given greater importance.

The problems of market failure occur in both developed and developing capitalist economies. Further, the three functions of government outlined by Musgrave provide a conceptual framework for the analysis of fiscal policy in any market economy. This chapter does not dispute the appropriateness of Musgrave's classification. However, my subsequent analysis is more concerned with the associated fiscal problems of economic development. Thus, issues relating to deficit financing, public expenditure, measures to deal with poverty and inequality, human resource development, public debt, and tax revenue insufficiency are analyzed from a development perspective. Further, stabilization policy can be viewed as an instrument to keep the economy on its long-term development path by correcting certain short-run imbalances. Finally, equitable income distribution is not regarded as a separate objective here, but as a component part of the development process. The next section therefore discusses the concept of economic development.

THE DEVELOPMENT ROLE OF GOVERNMENT

Economic development is a normative concept. It is defined here as a dynamic process of structural change which guarantees a more equitable income redistribution and increased welfare levels for the poor majority of the population. The first element of my definition is that of structural change, which is central to the work of economists such as William Demas (1965) and Hollis Chenery (1979). Structural change relates to diversification of the productive base, reflecting a movement of factors of production and output between primary, secondary, and tertiary economic activities. However, for development to take place, structural change must be accompanied by income redistribution.

Fiscal policy to redistribute income must be given a priority ranking in the process of economic development. Income redistribution was assigned a low status in the early efforts of many of the development economists of the 1950s, but more recently, as in the work of Dudley Seers (1979), the need for income redistribution has been emphasized. The disenchantment with the 1950s strategy of growth, with its "trickle down" redistribution, has led to a new interpretation of development as a process which should redistribute income to the poor. Thus, economic development should be conceived as an improvement in the level of welfare in a society.

Development policies to improve welfare levels should also emphasize increased local economic decision making. Some measure of indigenous development in terms of domestic food production, mobilization of domestic savings, and entrepreneurship should be pursued as a means of increasing the resilience of the developing economy. Further, the pursuit of indigenous development should also be interpreted as the acquisition of a reasonable degree of local ownership of key sectors of the economy, such as agriculture, manufacturing, banking, and public utilities. A caveat is necessary here. Although some degree of indigenous development is highly desirable in small economies, a type of development can also be achieved with the use of large external resources. This process is sometimes known as dependent development. Many small countries have relied on foreign resources to supplement domestic savings and accelerate their development process. This does not mean that the creative energies of the population should not be harnessed to generate self-sustaining development.

Other fiscal policy implications flow from our welfare-oriented approach to development. Clive Thomas (1988) contends that development requires a system of production oriented toward satisfying the basic needs of the poor. The basic needs approach is not new and is nothing more than a modification of merit goods theory. Most governments in the region have adopted some type of basic needs strategy, based on the provision of merit goods, such as health services, sanitation, housing, and education. This approach, and its implications for public expenditure, are discussed in Chapter 3.

Since development is concerned with people, the improvement of human resources is a key to growth and development. Courtney Blackman (1979) correctly argues that the dynamics of economic development must be sought in the capacity of a nation's people to adopt the appropriate attitudes, and make the decisions, needed to effect economic transformation. Blackman's thesis implies that local decision making in these countries requires a managerial approach which emphasizes the development of appropriate attitudes and skills in the work force. The role of government expenditure in stimulating human resource development is also investigated in Chapter 3.

Arthur Lewis (1955) provides a comprehensive statement on the role of government in economic development. Although most of the functions he identifies can be subsumed under Musgrave's classification, Lewis's real contribution highlights the role of institutions in public policy. According to Lewis (1955: 57), "institutions promote or restrict growth according to the protection they accord to effort, according to the opportunities they provide for specialization and according to the freedom of manoeuvre they permit."

Firstly, governments need to safeguard institutions to protect effort. An important example is property rights. For purposes of economic growth, government must protect public property from private abuse and private property from public abuse. The institution of foreign investment is highly vulnerable in some developing countries, where the governments do not adequately enforce private property rights.

Secondly, governments must create new institutions to accelerate growth. In the early stages of development the governments of many small countries devote large sums of money to the building of development banks, industrial development corporations, agricultural extension services, and so forth. In later stages, the creation of stock exchanges and venture capital funds are necessary to stimulate the capital market.

Another caveat. If a government imposes undesirable institutions on individuals, this can retard the process of growth. Thomas (1989: 219) has shown how the implementation of cooperatives in Jamaica during the 1970s was badly administered and opposed by members of the government. Thomas argues that the inefficiencies of the sugar cooperatives and the uncoordinated expansion of state property were some of the factors adversely affecting Jamaica's development during the 1970s. According to Lewis (1955: 413), overregulation and haphazard institutional development prevent people from exercising initiative and common sense and restrict economic growth.

Although I have identified areas for government intervention, during the 1960s and 1970s many governments in developing countries became highly intrusive in the economic affairs of their citizens. Extensive nationalizations and barriers to free trade reduced the freedom of the market mechanism. In Guyana, the state's heavy hand in economic management denied citizens some of their individual liberties in the pursuit of socialism. Modern economic thought suggests that the private sector should be allowed to play a more dominant role in the economies of fledgling nations. The private sector is more efficient in areas where high levels of competition are required, and where the opportunity costs of investment are lower than in the public sector.

Despite the weakness of the neoclassical marginal conditions, the market mechanism is still an important institution for resource allocation. The market works best when regulation such as price controls and subsidies, is at a minimum. Governments should increase the efficiency of the market by creating an environment where property rights are respected. Further, a leaner public sector is necessary to stimulate the growth of an efficient market mechanism. This is the most important aspect of the changing role of the state in the 1990s.

THE SIZE CONSTRAINT

Economists since the days of Adam Smith have regarded size as a constraint on economic activity. Smith himself stated that the division of labor was limited by the extent of the market. Neoclassical economists have been concerned with the economies of large-scale production. This section addresses the issue of country size and its influence on the scope of development policy. We will look first at the implications of small size for the economy as a whole, and second at the relation of size with the costs of public sector administration and with public sector revenues. My discussion of size is important for an understanding of public sector decision making.

The theoretical contribution of Demas (1965) was to relate the physical concept of size to dependence and the development process, showing that size limits the range of policy options available to the government in small countries and is therefore a binding constraint on the rate of structural transformation. Demas is prepared to analyze the size parameter while abstracting from historico-institutional variables. Even though he is aware of these factors, his argument is that size provides the structural context and is unalterable. Size also increases dependence on the world economy.

Demas's central position is really derived from the classical thesis that economies of scale are limited by the size of the market. The size constraint is operative not only in manufacturing, but also in public administration, public utilities, and some kinds of services, such as education and health. Although population size is not the only variable affecting the size of the market, it defines the physical upper limit for expansion of the domestic market. Further, scale constraints affect the growth of the domestic capital market. The small capital market is characterized by a narrow range of financial instruments, which impose restrictions on the mobilization of internal finance for development. The theoretical implication is that the small economy will depend on capital inflows.

Scale constraints stemming from the small size of a domestic market limit the internal range of backward and forward linkages. Linkage effects are generated outside the geographical confines of the economy, because the small size of the domestic market orients the economy toward exports, which maximize the benefits of economies of scale. The highly skewed resource base implies that the economy will rely heavily on imports of intermediate goods and raw materials. The high import coefficients in a small economy also result from the divergence between the narrowly based structure of production and domestic demand. The physical size constraint also implies that the small country will not be able to generate its own endogenous growth dynamic, because its capital goods sector is likely to be small or nonexistent. The absence of a capital goods sector will considerably limit the gains to be derived from import substitution industrialization. Demas's (1965) analysis rationalized the urgent need for policies to promote regional integration, and it influenced theoretical investigations in this area.

The small economy thesis has shed some light on the constraints on development in the typical staple economy. However, the concept of size as a purely physical phenomenon needs some modification, because some physically large economies display similar behavioral patterns. We identify two dimensions of size, namely size as a physical phenomenon and size as a theoretical construct. This latter conceptualization is advanced by Martin Prachouny (1975) and Stephen Turnovsky (1977), both of whom view size as a theoretical abstraction that has no physical properties. Prachouny, for instance, argues that a small open economy is any country which treats the price of any internationally traded good or asset as exogenously determined and, given this constraint, aims to maximize some objective function. The relevant line of inquiry is whether a country can be regarded as small, and hence dependent, if it can treat variables such as the foreign interest rate, import and export prices, and the level of capital inflows and exchange rates as exogenous variables. The contention is valid that if a country cannot determine any of these variables by its own domestic activities, then that country should be considered small. However, there is a strong relationship between small physical size and small theoretical size. That is, the physically small economy, by reason of its structural constraints, is by necessity a price taker. The two aspects of size are relevant to our conceptualization of the Caribbean economies and help us to understand the persistence of certain structural and historical problems in the contemporary period.

A fundamental deficiency of the small economy thesis, however, is that it does not examine the role of management in the national economy. Given the invariance of the structural constraints, it is contended that the orientation of development policy, as well as the management of allocation and distribution, are significant determinants of the character of the small country's development path. The policies of the government and the efficiency of their implementation can impact on certain institutions, technology, and human resources and can therefore cause an outward shift in production possibilities. However, although there is a role for efficient management, the latter has its own limitations in open systems. This view is debated.

Blackman (1979) is not convinced that size is a constraint on fiscal policy. His thesis reflects the dictum of Ernst Schumacher (1974) that "small is beautiful." Blackman contends that large size increases the problems of economic management, and that small economies are more manageable than large economies. He cites Peter Druker (1973) in advancing the view that some large organizations are unmanageable. Blackman posits that small size leads to greater homogeneity of interests and aids consensus, and he maintains that size makes change easier to achieve, that since decisions involve change, small countries are likely to be more decisive and capable of change. Because the economies of small nations are highly manageable, their national decision makers can respond swiftly to their environment and reallocate resources as rapidly as required.

Blackman's argument ignores the economic factors relating to dependency mentioned above. Although there are benefits of small size, including greater social cohesion and consensus, managers in small countries lack bargaining power in the international arena. This is one reason why regional integration has been advanced as a solution to the lack of bargaining power of individual countries. Blackman opines that small countries are likely to be more decisive, but often public sector decisions are forced upon small-country managers as a result of events and developments in the large, industrialized economies. Smallness does not necessarily make a system easy to manage. Small systems are highly open and subject to random external shocks, which make it difficult for governments to forecast movements in economic variables. Indeed, openness augments the degree of managerial uncertainty for the governments of small countries.

Although small size may increase the administrative costs of government, its effect is difficult to quantify. Alison Martin and Arthur Lewis (1956), attribute high administrative costs to small size, from an absence of economies of scale in administration. A later pioneering work by Edward Robinson (1963) reached inconclusive results on the relationship between country size and cost of public administration. He concluded that, in terms of economies of scale in relation to administration, provision of public services and defense are probable advantageous to a large nation, but with the exception of defense, the advantage is probably not highly significant. The tendency to link high administrative costs with small country size stems from the fact that a small country is likely to have the same kind of central institutions as a large one. Further, the size of the public service, expressed as a percentage of total population, tends to be higher for small states (Jacobs 1975). Work on the post-World War II colonial fiscal system of Barbados (Howard 1979a) revealed high costs of administration for the public service. This appeared to result from the colonial type of administration. Colonial societies tend to have "top-heavy" administrations, with metropolitan officials paralleling and supervising the operations of local administrators. To the extent that the Caribbean inherited a colonial system, this may be a factor influencing the high costs of government in these countries.

A study by Harold Codrington (1989) showed that small countries tend to have higher tax/GDP ratios than large countries. Codrington (1989: 517) uses the tax/GDP ratio as a measure of the efficiency of the tax system, and suggests that small countries are more efficient in raising taxes than large countries. Codrington's study sheds light on the statistical relationship between size and tax revenues. The efficiency of a tax system is judged by the extent to which it minimizes excess burden, or the welfare loss of taxation. A high tax ratio may show that a country is able to increase discretionary tax rates in its budget year after year. High taxes are not necessarily an indication of elasticity which is the automatic response of taxes to income changes. Further, high taxes are not good for development, but in fact they may suppress private sector saving and investment and retard development. Many low-tax small countries, like Hong Kong, have been able to achieve high rates of economic growth.

THE BALANCE OF PAYMENTS CONSTRAINT

In small economies, foreign exchange is a binding constraint on fiscal policy. Foreign exchange is needed to purchase imports to construct government projects and for the maintenance of projects already completed. In an open economy, investment equals domestic saving plus the deficit in the balance of payments which must be financed by foreign borrowing (Kennedy 1966).

Therefore, the rate at which government investment expenditure grows is limited by the country's ability to earn foreign exchange through exports, or its capacity to borrow from abroad. Excessive foreign borrowing incurs a large debt which has to be paid by future generations. This is why governments of small countries need to save more, that is, achieve current account surpluses in order to finance capital expenditure. The analysis in Chapter 2 will show that the foreign exchange constraint on government spending was particularly binding in the economies of Jamaica, Barbados, Guyana, and Trinidad and Tobago during the 1980s. To some extent, the foreign exchange problems in these economies were influenced by failures in the export sectors. However, in Chapter 2 it will be shown that these countries' fiscal disequilibrium, deficits, and balance of payments difficulties not only were structural in nature, but can be explained by fiscal indiscipline.

Tables 1.1 and 1.2 give some idea of the balance of payments context of fiscal policy in the Caribbean. Net foreign reserves position (Table 1.1) is an indicator of a country's foreign exchange constraint. Current account balance of payments (Table 1.2) is a measure of the import surplus which has to be financed by capital inflows or by running down foreign reserves. For purposes of comparison I have used the Barbadian dollar as a numeraire (Bds$2.00 = US$1.00). The analysis shows that the net foreign reserves positions of Jamaica and Guyana were negative for the entire period of the 1980s, but that there was some improvement in the years after 1986. The only country to show positive reserves for the entire period up to 1990 was Barbados.

It must be noted, however, that the reserve liquidity available to Barbados

Table 1.1
Net Foreign Reserves Position of Selected Caribbean Countries, 1980–1990
(in millions Bds$)

Year	Jamaica	Guyana	Barbados	Trinidad & Tobago
1980	-979.2	-369.7	169.0	5,286.3
1981	-1,184.0	-443.7	128.1	6,405.7
1982	-965.0	-630.8	188.0	5,966.5
1983	-1,477.0	-828.4	231.5	4,165.2
1984	-1,065.0	-1,016.8	241.5	2,374.9
1985	-1,271.4	-1,275.2	328.0	1,988.6
1986	-1,307.6	-1,086.5	304.5	658.0
1987	-914.6	-955.0	296.8	158.3
1988	-573.0	-979.1	350.8	-12.5
1989	-891.8	-814.7	268.2	204.3
1990	-522.2	-798.1	165.9	397.4

Note: Bds$2.00 = US$1.00
Deficit (−)/Surplus (+)
Source: Central Bank of Barbados, *Annual Satistical Digest,* 1990.

Table 1.2
Current Account Balance of Payments Deficits of Selected Caribbean Countries, 1980–1990
(in millions Bds$)

Year	Jamaica	Guyana	Barbados	Trinidad & Tobago
1980	-332.6	-200.8	-54.3	787.2
1981	-673.6	-339.8	-250.7	626.1
1982	-775.8	-250.6	-84.3	-1,790.6
1983	-961.0	-264.2	-101.3	-2,053.3
1984	-595.0	-194.2	22.4	-1,114.0
1985	-591.6	-163.6	81.0	-216.4
1986	-85.4	-230.8	-31.8	-1,263.7
1987	-295.6	-206.4	-107.0	-494.7
1988	62.2	-173.4	54.8	-235.6
1989	-536.0	-	-5.2	-133.6
1990	-655.2	-	-75.1	808.8

Note: Bds$2.00 = US$1.00
Deficit (−)/Surplus (+)
Source: Central Bank of Barbados, *Annual Statistical Digest,* 1991.

was much less than indicated in the data. This is because Guyana owed Barbados Bds$140.0 million, which has been included in the Barbados reserves. Guyana has been unable to repay the full sum of this money because of its own financial problems. Therefore, the reserve liquidity of Barbados in 1989 was around Bds$128.2 million, or 2.5 weeks of imports. Trinidad and Tobago recorded a sharply declining reserves position because of the fall in oil prices in the early 1980s. The current account deficits (Table 1.2) were generally high for all these countries, revealing the weakness of their export sectors.

SUMMARY

Economic development is a major objective of fiscal policy in small countries. The allocation and income distribution functions of government identified by Musgrave (1959) should not be treated as separate goals, but as part of the development process. Governments in small countries should not attempt to dominate their economies to the extent that fiscal policy crowds out private sector initiative. Although I defined areas for government intervention, the free market mechanism still has an important role to play. I have also indicated two important constraints on the role of government in small countries. These are size and foreign exchange. Size limits economies of scale where production is geared for the domestic market. Although the evidence is inconclusive, size may increase the cost of government and also lead to high taxes. A small economy needs foreign exchange for growth, and governments can encounter serious balance of payments deficits if public expenditures exhaust the available foreign exchange reserves.

2

DEFICIT FINANCING IN THE CARIBBEAN

In their efforts to accelerate their rates of economic development, one of the most serious problems encountered by governments in the Caribbean is fiscal disequilibrium. Fiscal disequilibrium is reflected in the size and rate of growth of a country's fiscal deficit. An overall fiscal deficit of around 5 percent of GDP is sometimes considered manageable for small countries. Deficits which exceed this amount may require demand management policies. The first half of this chapter is concerned with fiscal disequilibrium, that is, with the causes of large fiscal deficits. The second half presents an empirical investigation of the behavior of fiscal deficits in the Caribbean. The thesis advanced in the second part is that during the 1970s and 1980s heavy use of central bank money creation to finance the fiscal deficits of Jamaica, Guyana, and Barbados was a significant proximate cause of balance of payments difficulties in these countries.

CAUSES OF LARGE FISCAL DEFICITS

Vito Tanzi's (1982) concepts of fiscal disequilibrium and fiscal disequilibrium scenarios provide a conceptual framework for understanding the causes of large fiscal deficits. According to Tanzi, fiscal disequilibrium arises from a divergence between "permanent" government revenue and "permanent" government expenditure. For example, permanent (or maintainable) revenues are sustained over a period of time, and do not include transitory, or windfall, components. Transitory revenue, for instance, might be from a petroleum or coffee export boom. Permanent expenditures are those which become internalized in the budget over time; current expenditure has a tendency to be more permanent than capital expenditure. Fiscal disequilibrium is a dynamic concept and must be analyzed in a long-term context. Analysis of a country's fiscal system for a single year cannot say very much about the nature of fiscal disequilibrium.

Following Tanzi (1982), a fiscal disequilibrium scenario can be described as a fiscal situation where a particular pattern of fiscal behavior or causation predominates. In his analysis of developing countries, Tanzi identifies five dominant scenarios, which he calls export boom, public enterprise, inelastic tax system, terms of trade, and growth of public expenditure. The first and perhaps most important is the growth of public expenditure scenario, which is specific to Jamaica and Guyana but also has application to Barbados. The second, which applies to Trinidad and Tobago, is the petroleum export boom/slump scenario. Contributory, but weaker, is the tax inelasticity scenario. I believe that Tanzi's public expenditure and public enterprise scenarios are related, since public enterprises increase government expenditures. His terms of trade and export boom scenarios also cannot really be treated separately, because export price movements determine the terms of trade.

For structural and political reasons, in developing countries it is critically difficult to control public expenditures. This explains why government expenditure growth is a primary generator of large and persistent fiscal deficits in the Caribbean. Governments face significant pressure from their electorates to provide education, infrastructure, low-cost housing, welfare and health services. Heavy government expenditure, financed by money creation, was a principal cause of fiscal deficits and balance of payments pressures in Barbados and Jamaica between 1974 and 1984 (Howard 1989a). Strong public expenditure growth also characterized the fiscal systems of Jamaica, Barbados, and Guyana during the late 1980s. In Jamaica the disequilibrium was particularly severe with a 37.4 percent increase of the fiscal deficit, stemming primarily from a 20.5 percent rate of growth of public expenditure.

Although it is desirable to curb the rate of growth of total expenditures, it is not always easy to achieve an absolute cut over a fiscal year. There has been a tendency in Barbados, for example, to overestimate current expenditure and underestimate revenue, so that the government's saving is sometimes much larger than projected. However, the recurrent costs of welfare services, foreign debt repayments, and salaries of civil servants create a built-in tendency for permanent expenditures to rise. An outcome below estimated levels may not necessarily indicate a genuine expenditure cut.

Premchand (1983) has suggested a number of ways in which expenditure control can be achieved. These include either across-the-board cuts or specific sector cuts in expenditure. Across-the-board cuts imply that all expenditures are treated equally. In the context of the severe disequilibrium in Jamaica and Trinidad and Tobago during the 1980s there were severe cuts in the salaries of public servants, as well as a reduction in public service personnel. These issues of public expenditure will be examined in more detail in Chapter 3.

Another factor responsible for the rapid growth of public expenditure and high fiscal deficits in these countries is poor performance by public enterprises. Many of these enterprises are inefficient, and they are financial burdens for governments in small economies. Many are heavily subsidized. As will be shown in Chapter 4, public enterprises were highly significant in Guyana, Jamaica, and Trinidad and Tobago. In the mid-1970s, for example, the Guyana government's share of total investment in the economy was around 70 percent (Adlith Brown 1981). Although privatization has been advanced as a means to reduce government ownership and control, less developed countries sometimes encounter difficulties in selling these enterprises, especially when they are not considered profitable ventures. However, the privatization argument is highly plausible for industries which can function more efficiently under private enterprise. The heavy financial burden of public enterprises also forces governments to raise new taxes, which may have severe welfare costs.

Trinidad and Tobago presents the special case of export slump fiscal disequilibrium. Analyses by David Morgan (1979), Tanzi (1982) and Terrence Farrell (1981) all point to the impact of oil price movements on the government's domestic budget deficit, that is on the difference between domestic expenditure and domestic revenue. In the case of Trinidad and Tobago, the difference between foreign expenditure and foreign revenue represents the budget surplus on foreign exchange account. Oil revenues accrue in the form of foreign exchange, which is surrendered to the central bank, which credits the central government with the domestic currency equivalent in the form of deposits. The domestic budget may be in deficit during an oil export boom, even though the overall budget may be in surplus. Farrell (1981) estimated that in 1980 the domestic budget deficit was TT$2,140.7 million even though the overall surplus was TT$850.1 million. After 1981, decreasing oil prices reduced the surplus on foreign exchange account and created overall deficits.

Table 2.1
Export Slump Scenario: Trinidad and Tobago, 1984/85 – 1987/88
(percentage of change)

	1984/85	1985/86	1986/87	1987/88
Petroleum output	– 5.0	– 21.6	– 4.2	– 12.0
Total government expenditures	– 8.3	– 14.6	– 2.4	– 5.3
Tax revenue	– 4.5	– 22.2	+ 0.6	– 6.2

Source: Trinidad and Tobago, Central Statistical Office,
    Review of the Economy, 1988.

The fiscal disequilibrium of Trinidad and Tobago is shown in Table 2.1. The decline in petroleum output in the late 1980s was associated with a sharp drop in tax revenue; the drop was steepest in the period 1985 to 1986. To prevent the fiscal deficit from widening, the government was forced to implement drastic cuts in expenditures. The cuts comprised wage and salary reductions and removal or reduction of subsidies. Despite these measures, the fiscal deficit expanded at an annual rate of 9.7 percent. The fiscal disequilibrium also contributed to the devaluation of the Trinidad and Tobago dollar in 1985 (see Chapter 5). During the export boom period (1974–1981), wages were allowed to rise sharply, contributing to disequilibrium in the period of petroleum export slump (post 1984).

In petroleum export-led economies, fiscal policies cannot address the source of the fiscal disequilibrium. This is so because permanent or maintainable domestic revenues are determined by the effects of oil expansion on the non-oil sectors of the economy. In the long run, the economic problems which emerged in the Trinidad and Tobago economy during the oil export boom can only be corrected by structural adjustment policies to diversify the non-oil sector, in terms of increased manufacturing output, food supplies, and output of services. In the short run, fiscal disequilibrium requires demand management policies, such as credit and wage controls and reductions in government expenditures.

The final scenario is the tax inelasticity scenario. In Chapter 8, moderate to low tax buoyancies are estimated for Barbados, Jamaica, and Trinidad and Tobago. Barbados registered an overall low tax buoyancy of 0.68, which implies a low elasticity. The tax systems of Barbados and Jamaica are considered inelastic because the buoyancies were only maintained by heavy and sustained discretionary indirect tax increases. Although we shall discuss these issues in the chapter on Caribbean tax structures, it is necessary to state the implications of an inelastic tax system for the fiscal deficit. Firstly, a significant lag in tax collections means that a government has to rely more heavily on central bank financing. In the case of Trinidad and Tobago, falling tax revenues also led to reductions in government expenditures. Over time, an inelastic tax system will sustain the level of the fiscal deficit.

The impact of worsening terms of trade on the overall budget deficit is difficult to quantify. The deterioration can be caused either by a sharp fall in export prices or by increases in import prices which help to generate domestic inflation. In the Caribbean, increasing oil prices in the 1970s played an important role in terms of trade deterioration. Imported inflation causes an increase in the nominal value of government revenues, especially when the indirect tax system is based on ad valorem rates. However, higher import and domestic prices also raise the nominal value of government expenditures. If the rate of change of government expenditures on public sector wages and capital projects exceeds the rate of change in the inflation tax, the government's deficit will worsen. The degree of fiscal disequilibrium will therefore depend on the size of the inflation tax as a result of higher import prices. Goode (1984) has argued that two significant considerations relating to the impact of inflation on the budget are the collection lag and tax elasticity. A long lag and low elasticity will most likely worsen the budget deficit. However, studies of inflation and budget deficits, such as those of Bijan Aghevli and Moshin Khan (1978) and Peter Heller (1980) attest to the unpredictability of the impact of inflation on the budget deficits of small countries.

DEFICIT FINANCING: SOME THEORETICAL ISSUES

Most economists agree that deficit financing affects inflation, the balance of payments, or both. The relative impact of deficit financing on these variables is, however, difficult to quantify. This is because other factors exert separate influences both on the balance of payments and on inflation. Much attention has been focused on the relationship between central bank money creation to finance a fiscal deficit and the revenue from inflation. Studies by Aghevli and Khan (1978) and Tanzi (1978) have examined this relationship in developing countries. In the Caribbean James Sackey (1981) found a positive relationship between the money supply and revenue from inflation for Trinidad and Tobago. Given Sackey's results, it is necessary to comment on whether the evidence supports the relationship for other Caribbean territories.

Tanzi (1978) utilizes an analysis based on certain restrictive assumptions. Firstly, he assumes that the fiscal deficit is financed only by central bank money creation. Secondly, the money supply is assumed to change only as a consequence of the financing of the deficit, rather than for other reasons, such as accumulation of foreign reserves or extension of credit to the private sector. Thirdly, the rate of inflation n is assumed to be equivalent to the rate of change of the money supply and also equivalent to the tax rate. Fourthly, he assumes that the tax base is equivalent to the real cash balances held (M/P). Therefore, the inflation tax revenue R is

$$R = n \ (M/P)$$

Tanzi found that there was a positive relationship between money creation and revenue from inflation for Argentina, but this was affected by lags in revenue collection.

Following Aghevli and Khan (1978), the link between the government deficit and the money supply can be defined precisely. The money supply M is a multiple of the monetary base H and the money multiplier m, such that

$$M = m \ H \qquad (1)$$

Changes in the monetary base H occur through changes in international reserves, changes in central bank credit to the government and changes in the central bank's claim on commercial banks and the private sector. Let us assume that changes in central bank lending to government are caused by the fiscal deficit then

$$H = G - R + E \qquad (2)$$

where E comprises changes in international reserves and the central bank's claims on the private sector, and $(G - R)$ is the fiscal deficit financed by money creation. The money supply becomes

$$M = m (G - R + E) \qquad (3)$$

For inflationary financing to take place, the domestic price level P must be a significant function of M, and other variables.

Sackey's (1981) study did not make the same restrictive assumptions as Tanzi's nor did Sackey formulate his approach in the manner of Aghevli and Khan (1978). Sackey does not assume that central bank money creation is the instrument used to finance the deficit. Rather, following Patrick Baptiste (1977), he investigated the relationship between the money supply and changes in the price index. He concluded that the financing of the inflation-induced deficit had led to an increase in money supply and generated further inflation. Thus, in Trinidad and Tobago, the increase in the supply of money contributed to the inflationary process. Sackey did not distinguish between the sources of government finance and the sources of monetary base expansion. He also concluded that for both Barbados and Jamaica, lagged values of the rate of growth of money supply were not significantly correlated with the current values of the price level. His conclusions suggest that for Jamaica and Barbados, the fiscal deficit was not inflationary.

Other studies suggest that inflation in the Caribbean is generated by external factors, rather than by central bank money creation. Eric St. Cyr (1979) found that import prices led to domestic inflation, as well as increases in wages and salaries. Most writers on Trinidad and Tobago, including Farrell (1984) and St. Cyr (1979), include a money supply variable in their tests, although they do not investigate the relationship between central bank money creation and inflation. This may be because money supply behavior in Trinidad and Tobago is the result of a complex interplay between petroleum receipts, the government's domestic budget deficit, and commercial bank credit (Farrell 1981). Andrew Downes (1985) did not see a role for money creation as a generator of inflation in Barbados; inflation was caused primarily by import prices, which accounted for 73 percent of the total domestic inflation.

Another fruitful line of inquiry in small, highly open economies is the relationship between central bank financing of the fiscal deficit and the balance of payments. The monetary approach to the balance of payments maintains that, assuming a fixed exchange rate, a stable demand for money, and an endogenously determined money supply, net foreign exchange receipts will vary inversely with domestic credit expansion. Analyses by Jacob Frenkel and Harry Johnson (eds. 1976), Mordechai Kreinin and Lawrence Officer (1978), and the International Monetary Fund (1977) all lend strong support to this view. This theoretical approach will be discussed later in this chapter. Further, to the extent that central bank money creation constitutes a high proportion of domestic financing of the fiscal deficit in these countries, one can conduct a historical analysis informed by the monetary approach. My investigation sees money creation as a determinant, though not the only, cause of the deterioration of foreign reserves in some Caribbean countries. The following paragraphs attempt to elucidate the relationship between central bank money creation and the balance of payments.

The monetary base *(H)* is defined on the liabilities side of the central bank's balance sheet as currency, with the non-bank public and commercial bank reserves. This concept can be employed in any economy where commercial bank deposits at the central bank are used to settle interbank debt and the conversion of the monetary liabilities of the banks is in the form of currency. Expansionary monetary policies, especially central bank lending to government in an open economy, expand the monetary base and lead to balance of payments deficits through reduction of the central bank's foreign assets. The effect may be particularly severe because money creation by the central bank does not reduce the resources of the private sector. Deficit financing by the commercial banks reduces bank reserves and leads to a resource transfer from the private to the public sector. The impact on the balance of payments is less than the impact of deficit financing by the central bank. Borrowing from the non-bank public by the government results in a direct transfer of resources to the government and reduces the external leakage by the non-bank public.

Foreign reserve movements also influence the government's borrowing requirements. Foreign exchange receipts, either by way of foreign borrowing or export earnings, represent inflows into the economy, but the creation of money seriously affects those receipts. Conversion of foreign exchange into domestic money augments the level of bank reserves and commercial bank deposit liabilities. However, an initial decline in the inflow of foreign money (for instance, a sharp decline in tourist receipts, or in the case of Jamaica, bauxite revenues) may reduce the part of the government's tax take that is in the form of indirect taxes on goods and services, and lead to an increase in the public sector borrowing requirement. Therefore, a decline in the real export sectors usually brings about an increase in central bank money creation. This effect was operational in Guyana, Jamaica, and Barbados during the 1970s and 1980s; the combined effects of real export sector decline and money creation led to foreign exchange deterioration.

It is now possible to discuss formally the monetary approach to the balance of payments. I make the assumption that central bank money creation is a strong component of domestic credit expansion, and I also assume that fiscal policy plays a more active role in small countries than monetary policy. In these countries, the effect of fiscal policy on the balance of payments is through the mechanism of money creation. Many monetarists and supporters of the monetary approach assume that fiscal policy plays a passive role.

The basic proposition of the monetary approach is that a balance of payments deficit reflects disequilibrium between the supply of and demand for domestic money. Following Kreinin and Officer (1978: 5–12), this model can be presented using the following equations:

$$Md = 1 \ (P, \ y, \ i) \tag{1}$$

where the demand for nominal money *(Md)* is a function of the price level *(P)*, real income *(y)* and the interest rate *(i)*. Stable demand functions have been found for Barbados (McClean 1982, Howard 1979b).

$$Ms = m \ (H) \tag{2}$$

where *Ms* is the nominal money supply and *m* is the money multiplier. The monetary base *H* has two source components, domestic credit *(D)* and the international reserve of the government and the central bank *(R)*. Therefore

$$H = R + D \tag{3}$$

Monetarists posit that stock equilibrium tends to prevail in the money market, such that

$$Md = M \ (R + D) \tag{4}$$

Further, the law of one price states that there is only one price operating in the market, such that

$$Pd = Pw \ E \tag{5}$$

where *Pw* = the world price level and *E* is the exchange rate.

If we denote foreign reserve changes as constituting balance of payments deficits or surpluses, then from equation (4) reserve changes vary inversely with changes in domestic credit *D*. These changes are changes in stocks rather than flows. A deficit in the balance of payments will occur if changes in *Ms* exceed changes in *Md*. This can happen if the central bank allows *D* to expand faster than the public's desire to accumulate money balances. These excess balances are off-loaded through a reduction of foreign assets, either by increasing imports or by exporting capital. Monetarists view the deficit as self-correcting; if the monetary authorities do not create new money, stock equilibrium would be restored in the money market. According to Kreinin and Officer (1978: 9), the monetary approach says nothing about the time period necessary to reach money stock equilibrium.

My analysis assumes that the government's fiscal deficit is a fundamental mechanism disturbing money stock equilibrium. The monetarists' literature tends to ignore the composition of *D*. However, Hyginus Leon (1988) and Robert Looney (1991) have shown that the monetary approach has some application to the Caribbean. My subsequent discussion looks at the size of the fiscal deficits and the rationale for heavy government borrowing in these economies under recessionary conditions.

THE SIZE OF THE FISCAL DEFICIT

For purposes of intercountry comparisons, the absolute magnitude of a country's fiscal deficit is not a meaningful concept. The relative size of a country's deficit can be gauged by relating it to some national income aggregate, and in small countries, the GDP is perhaps the best aggregate for this purpose. In this study, the ratio of fiscal deficit to GDP is used for comparing the sizes of the deficits of the four countries studied.

Table 2.2 shows the deficit/GDP ratios over time. The Guyanese economy recorded unacceptably high ratios in the 1980s, the years for which reliable data are available. The ratio reflects high total government expenditures, which exceeded the country's GDP for some years during the 1980s. For instance, total government expenditure was 101.4 percent of GDP in 1988. Current expenditures were normally higher than capital expenditures, revealing the high cost of the state bureaucracy and nationalized enterprises. The

Table 2.2
Fiscal Deficit as a Percentage of GDP for Selected Caribbean Countries, 1974–1990

Year	Barbados	Jamaica	Trinidad & Tobago	Guyana
1974	− 5.3	− 7.7	9.7	-
1975	− 2.6	− 7.8	8.1	-
1976	− 7.0	− 15.4	5.8	− 39.3
1977	− 8.3	− 14.3	8.3	− 24.3
1978	− 2.8	− 16.6	2.0	− 17.1
1979	− 3.4	− 13.4	− 2.5	− 23.9
1980	− 5.2	− 20.8	5.8	− 35.0
1981	− 8.1	− 15.6	1.0	− 42.0
1982	− 6.0	− 12.6	− 13.8	− 83.2
1983	− 3.4	− 18.7	− 12.2	− 55.9
1984	− 5.8	− 10.5	− 6.9	− 52.4
1985	− 5.5	− 8.9	− 7.4	− 40.7
1986	− 7.1	− 8.7	− 8.0	− 71.7
1987	− 7.6	− 6.6	− 7.3	− 50.0
1988	− 5.5	− 11.6	− 6.5	− 36.4
1989	− 0.9	0.7	− 3.8	− 20.6
1990	− 8.8	3.7	-	− 35.3

− denotes deficit; + denotes surplus

Sources: Central Bank of Trinidad and Tobago, *Annual Reports,* 1980–84; *IMF Financial Statistics,* 1985.

nationalization of the Guyanese private sector is also reflected in the high ratios of fiscal deficit to GDP.

The second-highest deficit/GDP ratio was found in the Jamaican economy. This ratio reached a high of 20.8 percent in 1980 and declined thereafter. As discussed below, the lower deficit/GDP ratios in the late 1980s reflect fiscal policies that had been tightened to deal with fiscal disequilibrium.

The relatively low deficit/GDP ratios for Barbados represent relatively more efficient fiscal management up to 1986. The Barbadian ratios tend to rise during election years, for instance 1976, 1981 and 1986. The ratio also rose in 1990, the year preceding the general elections in January 1991. Since 1974 Barbadian policymakers have pursued contractionary fiscal policies, except in election years. The deficit/GDP ratio was held to manageable levels, below 10 percent during the period.

In contrast with Jamaica and Barbados, expansionary expenditure policy in Trinidad and Tobago was supported by budget surpluses for most years up to 1981. Thereafter, with the fall in oil prices, the Trinidad and Tobago budget went into deficit, and the ratio of fiscal deficit to GDP peaked at 13.8 percent in 1982, after which some fiscal restraint was exercised to reduce this ratio. The case of Trinidad and Tobago is discussed in a later section of this chapter, as a special case of a petroleum export economy in recession.

EXPENDITURE-INDUCED DEFICITS: GUYANA, JAMAICA, AND BARBADOS

Guyana

Of the four countries studied, Guyana presents the most serious case of fiscal disequilibrium. An analysis of the political and economic context in which the deficit financing took place is necessary for an understanding of this. The following interpretation, therefore, relies on the work of Thomas (1989) and Donna Danns (1990). The examination here looks first at the political context of fiscal policy.

According to Thomas (1989), the declaration in 1970 of a cooperative socialist republic in Guyana by the People's National Congress (PNC), implied four policy initiatives. The first was the nationalization of foreign property, and by the mid-1970s, sugar, bauxite, the import trade, public transport, and sections of distribution and communication had been nationalized. The second was a type of basic needs program under which the government attempted to feed, clothe, and house the nation by 1976. Thomas argues that the development program of 1973, which embodied these goals, was never revised or presented for public scrutiny. By the third policy initiative, it was intended that the cooperative sector would dominate the economy; however, Thomas is of the view that the Guyana cooperative sector remained a minuscule part of the economy. In the fourth part of the declaration, the ruling party, the PNC, proclaimed itself pre-eminent. Thomas maintains that since the government did not achieve power by free and fair elections, the claim of pre-eminence was, in effect, a thinly disguised proclamation of dictatorship. These political factors enabled the state machinery to exercise authoritarian control over economic and financial institutions, particularly the central monetary authority, the Bank of Guyana.

The Guyana economy experienced serious recessionary conditions dating from the mid-1970s. Output declined, and the balance of payments came under considerable pressure.

Table 2.3 shows that foreign reserves started to decline in 1976. From a peak of G$197.3 million in 1975, foreign reserves became negative, falling at a rapid rate to minus G$13,442.6 million by 1989. This sharp decline in foreign assets was occasioned by two factors: failures in the nationalized export industries and heavy central bank money creation to finance the public sector deficit. Danns (1990) describes 1976–1988 as the period of accommodative monetary policy, when central bank credit to government had become the greatest source of monetary base expansion in the Guyana economy.

Table 2.3
Central Bank Lending: Guyana, 1974–1989
(in millions G $)

Year	Central Bank Claims on Government*	Net Foreign Reserves
1974	28.4	105.4
1975	44.5	197.3
1976	254.8	− 31.4
1977	346.8	− 100.2
1978	396.1	− 109.2
1979	612.6	− 251.3
1980	850.3	− 471.4
1981	1,038.1	− 620.0
1982	1,467.3	− 946.2
1983	2,357.1	− 1,263.6
1984	2,825.6	− 1,902.4
1985	3,228.4	− 2,182.2
1986	4,332.6	− 2,451.5
1987	9,537.8	− 4,774.7
1988	10,449.1	− 4,895.6
1989	24,158.8	− 13,442.6

* Denotes central bank credit outstanding to government.

Note: G$122.00 = US$1.00 at December 1991.

Source: Bank of Guyana, *Statistical Bulletin,* December 1989.

Table 2.3 shows the cumulative expansion of central bank claims on the government, which by 1989 had reached G$24,158 million. In 1983 the government's domination of the Bank of Guyana was shown by its deletion of the section from the Bank's Act which stated that the amount of Guyana securities held by the bank was not to exceed 30 percent of the annual revenue of the central government for the preceding three years. Danns (1990: 106) contends that these limits had actually been exceeded as far back as 1976. One can agree with Danns that the bank's role in the Guyana economy was reduced to that of a "spectator and constrained ally" of the government.

The actual financing of the Guyana fiscal deficit is shown in Table 2.4. Borrowing from the banking system is the largest category, followed by borrowing from the public. Guyana became increasingly unable to secure foreign financing, mostly because of its large foreign debt and balance of payments problems, which reduced its credit rating in international financial markets. The role played by the IMF in implementing fiscal policy changes to reverse the balance of payments is discussed in Chapter 5.

Jamaica

As with Guyana, the fiscal problems of Jamaica originated in the mid-1970s. The expansionary expenditure policy adopted by the Manley government after the election of 1972 was the fundamental reason for persistent budget deficits in the 1970s. To some extent these deficits also had structural causes, since they were related to the decline of the Jamaican economy, particularly in tourism and bauxite. This decline led to increased state spending to prop up the economy. The policy of democratic socialism adopted

Table 2.4
Deficit Financing: Guyana, 1984–1989
(in millions G $)

Year	Total Deficit	Borrowing from the Public	Foreign Borrowing	Borrowing from Banking System
1984	− 739.8	220.7	54.0	1,230.3
1985	− 663.9	330.2	62.2	541.9
1986	− 1,305.8	348.0	106.0	1,358.9
1987	− 1,421.8	40.0	97.0	4,410.0
1988	− 1,309.0	191.0	− 245.0	1,258.0
1989	− 1,065.0	773.0	98.0	2,039.0

Note: G$122.00 = US$1.00 at December 1991

Source: Central Bank of Guyana, *Statistical Bulletin,* December 1989.

by Manley was also designed to increase the role of the state through social service expenditures and by way of an expanded role for public sector enterprises. This policy over time led to excessive consumption expenditures. Between 1974 and 1978 the ratio of total expenditures to GDP in Jamaica rose from 32.8 percent to 49.2 percent. The fiscal deficit expanded, and central bank financing began to play a significant role (Table 2.5).

The Bank of Jamaica advanced the view that in the absence of any significant foreign financing, money creation was necessary in order for the public sector to maintain economic momentum, given a sluggish private sector. The annual change in central bank money creation as a ratio of domestic borrowing was 62.8 percent in 1975 and 73.5 percent in 1976. During the years 1978 and 1979, under the IMF Extended Fund Facility Program of 1978, restrictions were placed on domestic borrowing from the banking system. After 1979, as financing from foreign sources failed to materialize central bank money creation was again relied upon (Table 2.5).

Table 2.5
Deficit Financing: Jamaica, 1974–1989
(in millions J $)

Year	Total Deficit	Central Bank Claims*
1974	− 167.9	-
1975	− 206.0	− 31.5
1976	− 418.3	147.9
1977	− 428.2	207.2
1978	− 625.0	89.8
1979	− 635.8	− 5.0
1980	− 986.0	940.1
1981	− 916.7	465.5
1982	− 957.1	263.9
1983	− 1,333.6	985.9
1984	− 988.7	737.5
1985	− 1,022.5	-
1986	− 1,164.1	664.7
1987	− 1,063.4	− 1,581.9
1988	− 2,178.7	9.5
1989	157.2	392.7

*Denotes annual changes in central bank credit to government

Note: J$21.00 = US $1.00 at December 1991

Sources: IMF International Financial Statistics, 1985;
          Economic and Social Survey of Jamaica, 1984, 1985, and 1989.

After 1980 there was a shift in economic policy toward revitalizing the private sector and reducing the size of the fiscal deficit. To reduce the tax burden and stimulate private sector enterprise, income tax reforms were adopted in 1985; these reforms are discussed in Chapter 9. However, the most drastic policy initiatives were taken on the expenditure side. In the public sector, there was substantial labor retrenchment in fiscal 1984/85 and 1985/86. According to Roger Robinson and Lelde Schmitz (1989), considerable attention was directed to the public enterprise sector, which suffered from poor management practices. Toward the end of the 1980s, to reduce the size of the public sector, the government adopted a policy of privatization of several areas of the economy. Although the nominal size of the fiscal deficit continued to rise, partly because of large amortization payments, the ratio of fiscal deficit to GDP actually fell from its high level of 20 percent in 1980 to a low of 6.6 percent in 1987. A small surplus was projected for 1989.

Jamaica's fiscal policies in the 1970s and 1980s worsened its foreign reserve levels. In 1980 the reserves were minus US$489.6 million, and by 1983 they had fallen to their lowest level, of minus US$738.5 million. By 1989 the reserves had stabilized at minus US$445.9 million (calculated from Table 1.1). Jamaica is yet another case of a country which failed to adjust its public sector spending quickly enough to deal with external shocks. In the pursuit of democratic socialism, Jamaica had also disregarded policies that would have increased the efficiency of its market mechanism.

Barbados

The principal fiscal problem facing Barbados after 1980 was management of the government's budget deficit. Prior to 1981 the deficit was reasonably well managed and was financed by domestic and foreign sources. Although the central bank contributed significantly in 1977 and 1979, central bank money creation before 1981 did not cause a serious problem for the balance of payments.

The year 1981 was a turning point in Barbadian fiscal management. In that year the overall fiscal deficit of Bds$181 million was financed mainly by foreign borrowing and money creation (Table 2.6). Because it was an election year, an unusually heavy government capital works program was financed, even though it had to be done against a background of recessionary conditions in the world economy. This massive capital expenditure, of Bds$173.1 million, was an important contributor to the fall in international reserves of Bds$40.9 million between December 1980 and December 1981.

Partly as a result of the expansionary monetary policies of 1981 and the deepening world recession of 1982, the Barbadian economy became locked into balance of payments difficulties which government stabilization policies were unable to solve. These policies were announced in two budgets: the "mini budget" of September 1981 and the annual budget of March 1982.

Table 2.6
Deficit Financing: Barbados, 1974–1990
(in millions Bds $)

Year	Total Deficit	Domestic Financing	Foreign Financing	Central Bank Claims*
1974	− 47.7	60.3	− 11.2	-
1975	− 25.8	− 0.9	1.2	− 7.3
1976	− 53.9	56.2	6.3	13.6
1977	− 89.1	77.1	6.2	45.0
1978	− 43.9	− 13.4	34.0	− 33.6
1979	− 55.4	28.7	22.9	33.4
1980	− 51.0	9.1	51.8	− 6.7
1981	− 181.0	71.4	94.7	21.9
1982	− 99.8	67.3	26.7	26.6
1983	− 87.4	23.4	59.4	− 11.5
1984	− 95.8	57.8	16.8	− 15.4
1985	− 119.6	4.2	77.7	− 46.4
1986	− 164.0	32.4	107.9	− 41.7
1987	− 189.8	58.0	154.3	− 8.9
1988	− 146.2	16.8	77.4	− 28.4
1989	− 26.0	12.8	27.0	24.0
1990	− 244.5	267.2	7.6	172.4

*Denotes annual changes in Central Bank credit to government

Note: Bds$2.00 = US$1.00

Source: Central Bank of Barbados, *Annual Reports.*

The Stabilization program emphasized measures designed to curb aggregate demand and reduce the negative pressure on the balance of payments. Particular stress was placed on wage and credit restraints in both the private and public sectors, on cuts in capital expenditures, and on control over the growth of current expenditures. Other fiscal measures included transport and health levies and a range of indirect taxes.

In 1982, the authorities were concerned that the widening of the current account deficit in the balance of payments would require the intervention of the IMF, which they considered to be the cheapest source of finance for balance of payments support. The government maintained that the problems of the Barbados economy were due primarily to the world recession, rather than to domestic monetary and fiscal policies.

Despite the defense by the government of its management of the economy, it is valid to say that the intervention of the IMF in the Barbadian economy in late 1982 partly reflected the effects of the heavy capital spending of 1981 and the accompanying policy of money creation. The standby agreement with the IMF set certain conditionalities. For the period from October 1, 1982, to May 31, 1984, Barbados was granted the right to make purchases from the IMF in an amount equivalent to Special Drawing Rights (SDR) 31.875 million, which was to be drawn in stages. The arrangement specified quantitative limits on central bank net domestic assets and on the net credit of the banking system to the nonfinancial public sector. Further, the arrangement did not rule out the possibility of exchange rate adjustments.

The Barbadian government also allowed its fiscal management to deteriorate in 1990, just before the general elections in January 1991. The deficit climbed to a record high of Bds$244.0 million in 1990 and was financed entirely by the domestic banking system, with the central bank contributing Bds$172.4 million. This financing was associated with a fall in the foreign reserves of Bds$100.0 million. Although real sector activity fell in 1990, the budget deficit was a contributory cause of the decline in foreign reserves.[1]

THE SPECIAL CASE OF TRINIDAD AND TOBAGO: PETROLEUM SLUMP-INDUCED DEFICIT

During the recessionary period 1974–1984 a completely different mechanism was at work in the case of Trinidad and Tobago. The rise in oil prices drove up the level of overall surpluses on the government account and also internalized a high level of wage increases in the economy. The government recorded cash surpluses for most years between 1974 and 1981, but after that the budget went into deficit. Large cash receipts had made it possible for the government to pursue expansionary fiscal policies without resort to the kind of central bank accommodation that had been the case in the other countries studied.

The slowdown in taxes from the oil sector after 1981 and sharp wage increases led to the adoption of a policy of fiscal restraint. In 1982, the deficit ratio to GDP was 13.8 percent. Current expenditures rose sharply in 1981 and 1982 as a result of wage and salary increases. Wage increases ranged between 30 and 37 percent in 1981 and from 10 to 11.5 percent in 1982. As a result, total public sector wages rose from TT$1,342.6 million in 1981 to TT$2,812.8 million in 1982.[2]

The Trinidad and Tobago government financed its deficits between 1982 and 1984 by the use of cash balances accumulated since 1974. Cash balances financed 85 and 78 percent of the deficits in 1982 and 1983, respectively (Table 2.7). Management of the deficits also focused on reduction of capital expenditures by 29.1 percent in 1983 and 23.3 percent in 1984. Advances from the central bank were used in the years 1986–1989.

Budgetary management in Trinidad and Tobago had relied heavily on direct subsidization of petroleum products as well as other basic commodities to cope with inflation. By 1984, in order to reduce the ratio of fiscal deficit

Table 2.7
Deficit and Surplus Financing: Trinidad and Tobago, 1979-1990 (Selected Years)
(in millions of TT $)

	1979	1981	1982	1983	1984	1989	1990
Overall surplus (+) or deficit (−)	−169	236.8	−2,652.4	−2,344.1	−1,392.8	−655.0	614.5
External financing (net)	130	27.0	258.7	228.1	437.5	−240.0	−238.0
Domestic financing	39	−236.8	2,393.7	2,166.0	955.3	896.0	852.5
a) Borrowing (net)	27	−30.6	129.2	277.4	61.1	505.0	-
b) Funds for long-term Development	−18	−48.6	554.0	1,153.2	−27.0	-	-
c) Cash balances (net)	30	−184.6	1,710.5	685.4	921.2	391.0	-

Note: TT $4.25 = US $1.00

Sources: Annual Reports; Central Bank of Trinidad and Tobago, Trinidad and Tobago, *Budget Speech,* 1989, 1990.

to GDP, the government embarked on a program of reducing various subsidies in order to finance development expenditures. This led to increases in
the price of petroleum products. Other subsidies were also removed or
reduced. In addition, the purchase tax was extended to cover several products
and import duties on building materials were introduced. Whereas in Barbados and Jamaica a rise in the indirect tax burden was directly related to
recessionary conditions and the oil shocks, the increase in indirect taxes in
Trinidad and Tobago was related to the impact of falling oil prices on the
total budget deficit.

After 1984 the fiscal strategy adopted by the government of Trinidad and
Tobago to deal with the fiscal deficit was part of a general adjustment program under the direction of the IMF (see Chapter 5). The budget of 1989
specified that the main policy strategy would be to close the fiscal gap through
increases in revenue collections and/or tighter control over recurrent expenditures. On the expenditure side, there was a need to reduce wages and
salaries, transfers to statutory boards and state enterprises, and non-priority
capital spending. The Trinidad and Tobago government achieved some
success at this in the late 1980s reducing the fiscal deficit from TT$2,300
million in 1984 to TT$709.6 million in 1989. A rise in the price of petroleum
in 1990, following the outbreak of the Gulf crisis, improved the balance of
payments position and further reduce the overall fiscal deficit. These developments again highlight the country's dependence on oil exports. In the case
of Trinidad and Tobago, although fiscal restraint was used after 1982 in the
context of falling reserve levels, the country does not appear to have adjusted
its standard of living fast enough to accord with its reduced foreign exchange
earning capacity. After 1973 it was necessary to address the issue of international competitiveness by increasing productivity in the non-oil sectors of
the economy. However this was not successfully done.

EVALUATION

This evaluation hinges primarily on the relationship of the fiscal deficit,
money creation, and the foreign reserves. In the Jamaican case, Keynesian
expenditure policy, to some extent necessitated by the decline of the mineral
sector and overall recession, was an important factor augmenting the monetary base through central bank money creation. This contributed to the running down of foreign reserves. This is not to say that other factors were
unimportant in the Jamaican foreign reserve problem; of course the decline
in real sector activity aggravated the problem. However, the Jamaican balance
of payments difficulties cannot be discussed apart from central bank money
creation.

In the context of the Barbadian economy, money creation appears to have
put pressure on the Barbadian balance of payments in the context of the
decline of the real sector. In 1981, for example, political expediency led to

new money creation because that year was an election year. The heavy expenditures on projects, which were closely bunched in order to secure an election victory, were made in the context of stagnating export earnings. Although such expenditures guaranteed increases in employment, they also led to a deterioration in foreign reserve levels. An expenditure program which was more carefully planned and stretched out would not have produced the same destabilizing effect on the economy. Similar political factors led to excessive money creation in 1990.

Guyana, Jamaica, and to a lesser extent Barbados had balance of payments problems that can be examined further within the context of political economy. Governments of small open systems ought to abandon the dangerous practice of obtaining credit from their central banks to accelerate the production of public goods. The central bank in a developing country cannot be regarded as an autonomous institution, since within the context of the power relationships and political realities implicit in the constitutional relationship between the two bodies, the bank is unable to resist the government's request for credit. Central bank financing should be a short-term mechanism of adjustment but in Jamaica and Guyana it became entrenched. The lack of autonomy of the central bank strongly reflects the aggressive role of fiscal policy.

In the Trinidad and Tobago case, the decline of the externally oriented mineral sector also had implications for public sector financing, and brought about the devaluation of the country's dollar in 1985. After 1982 Trinidad and Tobago tried to adjust its declining reserves problem by fiscal restraint, consequent upon the sharp public sector wage increases of 1981 and 1982. Trinidad and Tobago should be regarded as a special case of a small petroleum economy which failed to mobilize its oil surplus to increase the internal dynamic of the other sectors of the economy.

NOTES

1. For further details, see Central Bank of Barbados, *Annual Report,* 1990.
2. See Central Bank of Trinidad and Tobago, *Annual Report,* 1980–1985.

3

PUBLIC EXPENDITURE ANALYSIS

The size and growth of public expenditure is a complex process which cannot be explained by economics alone. Public expenditure determination is a political process which involves the political philosophy of the government, the demand for public goods, structural changes in the economy, and other non-quantifiable variables. This chapter reviews the main approaches to the determination of the size and growth of the public sector in order to identify those factors relevant to an analysis of the structure of public expenditure in the Caribbean. The term "size of the public sector" refers to the ratio of government expenditure to GDP (G/GDP). Although Musgrave's three branches of decision making, namely allocation, distribution, and stabilization, provide an operational framework in which the size of the public sector can be determined, this approach does not adequately explain increases in the G/GDP ratio. The following section looks at public choice theory, which has shed some light on the way the political process influences growth in the size of the public sector.

THE PUBLIC CHOICE APPROACH

The public choice literature is quite extensive, and no attempt is made here to survey this body of thought. Instead, some of the considerations raised by this theory will be presented, and then the implications of the theory for small democratic states will be discussed. The basis of public choice theory is its emphasis on the political process in the allocation of public expenditures. Following Premchand (1983), public choice theory can be described as the analysis of non-market decision making. The theory focuses on positive analysis of public goods determination. According to Boadway and

Wildasin, public choice theory "treats the political mechanism, especially voting behavior, as the means by which the preferences of individuals for public goods are rationally transmitted to policy makers and, as such, is an extension of economic analysis into political decision making." (1984: 138).

There are essentially two variants of public choice theory. The first variant appears to reflect a view of the state as a mechanism that transforms individual preferences into political outcomes (Mueller, 1987). Most classical work on public choice theory, such as that of Anthony Downs (1957) and James Buchanan and Gordon Tullock (1962), reflects this citizen over-state view of policy. The second variant focuses principally on bureaucracy. This line of inquiry rests on a view of the state as reflecting the interests of bureaucrats and political leaders. The theory of bureaucracy characterizes the work of William Niskanen (1971) and Thomas Romer and Howard Rosenthal (1979).

The first variant of public choice theory utilizes voting models to explain the political process, which enables policy makers to allocate spending in the interest of citizens. Buchanan and Tullock (1962) made an important contribution to this approach by analyzing the effects of logrolling on the political process. Logrolling is a form of vote bargaining in decision making. In this approach, the growth of government expenditure is linked to the activity of interest groups. This line of inquiry has been developed by North and Wallis (1982) and Dennis Mueller and Peter Murrell (1986). The latter work supports the view that interest groups in some countries have a positive effect on the size of government.

Downs (1957) advanced a model of political decision making emphasizing the role of political parties as the mechanism through which the interests of voters are articulated. However, political parties are vote maximizers, and they pursue their own interests when they attain political power. Downs's model has been subjected to extensive criticism, and it is not possible to do justice to his work in a few paragraphs. However, even though politicians may act in their own interests, they must also be conscious of the preferences of the public if they are to win elections. In many democratic governments, public expenditures expand rapidly as the date of elections draws near.

The theory of bureaucracy is a promising area of public choice theory. Bureaucrats pursue their own interests and have an impact on the determination of public expenditure. Niskanen (1971) argues that the bureaucrat's utility function, which includes the bureaucrat's salary, staff, perquisites, and public reputation, augments the size of the budget. Bureaucrats are viewed as budget maximizers and will have significant influence on the growth of public expenditure. Governments in the Caribbean have been characterized by significant expansions in their bureaucracies. Trade unionism has exerted upward pressure on public service salaries, and bureaucrats have become more conscious of their rights and privileges.

Public choice theory can best be described as a school of thought, rather than a unified theory of public expenditure growth. Although the theory has identified a number of fruitful areas of inquiry, the propositions of this school have not been tested and quantified for a large number of developing countries. Further, in small countries it is difficult to measure the relative weights of voter preferences, political party preferences, and bureaucratic pressure on the magnitude of public expenditure growth. Again, much of the analysis of the public choice school is static, often ignoring changes in the political philosophies of governments over time. I am not aware of any published study of public choice theory in the Caribbean; much of the analysis is confined to the United States. However, some of the concerns of this theory can be included in historical analyses of public expenditure growth in the Caribbean. A historical approach to public expenditure growth in small, structurally dependent economies seems preferable to approaches which attempt to isolate, in static fashion, specific determinants for analysis.

THE POSITIVE EMPIRICAL APPROACH

The positive empirical approach to the determination of public expenditure growth has focused primarily on the testing of Wagner's law of increasing state activity. Wagner's law suggests that the share of the public sector in the economy will rise as economic growth proceeds. Many of these tests used cross-sectional as well as time series analysis. The 1960s approaches by Jeffrey Williamson (1961) and Richard Thorn (1967) tested the proposition that a relationship exists between per capita income and the size and pattern of government expenditures. These studies were based on the view that the "stage of development" can be represented by the amount of per capita income. The studies concluded that (1) the share of government expenditure in the gross national product tends to increase with per capita income; (2) current expenditures as a whole increase their share of the national product with rising income; and (3) social expenditures tend to rise as a percentage of total government expenditure.

Cross-sectional studies revealed serious drawbacks. It should be noted that income per head is not a good indicator of development, since it says nothing about the distribution of income. Statistically, it is not good to extrapolate from cross-sectional studies for the purpose of time series analysis; that is, cross-sectional analysis may give misleading indicators for individual countries. Another shortcoming of these studies is that sociopolitical variables play no part in some regression analyses. A study for the Caribbean by Irving Goffman and Dennis Mahar (1971) identified other influences on public expenditure growth, including openness and changing internal political philosophies. However, as Maurice Odle (1976) notes, these studies put forward no systematic theory to explain the role of the state.

We can identify two types of models in the positive empirical tradition. The stages of development models, like those of Musgrave (1969) and Odle

(1976) focus on demand-side factors influencing expenditure patterns. On the other hand, Alan Peacock and Jack Wiseman (1961) utilized a supply-side approach, treating changes in government expenditure as consequences of social disturbances or wars. It is necessary to look closely at Musgrave's analysis, since it offers some insight into expenditure determination in small countries like those in the Caribbean.

Musgrave (1969) distinguishes between (1) the determinants of public expenditure development and (2) conditioning and social factors. According to Musgrave, allowance must be made for the political, cultural, and social factors that determine the environment in which budget policy operates. Musgrave concentrates his analysis on public capital formation, public consumption, and transfer payments. Capital formation in the form of infrastructure tends to be high in the early stages of development. As the economy develops, basic social overheads are created and additions are made at a slower rate. The structure of social overhead capital declines as a share of net capital formation. Therefore, the ratio of public to total capital formation may be expected to be high in the early stages of development and to decline, at least temporarily, after the "take off" is reached. However, there may be later periods in which capital expenditure rises as a share of total capital formation.

Musgrave's analysis is not conclusive with regard to public consumption and public redistribution. There is no clear theory that public consumption will rise as a share of government outlays. Furthermore, public redistribution depends on the objective of distributional policy, which varies from country to country.

Musgrave's analysis rests on safer ground with respect to the conditioning factors. Demographic factors are important influences on public expenditure growth, for obvious reasons. Expansion in the absolute size of the population leads to expansion in the level of public services. This is particularly so in urban areas, especially when population growth is combined with rural-urban migration. The age structure of the population also has an impact on distribution of services. For instance, an age structure which is highly skewed toward the very young will lead to more emphasis on primary and secondary education. As the population ages, pensions and various welfare services become more important.

Other factors, such as technological change and sociopolitical factors, are all discussed in a very generalized way by Musgrave. Musgrave proceeds to regress expenditure/GDP ratios on per capita income, a procedure which leads to misleading conclusions because the econometrics ignore the political factors. Musgrave's approach, while identifying some of the factors which influence government expenditures, is too general to provide a rigorous theory of public expenditure growth.

Peacock and Wiseman's (1961) displacement thesis maintains that public expenditure shows a gradual upward trend under normal conditions, but that increased outlays during war or social upheavals permit permanently higher postwar civilian expenditures. Public expenditure is financed by higher taxation during periods of stress, and this expenditure is displaced upward after the war or social upheaval. Peacock and Wiseman's analysis is essentially short term, since it explains the upward displacement of the expenditure function but does not provide a firm theory of the determinants of the displaced function.

A study by Sackey (1980) is an application of the positive empirical approach to expenditure determination in the Caribbean. Sackey's study provides an empirical investigation of Wagner's law, utilizing time series data on 12 less developed countries. The results support Wagner's law in the long run. Sackey examines various expenditure elasticities and expenditure growth rates. The weakness of Sackey's analysis is that it concentrates almost exclusively on the measurement of statistical magnitudes. He does not advance an explanation of the causes of the behavior of the expenditure variable. Sackey completely excludes non-economic factors. Further, he specifies real per capita government expenditure as a function of the level of real per capita income and the previous year's real expenditure per capita, ignoring politial explanations of expenditure growth.

THE BAUMOL EFFECT AND THE PUBLIC SECTOR

We now discuss the "Baumol effect" as one explanation of public expenditure growth. The Baumol effect may have some significance in explaining the heavy wage bills of some public services in the Caribbean. William Baumol (1967) divides the economy into two sectors, the progressive and non-progressive sectors. The progressive sector experiences productivity growth, while productivity in the non-progressive sector is constant. The basic difference between the two sectors resides in the role played by labor in the activity. In some cases labor is an instrument to produce the final product, while in others labor itself is the end product (Baumol 1967: 416). Manufacturing is an example of the former type of activity, whereas there are services, such as teaching, where labor is an end in itself. Services tend to be labor intensive and offer less scope for technological change that improves productivity. The concept of a non-progressive sector may apply to public service labor activity.

The Baumol model can be summarized in the following propositions:

1. The output of the non-progressive sector is produced only by labor with constant productivity. The output of the progressive sector is a function of labor productivity which grows at an exponential rate.
2. Wage rates are equal in the two sectors and increase at the same rate as productivity in the progressive sector.
3. The cost per unit of output of the unprogressive sector will rise without limit, while the unit cost of the progressive sector will remain constant. This is because productivity in the non-progressive sector is less than in the progressive sector.

Baumol's model, therefore, provides an explanation of expenditure growth in the public sector, if we assume that the public sector is labor intensive and experiences constant productivity, and that public sector wages move at a rate similar to that of wages in the progressive sector, which uses capital-intensive technology.

Baumol's model is intuitively appealing but difficult to quantify in the Caribbean, where the public service is popularly perceived as inefficient and cumbersome, more bureaucracy-oriented than service-oriented. Despite the difficulty of estimating productivity in the public service in the Caribbean, one can still regard the Baumol effect as a plausible explanation of the large wage bills of the public sectors of Barbados and Trinidad and Tobago in the 1980s. It is also true that trade unions in the Caribbean have placed heavy emphasis on inflation as the rationale for wage increases in the public sector, rather than relating wage increases to productivity growth. We also note the observation of Peacock (1975: 105) that productivity of government services may be markedly influenced not so much by the characteristics of supply along the lines of the Baumol effect, but "by the lack of incentive to introduce process and product innovations by bureaucratically organized production." Perhaps this lack of incentive in the Caribbean public services stems not only from the non-profit nature of many government services, but from the reality that public sector managers are ultimately responsible to politicians. As a result, the managers feel no compulsion to introduce new ideas. Productivity remains constant, and public sector wage costs rise under trade union pressure.

THE POLITICO-HISTORICAL STAGES APPROACH: ODLE AND HOWARD

The politico-historical thesis is perhaps the strongest explanation of the magnitude and growth of the G/GDP ratio in the Caribbean during the post-World War II period. I accept the thesis that the change in the role of the state was a dominant determinant of public expenditure growth. This approach is embodied in the work of Odle (1976), which is the first comprehensive analysis of the evolution of public expenditure in the Caribbean. Odle's work concentrated on Guyana, but had theoretical application to the entire Caribbean (Odle 1975). Odle's stages theory is applicable to the Barbadian case (Howard 1979a and 1982). This section discusses the work of Odle and its wider applications, to pave the way for an examination of the structure of public expenditure in the Caribbean.

Odle (1975) distinguishes three major periods of public expenditure growth: the traditional period, the transitional period, and the post-colonial period. The traditional period is the colonial period (pre-1960), when the tax system and the allocation of public expenditure in the Caribbean were designed to assist the operations of the foreign-owned plantations. In Barbados, Jamaica, and Trinidad, a heavy proportion of expenditure was allocated to road building, to link the sugar estates and aid the extraction and internal transportation of sugar. There was also considerable spending on ports and harbors, to facilitate shipments of sugar. The share of government spending on education and health was relatively low. Public expenditure patterns were modified after 1937, when the British government adopted a more benevolent approach to public policy in the colonies. This was seen in the passing of the Colonial Development and Welfare Acts of 1940 and 1945, which provided for increased loans and grants to improve the social and economic infrastructure. This provision for minimum social welfare and infrastructure increased the share of expenditure in the domestic product.

During the stage of internal self-government in the 1950s, or the transitional period before full political independence from Britain, emphasis was placed on reducing monoculture in the Caribbean. Governments adopted industrialization programs based on liberal tax incentives. There was an increase in the public expenditure share of public goods and infrastructure to support private enterprise. Statutory corporations were established during this period, including development boards and marketing and financial corporations. Thus, the change in the character of the state gave the political directorate more autonomy in economic management, which was reflected in rising public expenditures.

The post-independence period, which began in Guyana and Barbados in 1966, was characterized by sharp increases in public expenditures owing to the internal and external responsibilities of nationhood. This included increases in administrative expenditures to finance new ministries; increases in defense spending; and increased spending in areas which were neglected during the colonial period, such as secondary and university education and health. This increase in expenditures was financed by heavy income taxation, which began to rival import duties in importance.

In some territories, like Guyana, Jamaica, and Trinidad and Tobago, the state established a large number of public enterprises to counterbalance certain foreign-owned interests. These efforts were supported by the establishment of cooperatives in some territories to increase local participation in economic activity. This heavy emphasis on state ownership increased the share of government expenditures. These issues are discussed in Chapter 4.

The stages theory has been applied to Barbados (Howard 1982), with the colonial and post-independence periods differentiated. In the colonial period the high level of structural dependence led the government to adopt expenditure policies which re-enforced the dominant mercantile class and retarded the emergence of a public policy to diversify the productive base. The existing colonial monetary system during this period was a constraint on government spending, because the colonial government had no control over the money supply, credit, or the structure of interest rates. The government's power to spend was limited by the reserves at its disposal; therefore the policymakers budgeted for a revenue surplus in times of export boom in order to spend in times of slump.

The political philosophy during colonialism was that secondary as well as tertiary education were privileges set aside for the elite. This explains the low level of capital expenditure on education. Between 1953 and 1964, capital expenditure on education grew at an estimated annual rate of 0.8 percent in Barbados (Howard 1979a). The level of current spending was not even adequate. Most schools suffered from an acute lack of accommodation. The class-ordered educational system prevented the emergence of an expenditure policy geared to reallocate human resources.

The most important fiscal achievement of the colonial administration was the building of a deep water harbor, which absorbed a heavy proportion of capital expenditure. Capital spending on economic services grew at the rate of 15.7 percent between 1953 and 1964. The colonial development plans in Barbados recognized the need for improved roads, port facilities, and water resources. Despite this emphasis on infrastructure, the colonial government was concerned with economic growth as it related to sugar output, rather than with the wider concept of economic development which relates to re-allocation of resources to increase the flexibility of the economy (Howard 1982).

Political independence of Barbados from Britain brought a change in the role of the state, and an expenditure policy was adopted which was more egalitarian. Further, independence facilitated inflow of foreign capital from donor agencies, thereby enabling higher levels of public expenditure. The post-independence period in Barbados saw a rapid growth of spending on education, health, and social services. Between 1966 and 1978 education constituted the largest category of current account spending. Government became committed to the concept of "free education" up to the tertiary level. The government of the day stressed the concept of social democracy, by which all citizens should have the right to work, and free education was a vehicle to re-allocate human resources. There was heavy spending on social services, with the provision of national insurance and social security.

Governments in the Caribbean had become quite large (Howard 1989a). During the early 1980s they adopted aggressive expenditure policies, partly as a result of the crisis in the major export sectors (see Worrell 1987). In pursuit of the democratic socialist ideal, heavy government expenditure was designed to maintain employment and social welfare levels. As we have seen in Chapter 2, these policies led to heavy fiscal and balance of payments deficits. However, one can argue that structural weaknesses in Caribbean economies were playing a part in government expenditure growth. Other descriptive analyses of public expenditure growth have been carried out by Muriel Saunders and Delisle Worrell (1981) for Barbados and Ramesh Ramsaran (1988) for Trinidad and Tobago.

The above politico-historical sketch indicates that growth of government expenditure is a complex phenomenon which cannot be explained simply by the econometric method. Regression of government expenditure share on per capita income or some other variable does not take into account the complex nature of political decision making. I believe that a historical analysis which highlights the changing political stances of government is perhaps a better guide to understanding the growth of government expenditure in post-colonial economies. Although most studies using the public choice approach do not focus on the politico-historical process, the theory, nevertheless, identifies politico-bureaucratic parameters worthy of investigation. In this respect the role of political parties and bureaucracy in shaping government spending patterns would complement historical analysis. This is a fertile area for research in the Caribbean.

CARIBBEAN PUBLIC EXPENDITURE STRUCTURES

This section uses ratio analysis to discuss the structure of government in the Caribbean. The size of Caribbean governments, as measured by the G/GDP ratio, is shown in Table 3.1. For Barbados, the ratio is almost constant up to 1986, rising to its highest levels in 1987 and 1988. The Barbadian

Table 3.1
Size of Government (G/GDP) of Selected Caribbean Countries, 1978–1989 (in percent)

Year	Barbados	Jamaica	Trinidad	Guyana
1978	34.3	49.2	30.4	n.a.
1979	33.4	36.5	33.5	n.a.
1980	34.6	43.7	34.4	n.a.
1981	36.3	49.1	36.8	n.a.
1982	34.5	46.3	49.5	n.a.
1983	32.2	44.2	46.3	n.a.
1984	33.4	36.9	38.4	112.3
1985	35.2	41.6	43.4	95.9
1986	34.5	42.0	38.1	140.1
1987	37.9	40.6	37.3	104.1
1988	37.7	43.7	35.2	101.4
1989	36.4	34.6	31.9	111.7

Note: n.a. denotes not available

Sources: Bank of Jamaica, *Statistical Digest*, September 1990; Planning Institute of Jamaica, *Economic & Social Survey of Jamaica*, 1989; Central Bank of Barbados, *Annual Statistical Digest*, 1990; Central Bank of Trinidad and Tobago, *Annual Economic Survey*, 1989.

ratio is the lowest of the three countries studied; this is partly explained by the more significant role played by the private sector in Barbados in comparison with the other countries. The Jamaican ratio is over 40 percent for most of the period. Derick Boyd (1988) reports a decline in real public expenditures in Jamaica between 1981 and 1985, which could explain the decline in Jamaica's G/GDP ratio during this period. The ratio declined in Trinidad and Tobago in the late 1980s as a result of expenditure-reducing policies. In the case of Guyana, the ratio is exceedingly high, probably because (1) the miniaturization of the organized private sector partly explains the large size of government and (2) the GDP is likely to be underestimated, since the substantial underground activity in Guyana, is not recorded in the GDP figures. For an analysis of the Guyana underground economy, the reader is referred to Thomas (1989).

The main line of inquiry here is an examination of the functional distribution of expenditure which determines the G/GDP ratio. The purpose of this exercise is to compare the relative emphases placed on various categories of expenditures by the governments. Besides revealing government priorities, structural analysis may also help in a limited way to gauge the preferences of the public for public goods. Primarily because I was unable to obtain reliable and comparable information for Guyana, the analysis is carried out only for Barbados, Jamaica, and Trinidad and Tobago, using representative years for which recent data are available. The analysis for Trinidad and Tobago is also limited by the unavailability of certain categories of data. I have mainly used current expenditure, since this represents ongoing, or "permanent", expenditure and is a better guide to understanding the structure of public goods than capital expenditure, which is more variable over time.

The functional analysis of the structure of current expenditure is shown in Tables 3.2 and 3.3. Barbados allocates a greater share of its budget, 22 percent, to education than either Jamaica or Trinidad and Tobago. Table 3.3 shows that current spending on education constitues 6.6 percent of GDP in Barbados, compared with 4.4 percent for Trinidad and Tobago and 4.0 percent for Jamaica. The educational policy and philosophy contributing to these high expenditures shares are explained in this chapter.

Another feature of Tables 3.2 and 3.3 is that social spending, particularly on health care, is also given heavier emphasis in Barbados. This is partly explained by the impact of expenditure-reducing policies on the social services in Jamaica and Trinidad and Tobago. Boyd (1988) reported that vigorous deflationary policies in Jamaica between 1981 and 1986 reduced central government expenditure in real terms, and that expenditures for social services declined more than proportionately. He calculated that the proportion of current expenditure going to social services fell from 37 percent in 1981/82 to 30 percent in 1985/86. My analysis in nominal terms shows that social services expenditure in Jamaica was 33.4 percent in 1988.

Deflationary policies in Jamaica also affected the ratio of current spending on economic services. The ratio is 5.0 percent, compared with 15.6

percent for Barbados and 12.9 percent for Trinidad and Tobago (Table 3.2). It can be argued that in the economic crisis, the two priorities of the Jamaican government were to sustain the operation of the bureaucracy, as shown by the high ratio of expenditure on general services (25.7 percent), and meet heavy charges of debt. Public debt charges were 35.9 percent of Jamaica's current expenditure, or 9.5 percent of GDP, in 1988. The Jamaican debt problem is discussed in Chapter 6.

I also looked at the economic classification of current expenditure for Barbados and Trinidad and Tobago (Table 3.4). The public sector wage bill constitutes a roughly similar share of current expenditure for the two countries in 1989, that is, 42.4 percent for Trinidad and Tobago and 43.9 percent for Barbados. The Trinidad and Tobago ratio has been determined by a number of factors. Ramsaran (1988) has presented data to show that there was rapid growth in the wage bill of the Trinidad and Tobago public sector between 1973 and 1982, caused by the expanding government labor force and absolute increases in wages and salaries. Between 1976 and 1979, according to Ramsaran (1988), the number employed in the public service rose from 66,900 tp 80,810. Wage increases were also sharp after 1979. Public sector wages rose by 109.5 percent between 1981 and 1982. By 1985 the public sector wage bill as a ratio of current expenditure was 45.4 percent (Table 3.4).

Table 3.2
Functional Classification of Current Expenditures in Barbados, Trinidad and Tobago, and Jamaica, 1988 or 1989
(percent distribution)

Function	Barbados 1989	Trinidad & Tobago 1989	Jamaica 1988
General services	17.7	17.1	25.7
Education	22.6	13.6	16.8
Health	14.4	8.2	9.8
Social security and welfare	9.4	8.6	3.6
Housing	4.7	0.5	1.8
Other social services	1.4	4.8	1.4
Economic services	15.6	12.9	5.0
Public debt charges	14.2	16.7	35.9
Other	–	17.6	–

Sources: Bank of Jamaica, *Statistical Digest*, September 1990; Planning Institute of Jamaica, *Economic & Social Survey of Jamaica*, 1989; Central Bank of Barbados, *Annual Statistical Digest*, 1990; Central Bank of Trinidad and Tobago, *Annual Economic Survey*, 1989.

Table 3.3
Major Components of Current Expenditures in Barbados, Trinidad and Tobago, and Jamaica, 1988 or 1989
(percentage of GDP)

Function	Barbados 1989	Trinidad & Tobago 1989	Jamaica 1988
General services	5.1	5.5	6.1
Social services	15.5	11.5	8.0
a) Education	6.6	4.4	4.0
b) Health	4.3	2.7	2.3
Economic services	4.6	4.2	1.3
Public debt changes	4.1	5.4	9.5

Sources: Bank of Jamaica, *Statistical Digest*, September 1990; Planning Institute of Jamaica, *Economic & Social Survey of Jamaica*, 1989; Central Bank of Barbados, *Annual Statistical Digest*, 1990; Central Bank of Trinidad and Tobago, *Annual Economic Survey*, 1989.

Table 3.4
Economic Classification of Current Expenditures in Barbados and Trinidad and Tobago, 1985 and 1989
(percent distribution)

Category	Barbados		Trinidad & Tobago	
	1985	1989	1985	1989
Wages and salaries	42.5	43.9	45.4	42.4
Goods and services	11.2	11.8	6.0	8.6
Interest	11.2	14.2	4.6	15.0
Transfers and subsidies	35.1	30.1	44.0	34.0
a) Public enterprises and institutions	(22.7)	(17.0)	(16.4)	(6.4)
b) Households	(6.7)	(7.4)	(9.8)	(13.3)
c) Other	(5.7)	(5.7)	(17.8)	(14.3)

Sources: Bank of Jamaica, *Statistical Digest*, September 1990; Planning Institute of Jamaica, *Economic & Social Survey of Jamaica*, 1989; Central Bank of Barbados, *Annual Statistical Digest*, 1990; Central Bank of Trinidad and Tobago, *Annual Economic Survey*, 1989.

Efforts aimed at reducing expenditure on wages and salaries in Trinidad and Tobago were continued in 1989 and provided the single largest

contribution to the overall decline in current expenditure. The annual economic survey for 1989, published by the Central Bank of Trinidad and
Tobago, reported that a cut of 10 percent in the salaries of public servants,
and continued suspensions of cost of living allowances, resulted in expenditure on wage costs amounting to TT$2,134.2 million in 1989, 11.9 percent
lower than in 1988. During 1989 the Trinidad and Tobago government also
delayed the implementation of retroactive salary payments awarded to public servants by a special tribunal. These factors explain the fall in the ratio
of public sector wages and salaries, from 45.4 percent in 1985 to 42.4 percent in 1989 (Table 3.4). However, the Trinidad and Tobago budget of 1991
mandated 10 percent restoration of public sector salaries, a move that was
seen as a political imperative.

The other category of interest in the economic classification is transfers
and subsidies. The ratio of transfers and subsidies to current expenditure
is higher for the years studied in Trinidad and Tobago (Table 3.4). Transfers constitute pensions, unemployment benefits, and social welfare payments
to households. Subsidies are paid, mainly to public institutions. In 1985 these
payments were 44 percent of current expenditures. In the context of the
austere fiscal policies pursued after 1982, the Trinidad and Tobago government took steps to rationalize the state-owned and other parastatal enterprises by reducing transfers to these institutions. In 1989, total transfers and
subsidy payments by the central government were TT$1,712.0 million, or
13.1 percent less than in 1988.[1]

Although Barbados has fewer public enterprises than Trinidad and Tobago,
transfers to statutory bodies in Barbados constitute a significant proportion
of the current budget. These transfers include payments to non-financial
enterprises, such as the transport board, Barbados Industrial Development
Corporation, the post office, the water authority, and the National Housing
Corporation. Transfers to other public institutions include grants to the
University of the West Indies, tourism promotion, sanitation services, the
Barbados defense force, and the welfare agencies. The ratio of transfers and
subsidies fell to 30.1 percent of current expenditure in 1989, as the Barbadian
government also attempted to adjust its expenditure program.

EXPENDITURE ON EDUCATION

We now look more closely at educational budgets, principally for Barbados and Jamaica. Governments in the Caribbean have shown a commitment
to human resource development as a fundamental aspect of development
policy. In 1989 total expenditure on education as a ratio of GDP was 7.9
percent for Barbados and 5.6 percent for Jamaica. The principal rationale
for expenditure on education and training stems from the need to provide
human capital. Development requires adequate supplies of high-level manpower, doctors, agronomists, and so forth, as well as sub-professional and

technical personnel. Education contributes to national productivity as well as personal development, since it increases the earning capacity of the individual. The main constraint on the development of human resources is the problem of absorptive capacity, which relates to the maximum number of persons who can be employed without redundancy or serious under-utilization of skills. In the Caribbean, recessionary conditions have increased the problem of absorptive capacity. The supply of educated people has become more plentiful relative to the declining employment-generating capacity of some territories. The absorptive capacity problem has led to migration to North America, especially from Jamaica and Guyana. Some countries, like Jamaica and Trinidad and Tobago, have been forced to control their education budgets to cope with the problems of recession.

Governments in the English-speaking Caribbean contribute to the support of the University of the West Indies. However, during the 1980s some governments attempted to recoup their expenditure on education by resorting to educational taxation. For instance, education at the university level was no longer "free" in Trinidad and Tobago, where the government introduced measures obliging students at the tertiary level to contribute to the cost of their education. The Guyana budget of 1991 also announced plans to reintroduce fees, abolished in 1976, at the secondary and tertiary levels. Although Barbados did not introduce new educational taxes in the 1980s, other measures were taken to control the education budget, like the withdrawal of study leave, which had enabled public servants to attend the university during the early 1980s. However, in Barbados education remained "free" at the point of delivery, up to university level.

The present educational policy in Barbados dates from the 1960s, when the Democratic Labour Party (DLP) government introduced free secondary and tertiary education, which determined the cost structure of the educational budget. Table 3.5 shows that the largest proportion of spending goes towards secondary education (31.7 percent), followed by preprimary and primary education (28.6 percent). The government remains committed to the provision of technical education and devotes 3.9 percent of the current budget to administrative costs and teacher education. It should be noted that besides the financing of 21 public secondary schools in 1989, the government also provided bursaries for children to attend 15 approved private schools. The per capita costs of financing public secondary schools was Bds$3,252.0 million in 1989.

Jamaica introduced "free" secondary education in 1973. At present, Jamaican educational expenditure is influenced by the Human Resource Development Programme (HRDP), of (1989–1994), a five-year program designed to bring about qualitative improvement in the educational system. The education component of the project is financed by the World Bank and other leading agencies. Specific objectives under the project include the refurbishing of 390 basic schools, upgrading of 20 primary and all-age schools, printing and distribution of primary textbooks, and expansion of the school feeding program.[2] Specifically, the government's policy includes increasing the emphasis on primary and preprimary education and closer monitoring of educational programs, as well as increasing the supply of textbooks.

The structure of Jamaica's current educational budget is shown in Table 3.5. The highest proportion of spending (37.3 percent) goes to primary and preprimary education, followed by secondary education (32.1 percent). The estimated per capita cost of primary education was J$6.47 thousand in 1989, compared with J$1,891.5 for secondary education and J$16,881.3 for tertiary education. About 70 percent of the tertiary-level finance goes to the University of the West Indies.

The impact of Jamaican educational policy on human resource development is shown in Table 3.6. Human resource output is strongest in the areas of management and teaching, followed by field of medicine. The supply of nurses constitutes the largest proportion of medical medical personnel, but this proportion has fallen from 45.6 percent in 1987 to 32.5 percent in 1989. The output of doctors totaled 44, or 7.8 percent in 1987 and 54 percent, or 11.7 percent of total medical personnel output in 1989. Despite the increase in the output of trained manpower, migration to North America has averaged about 20,000 annually, and a large part of this consists of trained manpower.[3] Massive migration is a serious drain of the country's resources.

Table 3.5
Structure of Current Expenditure on Education in Barbados and Jamaica, Fiscal 1989/90

(in percent)

Program	Barbados	Jamaica
Preprimary and primary	28.6	37.3
Secondary	31.7	32.1
Tertiary	18.6	23.3
Technical and vocational	5.4	4.7
Administrative and teacher training	3.9	1.3
Other	11.8*	1.3

* Includes mainly primary school meals service.

Note: Estimated values are used.

Sources: Economic and Social Survey of Jamaica, 1989; *Barbados Estimates*, 1989/90.

Table 3.6
Professional, Technical, and Managerial Output of Manpower in Jamaica,
1987–1989

Occupation	1987 No. of Persons	1988 No. of Persons	1989 No. of Persons
Education	788	628	593
Medicine	562	555	462
Management and accounting	725	746	738
Engineering and technology	256	231	265
Social science	134	115	249
Physical science	172	183	169
Architecture and surveying	78	84	105
Law	36	34	39
Agriculture	63	56	79
Computing	–	–	97
All others	246	304	594
Totals	3,060	2,936	3,390

Source: Planning Institute of Jamaica, *Economic & Social Survey of Jamaica*, 1989.

One of the most serious challenges facing Caribbean governments is increasing and retaining the educational output at the tertiary level. The per capita cost of education is highest at this level and must be financed from taxation or borrowing. Finance is a constraint on the expansion of the university plant, although there is a need to expand enrollments in areas such as science and technology. Some of the governments of the smaller territories in the region have difficulty paying their share of the costs of running the university.

Table 3.7 shows the per capita economic costs paid by the governments of Barbados, Jamaica, and Trinidad and Tobago to the Cave Hill Campus of the University of the West Indies, on behalf of their nationals studying there. These per capita costs reflect wages, and maintenance as well as the other operational costs of running the university. They do not include tuition fees. The analysis shows that for all programs, the costs are high and rising. The cost for a medical student is highest of all. In most programs, per capita costs rose by over 30 percent between 1986 and 1990. These costs significantly augment the current account budgets of the governments.

Table 3.7
Per Capita Economic Costs: Cave Hill Campus, 1986/87–1990/91
(in Bds $)

Program*	1986/87	1987/88	1988/89	1989/90	1990/91
Arts and general studies	13,500	14,600	14,400	16,800	18,500
Natural sciences	18,800	20,200	20,200	23,000	25,300
Education	18,700	25,600	15,800	25,000	25,000
Law	17,000	17,000	17,000	19,500	21,400
Medicine	–	–	–	–	59,000

* Refers to full-time program.

Note: Bds$2.00 = US$1.00

Source: University of the West Indies, *Estimates for Annual Expenses for Undergraduate Degree Programmes at the Cave Hill Campus,* various years.

EXPENDITURE ON PUBLIC HEALTH

This section examines the costs of public health in Barbados and Jamaica. Public investment in health care in developing countries should lead to a decline in crude death rates as well as in infant mortality rates. Health care improvements should also increase labor productivity, which is a function of a large number of variables, including management, education, attitudes about work, and so forth. A healthy labor force is likely to increase output by spending more hours on the job than an unhealthy labor force. Disease is one cause of loss of working time and debility of the work force in developing countries. In Barbados the infant mortality rate fell from around 29.3 per thousand births in the 1970s to 15.5 in the 1980s. This can be attributed to rising levels of health care. In Jamaica, the infant mortality rate was estimated at 27 per thousand births in 1989, which is unacceptably higher that the Barbadian rate in the 1980s. The crude death rate in Barbados was not significantly affected by health improvements. It fell from an average of 8.7 per thousand in the 1970s to 8.2 in the 1980s. We note, however, that health care expenditure is only one factor influencing standards of living and longevity. Other aspects of social policy, such as housing, education, life-style, and physical activity also affect standards of living.

The analysis in Tables 3.8 and 3.9 shows the performance of the health budgets of Barbados and Jamaica. Secondary health care, or hospital services, accounts for the largest proportion of the health budgets: 49.1 percent of the total for Barbados and 43.0 percent for Jamaica in fiscal 1989/90. Primary health care represented a similar proportion of the budget in both countries, that is, 15.6 percent in Barbados and 15.3 percent in Jamaica in fiscal 1989/90. The most important feature of the budgets, however, is that the Barbados government spends 5.3 percent of the nation's GDP on health, whereas the Jamaican government spends only 3.0 percent.

Underfinancing of the health budget has been identified as a major problem facing the Jamaican government.[4] Underfinancing hampers the delivery of good-quality health care and was reflected in the inadequacy of the infrastructure and of diagnostic and support services. Further, there were severe shortages of staff in critical areas of health service. In 1989 there were an estimated 60 percent vacancies among pharmacists; 57 percent among medical technologists; and 43 percent, 40 percent and 42 percent, respectively, among registered nurses, enrolled assistant nurses, and public health inspectors.

In the 1980s Barbadian policymakers placed considerable emphasis on primary health care. This was reflected in the continued expansion of the multipurpose policyclinic service. Primary health care expenditure in 1989 went toward financing eight polyclinics, providing services free at the point of delivery. The upgrading of dental health services and the expansion of the national drug service, which provides drugs for certain chronic illnesses free of charge, were important objectives of the national health budget. Most capital expenditure on secondary health care went toward the expansion of the largest hospital, the Queen Elizabeth Hospital. Both primary and secondary public health care in Barbados are complemented by private enterprise in general practitioner and specialist services.

Table 3.8
Public Health Expenditures: Barbados, 1988/89 and 1989/90
(in millions Bds $)

	1988/89		1989/90*	
Category	$	%	$	%
Current expenditures	128.1	90.0	135.5	81.8
Central administration	8.4	6.0	6.5	3.9
Individual health service (primary care)	23.0	16.1	25.8	15.6
Hospital services (secondary care)	75.6	53.1	81.3	49.1
Sanitation services	21.1	14.8	21.9	13.2
Capital expenditure	14.3	10.0	30.0	18.2
Total	142.4	100.0	165.6	100.0
Total as percentage of GDP		5.3		5.3

* Estimate.

Note: Bds$2.00 = US$1.00

Source: Barbados Estimates of Revenue & Expenditure, 1990/91

Table 3.9
Public Health Expenditures: Jamaica, 1988/89 and 1989/90
(millions of J $)

Category	1988/89 $	1988/89 %	1989/90 $	1989/90 %
Current expenditure	483.1	79.4	536.9	78.5
Central administration	28.8	4.8	36.6	5.4
Primary care	85.1	14.0	104.0	15.3
Secondary care	282.6	46.4	291.1	43.0
Paramedical services	52.0	8.5	65.8	9.6
Training	5.6	0.9	6.9	1.0
Other	28.9	4.8	32.4	4.7
Capital expenditures	125.3	20.6	147.0	21.5
Total	608.4	100.0	683.9	100.0
Total as percentage of GDP		3.2		3.0

Note: J$21.00 = US$1.00 at December 1991

Source: Planning Institute of Jamaica, *Economic and Social Survey of Jamaica 1989*

CONCLUSIONS

The political philosophies of Caribbean governments during the post-independence era exerted a major influence on the growth and composition of public expenditures. The philosophy of democratic socialism, especially in Jamaica, and to a lesser extent in Barbados and Trinidad and Tobago, emphasized the importance of social expenditure, thereby internalizing a high level of recurrent costs in the social budgets. Cooperative socialism in Guyana also determined public expenditure because of its emphasis on state control of the economic systems. (See the discussion of the genesis of cooperative socialism in Guyana in Chapter 2.)

Heavy investment in public enterprises augmented public expenditures, owing to the dependence of these parastatals on transfers and subsidies from the central government. Even in Barbados, where there were fewer public enterprises, the statutory boards were recipients of numerous government grants and subsidies.

Real sector economic decline in the late 1970s and early 1980s exerted an influence on the growth and composition of public expenditure. The governments of Jamaica, Guyana, and Barbados pursued aggressive expenditure policies partly to compensate for the decline in real sector activity. In Trinidad and Tobago, the aggressive expenditure policy was supported by expansion in oil revenue prior to 1982. All the governments practised fiscal restraint in the second half of the 1980s. Expenditure-reducing policies in Jamaica and Trinidad and Tobago curtailed public expenditure growth.

The demand for public goods in the post-independence period also influenced the size of government. Certainly, the public's preferences for education, health care, and housing would have influenced the provision of these goods;[5] however, it is difficult to quantify the public's preference for public goods.

The growth in the size of government brought about higher charges of debt, which further influenced the composition of public expenditure. In Jamaica, for example, charges of debt were 35.9 percent of current expenditure, or 9.5 percent of GDP. In Barbados, debt charges were 14.2 percent of current expenditure, and in Trinidad and Tobago they were 16.7 percent. The public debt is analysed as a separate issue in Chapter 6.

Financing of education at the tertiary level presents a challenge to the governments of the region. Of all categories of current expenditure on education, tertiary education has the highest per capita costs. Recessionary conditions during the 1980s led to rising per capita expense of maintaining the University of the West Indies, given which, if the region is to retain its output of high-level manpower, the absorptive capacity of its economies must be increased.

Overall, this analysis shows the complexity of the factors influencing the size of government in small, post-colonial, dependent economies. Although there are broad similarities in the expenditure analysis of these countries, each country also has economic and political factors peculiar to itself.

NOTES

1. See Central Bank of Trinidad and Tobago, *Annual Economic Survey 1989*, p. 30.
2. Planning Institute of Jamaica, *Economic and Social Survey Jamaica 1989*, p. 185.
3. Ibid., p. 154.
4. Ibid., p. 201, for points mentioned in this paragraph.
5. The growth of mass-based political parties rooted in the trade union movement after 1945 played an important role in articulating the interests of the broad masses of people.

4

PUBLIC ENTERPRISE AND PRIVATIZATION

The public enterprise model had considerable influence on economic thinking in the 1960s and 1970s. In many developing countries, emphasis was placed on controlling the "commanding heights" of the economy. In the Caribbean, structuralist economists recommended nationalization as a means of establishing ownership and control over the key sectors of the economy. Nationalizations were numerous in Jamaica, Guyana, and Trinidad and Tobago. In other developing countries, such as Brazil, Tanzania, India, and Mexico, the state established a large number of public or state-owned enterprises as a means of strengthening the productive sectors. Public enterprises were set up in manufacturing, mining, telecommunications, and services. Public ownership was not confined to socialist regimes. Many democratic, developed countries also established public enterprises.

Increased state ownership led to large public sectors, which expanded the cost of government. The result was huge public sector deficits, heavy taxation, and foreign borrowing. The 1973 and 1981 world recessions increased the financial burdens of governments in both developed and developing countries, and led policymakers to question the efficiency of the state ownership model. Some of these enterprises had had significant losses and had been unable to adjust to the risks of a changing world economy. Some countries with relatively large state sectors did not experience as high a rate of growth as did countries with resilient and competitive market economies.[1]

This chapter examines the rationale for public enterprises in the Caribbean, as well as the functioning of these institutions and the different policy positions adopted by the governments to deal with inefficient public enterprises. The policy of divestment in the Caribbean is relatively new, and at this stage it is not possible to evaluate its economic impact. Further, I was unable to acquire adequate and reliable information on divestment in Guyana.

In Trinidad and Tobago, the government's divestment policy has not been as strong as in Jamaica, and in Barbados privatization was not implemented as an instrument of development policy before 1991.

RATIONALE FOR PUBLIC ENTERPRISE IN THE CARIBBEAN

Following George Mills (1981), we can identify two dominant justifications for public enterprise in the Caribbean. These are the pragmatic nationalist approach and the ideological argument. The pragmatic nationalist approach, which emerged during the 1950s and 1960s, embraced a wide range of arguments for nationalization. This chapter considers the active internal and external economic and political factors which influenced the public enterprise movement in the Caribbean just after World War II. Further, the chapter identifies the political philosophies of public ownership which exerted a strong influence in some Caribbean countries, primarily in the 1970s and early 1980s.

The British nationalization precedent gave impetus to the few Caribbean nationalizations during the colonial postwar period, as well as to the establishment of state-owned corporations and enterprises. The British Labour government announced a nationalization program in 1945, involving the nationalization of coal, gas, transport, and electricity.[2] The nationalization of natural gas in Barbados during the colonial period was influenced by these precedents (Emtage 1969: 203). Odle (1979) argues that some of the pre-independence nationalizations elsewhere in the Caribbean also constituted moves on the part of the property-owning class to get rid of financially burdensome undertakings. He cites the nationalization of the Guyana railways and the Trinidad government's acquisition of the Hilton Hotel and BOAC's BWIA. The British precedent included nationalization of industries with outdated structures, such as coal and gas.

The establishment of public enterprises in the Caribbean during the early postwar period rested on the argument that what was good for Britain was also good for the colonies. John Lee (1967) contends that the discussion of the form public corporations should take in the colonies largely reflected the discussion of the nationalization issue in Britain. With respect to nationalization, the left wing of the Labour Party was impatient with arguments that colonial conditions were not suitable for large-scale nationalizations. The view is advanced by Lee that the colonial governments had enough autonomy to pursue large-scale nationalizations. However, in Barbados, the mercantile and planter interests still exerted some influence on government policy, thereby curbing the extent to which the government could pursue nationalization policies.

In the post-independence period the Caribbean public enterprise movement was also conditioned by political nationalism in other third-world countries. This nationalism was reflected in a spate of nationalizations, which included the Mexican oil nationalization of 1938, the Persian oil nationalization of 1952, Egypt's nationalization of Suez in 1956, the Cuban nationalization of 1960, and the Chilean and Zambian copper nationalizations of 1969. Norman Girvan (1971b) has cited these nationalizations, stating that they should have provided guidance for the Caribbean.

According to Odle (1979), this confluence of effort made it impossible for the multinational corporations or their home governments to concentrate repressive attention on any one developing country. The international political climate was therefore conducive to nationalization, and this was reflected in the recommendation by the United Nations that home countries should refrain from involving themselves in disputes between multinational corporations and host countries.[3]

The New World group of Caribbean economists of the 1960s proposed nationalization and indigenization as a logical countermeasure to foreign domination. Plantation economists recommended nationalization of plantations, foreign banks, and the mining industry.[4] Their reform program also favored creation of indigenous banks. Further, Alister McIntyre and Beverly Watson (1970) recommended the use of legislation to discriminate in favor of national ownership, by varying the incentives granted to correspond with the degree of local share in the equity. It was recognized that changes in the pattern of ownership would not lead to instant economic transformation, because the process also depended on development of adequate local personnel.

The theoretical argument for ownership and control had both micro and macro economic implications. At the micro level, nationalization was encouraged, to establish effective control over the pricing and marketing of commodities, as well as the purchasing and processing of raw material supplies. At the macro level, public ownership and control were designed to arrest the outflow of the domestically generated economic surplus. As a welfare instrument, nationalization was also conceived as a means to redistribute income and wealth, particularly in the rural sectors of the economy dominated by foreign-owned plantations.

The tendency to establish state-owned institutions to compete with foreign-owned multinational corporations has been criticized as leading to duplication and waste (Thomas 1974). The publicly owned competitor model was subject to careful scrutiny in the banking sector. Evidence advanced by Compton Bourne (1974) shows that such duplication is possible, and that an ideology of development based on public ownership is not a sufficient condition to trigger development in an economy dominated by profit-maximizing banks.

The pragmatic nationalist approach had its strongest expression in Trinidad and Tobago. According to Mills (1981: 51), the public sector was assigned the role of creating new jobs and developing new areas of production. Nationalization was to protect the national interest against foreign domination. During the 1980s this nationalist justification of state ownership was embodied in the analysis of Frank Rampersad (1988: 15), who argued that the weakness of the indigenous capitalist class and the marginal role of foreign investment justified involvement of the state in the production process. According to Rampersad, the indigenous investors had not demonstrated a willingness to extend the frontiers of production. Foreign investment was mainly involved in resource-based industries. Primarily because of the lumpiness of capital in certain types of investments, the local private sector was unable to mobilize the resources required to sustain these investments during the gestation period. However, despite the above analysis, both Rampersad and the government of Trinidad and Tobago were aware of the need for divestment in areas where public enterprise was a financial burden.

The government of Barbados, between 1966 and 1976, favored a very limited form of direct state participation. The government instituted statutory corporations in areas where the state could provide an impetus to private development in certain leading sectors, or in sectors where private investors were unwilling to become heavily involved. Thus, the building of the Hilton Hotel and the creation of the Barbados Industrial Development Corporation were really initiatives to encourage further private sector investment. The establishment of the Pine Hill Dairy in 1966 and the Agricultural Development Corporation was intended to provide institutional support for agricultural diversification. The Agricultural Development Corporation was designed to stimulate development in the private sector, as well as to manage government-owned estates.

The Barbados government's aversion to heavy state ownership of commercial ventures in the 1960s and early 1970s is also seen in the attitude toward establishment of indigenous commercial banking. Errol Barrow, the prime minister of Barbados between 1966 and 1976, argued that an indigenous state-owned commercial bank was not necessary in Barbados because there were sufficient institutions concerned with financing commercial ventures. He had believed in the 1960s that the nature of the Savings Bank of Barbados should remain unchanged, that is, as an institution for mobilizing small savings. Further, he stated that the government had no intention of financing imports, which was a principal function of foreign commercial banks. His preference was for development banking rather than indigenous banking.[5]

In the late 1970s and 1980s the Barbadian government owned and controlled a number of commercial ventures which ultimately became financial failures. They were Caribbean Airways, a national airline; the Arawak Cement Plant; and Caricargo. The government held the view that the public sector had to intervene in the economy during recessionary conditions to prop up the private sector. Government policy in the early 1980s appeared to give greater support to ownership of commercial ventures, than in the 1960s.

The ideological approach to state ownership influenced public enterprise expansion in Guyana and Jamaica. According to Edwin Jones (1981: 18), "control of the commanding heights" was a socialist notion advocated by the Jamaican government during the 1970s, influencing public ownership of utilities such as bus transportation, telephones, and electricity, as well as hotels. In Guyana, the regime of cooperative socialism focused on nationalization of foreign property, which aided the expansion of the state bureaucratically, ideologically, and militarily (Thomas 1988: 225).

Thomas (1988) advances the view that the expansion of the state sector in Jamaica in the 1970s was at too high a cost. The nationalizations were paid for promptly and in full. The expansion of public enterprise was also accompanied by a severe shortage of the trained managers needed to ensure that the enterprises were efficiently run. Thomas also argues that in the Caribbean the purchases to effect nationalization increased the countries' foreign debt. The resort to management contracts after nationalization also led to a drain of income.

ARE PUBLIC ENTERPRISES INEFFICIENT?

A central argument used to support privatization is the "inefficiency" of public enterprise. Various explanations for such "inefficiency" have been advanced by economists, such as Heidi Vernon-Wortzel and Lawrence Wortzel (1989), Steve Hanke (1987a), and Richard Hemming and Ali Mansoor (1987). Firstly, they argue that the performance of a state enterprise is not only a function of state ownership per se, but also a function of the type of management and the appropriate culture in the firm. Some state-owned enterprises function efficiently. Nevertheless, the organizational culture of state enterprises tends to be government oriented rather than customer oriented. This is reflected in political interference in day-to-day decision making, which in many cases prevents public sector managers from pursuing strategic planning.

Secondly, a view is advanced from property rights theory. According to Hanke (1987a), different forms of property ownership give rise to different economic incentives and different economic results. Private enterprises are free to use and exchange their private property rights, which give individual owners a claim on the assets of the enterprise. Private-sector managers ultimately face the bottom line, which measures the profits or losses that owners claim. On the other hand, public managers and employers allocate assets that belong to taxpayers. Such managers do not bear the costs of their inefficient decisions, nor do they gain from efficient behavior. Only the politicians are ultimately accountable to the taxpayers. The political interference and property rights theories are generally strong in explaining the managerial drawbacks of public enterprise. Privatization is seen as a means of improving the efficiency of enterprises by limiting the scope of political interference.

The principal economic problem facing public commercial enterprises in the Caribbean is financial inefficiency. A full study of financially inefficient public enterprises is beyond the scope of this book, but it is still appropriate to discuss a few of these unprofitable ventures. An interesting example is the Caribbean Air Cargo Company (Caricargo), which commenced operations in February 1981. Total share capital at commencement was Bds$9.0 million, which represent equal shareholding between the governments of Barbados and Trinidad and Tobago. In the first year of operations the company's capital requirements were Bds$17.9 million, to be financed by equity capital and loans.[6]

The Caricargo venture, which depended on two B707 aircraft to transport cargo, was undercapitalized from the start. By December 1982 the company had a debt burden of Bds$17.6 million; it had already approached its shareholders in October 1982 requesting an equity injection, outlining the increasing debt to equity ratio. However, an equity injection of Bds$5.0 million was not disbursed until 1984, by which time the company had increased its overdraft with the Barbados National Bank (BNB) in Barbados to finance the working capital deficiency. This heavy dependence on the BNB continued up to 1990. During the early 1980s the Trinidad and Tobago market had accounted for 80 percent of the airline's freight, but toward the late 1980s this market accounted for only 35 percent thereby reducing the company's earning capacity.

By September 30, 1989, the debt of Caricargo stood at Bds$51.1 million to the BNB, Bds$1.7 million to the National Commerical Bank of Trinidad and Tobago, Bds$7.7 million to the Caribbean Development Bank, and Bds$16.0 million to other creditors. The major contributor to this debt was the high cost of maintaining the two aircraft, which came to Bds$16.9 million between 1981 and 1988. From very early in its operations the airline was insolvent.

In the case of Caricargo, the public sector attempted to run an undercapitalized airline. The private sector has greater experience in cargo handling and lifting as well as airline management. By the end of 1990 Caricargo had ceased flying, and its two airplanes had been sold. However, the company remained in existence, with large liabilities to its major creditors, especially BNB.

Other examples of unprofitable state enterprises can be drawn from the Trinidad and Tobago experience. The available evidence shows that in 1985 the non-petroleum state enterprises in Trinidad and Tobago were very large dissavers, with expenditures exceeding revenue by almost TT$700.00 million (Ryan 1988: Appendix 4). Dennis Pantin (1988: 33) had identified a number of natural gas based projects which recorded accumulated net losses between 1982 and 1986. The Urea Company and the Methanol Company registered net losses of TT$106.7 million and TT$125.7 million, respectively. The Iron and Steel Company of Trinidad and Tobago (ISCOTT) also made accumulated losses of TT$1,132.7 million between 1982 and 1986, with losses being recorded in each of the five years. According to Pantin (1988: 37), capacity utilization was less than optimal at ISCOTT, resulting in high unit costs of production. This was worsened by a downward trend in steel prices and increased protectionism on the part of the United States. The operation of these inefficient enterprises had resulted in considerable domestic resource costs, as well as foreign exchange losses.

THE ECONOMICS OF PRIVATIZATION

The major economic issue involved in privatization is that of efficiency. Property rights theory suggests that public enterprises operating in competitive markets should be privatized. The argument applies to manufacturing industries, airlines, and other competitive service industries. Competition provides greater incentive to private managers to increase allocative and productive efficiency.[7]

The replacement of a public monopoly by a private monopoly may not necessarily lead to significant efficiency gains. However, it is generally recognized that privatization can reduce political interference and enhance the quality of management. In any case, a private monopoly in the field of public utilities has to be regulated, to guarantee social efficiency by way of equitable pricing arrangements.

The above arguments need some modifications. Some governments are not inclined to privatize, by way of divestiture, enterprises which are profitable or socially efficient, where social efficiency is a highly valued objective. It is contended that privatization should be considered mainly for those commercial enterprises which have become a financial burden on the taxpayers. Continued maintenance of such loss-making enterprises also increases their financial inefficiency, because public sector firms have easy access to credit and government subsidies and are protected from competition.

There are also political constraints involved in privatization. The political directorate may regard certain public utilities as employment agencies. Privatization reduces such political influence. Trade unions, too, may fear that privatization would result in increased unemployment, thereby reducing their political influence. One must, therefore, address the political economy of privatization, rather than confine the analysis mainly to economic efficiency arguments (Poole 1987).

Although economic theory gives general guidelines to privatization, the political decision to privatize an enterprise should be based on the application of specific economic and political criteria to the special case. Such criteria would include economic and social efficiency, financial viability, managerial performance, and the perceived impact of the privatized enterprise on employment, prices, and output.

Privatization, in my view, is not recommended for certain public goods or public utilities in small developing countries, where social efficiency is the objective function of government. This argument applies to the areas of water management, primary and secondary education, health and social security, sanitation, infrastructure and rural transport. These services are subject to market failure, and government has a responsibility to provide them in the interest of social efficiency and income distribution. The private sector can complement the government's provision by contracting certain services, for instance, low-cost housing. The Barbadian private sector, for example, is already heavily involved in transport and communications, although rural public transport should not be left to the whims and fancies of the market mechanism. Private provision of health services should complement public provision.

The theory of property rights suggests that financial institutions develop more efficiently when left to the private sector. Historically, financial institutions tend to be more operationally efficient in competitive markets driven by the profit motive. However, a private development bank is not likely to be socially efficient if it attempts to maximize profits in pursuit of its shareholders' interests. Privatization of an ailing development bank may not be the solution to the problem of long-term development finance in small systems.

Barbados presents the case of a small open economy where privatization is recommended in a few cases of financially unviable commercial enterprises. Barbados did not adopt the state ownership model on a scale as extensive as Jamaica, Guyana, or Trinidad and Tobago. By following a conservative plan of development, Barbados remained predominantly a market-oriented service economy. The private sector dominates tourism, manufacturing, agriculture, commerce, banking, financial services, and general consumer services, while the state is entrenched in the area of public goods the provision of which should not be left completely to the market mechanism.

Kenneth Wiltshire (1987) has identified a number of lessons from the British experience which are important for small Caribbean countries considering privatization. The first lesson of the British privatization process is the concept of "dressing up" the enterprise for sale. This involves restructuring the enterprise until it can compete in the private sector. Dressing up normally involves a cost, since revenues are taken from the consolidated fund. It also involves a redistribution of income from taxpayers to ultimate shareholders. However, in a small country like those in the Caribbean, a government with a heavy fiscal deficit is not likely to undertake any substantial restructuring of an enterprise before sale. The dressing up process is also likely to encounter serious political opposition.

The other issue in the British experience noted by Wiltshire concerns the price at which the enterprise is sold to the private sector. British enterprises were usually sold on the share sale method. Wiltshire (1987: 66) maintains that this type of pricing has been intensely criticized because of the rapid rise in share prices after the sale. Criticism of the process implies that in order to give the privatization program increased momentum, the British government undervalued the enterprises before sale by underpricing the shares. Although the share sale method helps to broaden the structure of private ownership, as well as enable employee shareholding, there is one constraint on this method in small Caribbean countries. The share capital market is relatively small, and the countries' stock exchanges are embryonic. Therefore, if privatization is pursued on a large scale using this method, efforts will have to be made to increase the capacity of the markets to take the float. In the Caribbean the promotion of a regional stock exchange has been one step in the direction of overcoming the small size of national stock exchanges.

Wiltshire (1987: 58–103) outlines a number of criticisms that have been made of the British process. One of these is that the process failed to ensure competition in the industries where privatization occurred, thereby appearing to convert public monopolies into private monopolies. As we have seen, an argument for privatization is that it increases efficiency by fostering competition; however, privatization of a public monopoly can hardly ensure increased competition. The possibility of increased competition after a privatization program usually depends on the type of market in which the industry operates. In the case of small open economies, this will depend on whether the industry is import substitutive or export oriented, on the degree of protectionism offered to the industry in reducing external competition, and so forth. Given the high levels of protectionism in Caribbean manufacturing, the greatest opportunities for competition offered by privatization seem to be in the area of tourism services.

Another criticism of the British process is that it "sells the family silver," that is, that the revenue from the sale of a public asset should not be placed in the consolidated fund, but should be earmarked for future generations and future public uses (Wiltshire 1987: xiii). There is some support for this position in small countries, in the sense that a sale of real assets should not be used to finance current expenditures such as wages and salaries, but should be placed in a fund for futher capital accumulation. The British experience also suggests that in the pursuit of privatization, the governments of small countries should adequately safeguard their national interest from foreign influences. Selling the family silver to the local private sector is preferable to selling a country's assets to foreigners.

DIVESTMENT POLICY IN THE CARIBBEAN

Trinidad and Tobago

The Trinidad and Tobago divestment policy in the late 1980s and early 1990s was a response to the gross inefficiency of the state enterprise sector. The National Alliance for Reconstruction (NAR) government, which came to power in December 1986, was committed to a policy of divestment. However, this policy was only part of a comprehensive strategy to reform the public enterprise sector, a strategy that was fully articulated in the budget speeches of 1989 and 1990. The government's policy was guided by the need to restructure certain enterprises as well as implement the divestment of others. The 1989 budget speech delivered by Arthur Robinson, minister of finance, stated:

> The Government will continue in the ownership of certain large scale and medium-scale economic activities, particularly in the energy sector and down stream industries. It will also seek through divestment, joint ventures with both the local and foreign private sector investors in several areas in which it now participates as sole owner.[8]

The 1990 budget of Selby Wilson restated the government's policy with regard to public enterprise to include the following objectives:

1. to prune the sector of enterprises that are clearly considered non-viable and cannot be justified on social grounds;
2. to reduce our participation in other enterprises where a greater private sector involvement seems to provide the opportunity for greater benefits for the society as a whole;
3. to restructure the remaining enterprises so that they operate more efficiently and more in keeping with accepted business practices.[9]

The 1990 Trinidad and Tobago budget speech also identified some of the achievements of the above program. The level of government transfers and loans to state enterprises and public utilities was reduced from TT$1,135.5 million in 1983 to TT$438.5 million in 1989.[10] Further, two state enterprises, the Methanol and Urea Companies, benefited significantly from internal restructuring and internal productivity improvements. The Methanol Company went from a deficit of TT$30.7 million in 1986 to a net profit of TT$129.1 million in 1988 and a projected profit of TT$95.3 million in 1989. The government also divested part of its equity in the Telephone Company (TELCO), Trinidad Cement Limited (TCL) and the National Commercial Bank. In the last two companies, the objective was to spread equity among a cross-section of people, including the employees of the companies. In the case of TCL the government limited individual shareholding to 10 percent of the issued share capital. ISCOTT was also leased, at a fixed rental of US$10.8 million per year.[11]

The Trinidad and Tobago program emphasized restructuring of the state enterprise sector rather than complete privatization. It was envisaged that there would be greater participation of citizens in the share ownership of enterprises; however, the government never intended to transfer a high degree of control to the local private sector. Indeed, the government's Public Sector Investment Programme (PSIP) was designed to stimulate the economy. It was estimated that for the year 1990, expenditure on the PSIP would total

TT$1,001.7 million, divided between government capital projects and invest-ments by the state enterprises.[12] Indeed, this concern of the Trinidad and Tobago government with preserving the "family silver" is a consequence of an economic history characterized by foreign domination. Implicit in the government's policy on public enterprise is a commitment not to revert to the type of foreign ownership of the pre-independence period.

Barbados

Between 1986 and 1991, the Barbadian government adopted an ambiva-lent attitude toward divestment. The manifesto of the DLP government, which assumed power in 1986, stated that the public sector must continue to play a role in the provision of private goods and services for purchase by individuals. It was the intention of the DLP government to invest in and promote the production and distribution of private goods, in areas where government initiative is required.[13] The government's strategy had three major objectives:

1. to emphasize joint ventures between government and the private sector;
2. to put an end to the practice of allowing publicly owned businesses producing non-strategic goods to continue to incur losses;
3. to undertake complete divestment in cases where analysis reveals that such action is appropriate.[14]

There is strong evidence to support the view that the DLP government was in favor of a plan to privatize the Hilton Hotel, the Heywoods Holiday Village Hotel, and the Arawak Cement Plant. This position was articulated by Errol Barrow, the prime minister at that time. His plan rested on the view that the taxpayers should be relieved of the burden of supporting these enter-prises, since the tax money could be more effectively used for providing hous-ing.[15] Further, Barrow sanctioned the discontinuation of the government-owned Caribbean Airways in 1987, because the national airline was losing at the rate of Bds$9.0 million a year, on two flights a week to Britain from Barbados.[16]

Barrow's approach to divestment rested purely on the argument that it was necessary to reduce the high costs to the government of operating in-efficient parastatals. However, it should be noted that the Barbados Transport Board, which operated with large annual deficits, was not on the govern-ment's agenda for divestment. Perhaps the government regarded the Trans-port Board as a strategic good in a social sense. Shortly before his death in 1987, Barrow decided against privatization of the Hilton and Heywoods Hotels and the Arawak Cement Plant. For the period between 1987 and 1990, there does not appear to be any documentary evidence to suggest that the Barbados government was firmly in favor of divestment of public sector enter-prises. The IMF program in Barbados in 1991 required the Barbados government to reduce its transfers to statutory corporations, and the government appeared to be under pressure from the IMF and World Bank to privatize certain public enterprises. The IMF letter of intent of October 1991 acknowledged the government's intention of divesting certain private interprises, including the Arawak Cement Plant, the Pine Hill Dairy, and Caricargo.

Jamaica

This section draws on Mills (1989) to interpret Jamaica's divestment policy after 1980. Mills (1989: 386) states that divestment in Jamaica was really initiated under Edward Seaga's Jamaica Labour Party (JLP) government, which had established a divestment committee by March 1981, to pursue divestment of equity and control in commerical enterprises at prices based on commercial criteria and the national interest. Certain objectives and priorities guided this approach. Divestment policy should ensure that public funds were not misallocated to inefficient enterprises. Seaga's government also believed that the policy would reduce the burden on the government's budget. The priorities for divestment would be determined by the budgetary impact of the policy, by the economic impact, by employment and linkage, and by the social impact. This approach was part of an overall program by the JLP government that was based on liberalizing the market system through deregulation and the removal of import restrictions. The JLP program represented an ideological shift from the previous regime, that of Michael Manley's People's National Party (PNP, 1972–1980). Manley's policy emphasized state control of the economy. The JLP approach was also driven by the need to ease the economic recession in Jamaica, which became an IMF-controlled economy during the 1980s (Mills 1989: 387–388).

By 1990 Jamaica's experience with divestment was more extensive than that of Trinidad and Tobago. I was unable to obtain reliable, detailed information on the Guyanese experience, and so cannot make definitive statements on the extent of divestment in that country. The National Investment Bank of Jamaica (NIBJ) is the divestment/privatization arm of the government. However, it should be noted that privatization is not the only role of this institution, which is responsible for the management of new and existing investments by the government and the provision of commercial investment banking services.[17] This institution has played a pivotal role in the success of some divestments in Jamaica.

Perhaps the most successful privatization in Jamaica was the National Commercial Bank (NCB) in 1986. This was one of the largest companies to be handled by the NIBJ, which effected the sale of 51 percent of its shares, for J$91.0 million. Mills (1989: 394) advanced the view that the success of this privatization was due to "a well thought-out study of the potential market, the Bank's earning record, an attractive share price, an advanced publicity and public education campaign and the state of the market at the time."

The privatization of NCB may become a model for commercial bank privatization in the Caribean.

Other divestments in Jamaica before 1990 are also worthy of note. The Caribbean Cement Company was divested by the NIBJ, which sold 71 percent of its shares in 1987. In 1989 the NIBJ divested three companies. West Indies Pulp and Paper, Jamaican Gypsum and Quarries, and Jamaica Aqualapia.[18]

CONCLUSIONS

The economic circumstances of the 1980s forced most Caribbean governments to change their attitude toward ownership of public enterprises. These enterprises were unable to pay their way during the recessionary conditions, and many of them became a burden on taxpayers. Public enterprises showed high levels of inefficiency and reported large losses. The movement toward privatization also reflected a new attitude world wide to the importance of the free market mechanism. This was associated with the demise of many socialist regimes and with changing perspectives on democracy and freedom. In this context, Caribbean governments had no other choice but to reduce the degree of regulation in these small economies to restimulate private sector enterprise.

NOTES

1. For useful comments on the extent of state-owned enterprises in developing countries, see Berg (1987).

2. From the large literature on British nationalization, see Kelf-Cohen (1969).

3. See United Nations, *The Impact of MNCs on Development and on International Relations* (New York: the UN, 1974).

4. For an informative analysis of the views of this school of thought, which comprised West Indian economists including George Beckford, Norman Girvan, Lloyd Best, Owen Jefferson, and Alister McIntyre, see Richard Bernal et al. (1984).

5. The evidence to support this position is contained in a statement by Errol Barrow to the Barbados Parliament in 1972. See *Barbados, House of Assembly Debates, First Session of 1971-76*, p. 408.

6. Based on a ministerial statement delivered by the Minister of International Transport, Philip Greaves, to the Barbados House of Assembly on November 21, 1989. See *Barbados, House of Assembly Debates (Official Report)*, November 21, 1989, pp. 4385-4387.

7. For good surveys of the economic and political issues involved in privatization see Van de Walle (1989) and Vernon Wortzel and Wortzel (1989).

8. Trinidad and Tobago, *Budget Speech and Taxation Measures 1989*, December 16, 1988, p. 17.

9. Trinidad and Tobago, *Budget Speech 1990*, December 22, 1989, p.5.

10. Ibid., p. 6.

11. Ibid.

12. Ibid., p. 12.

13. *Manifesto of the Democratic Labour Party 1986,* Barbados, p. 7.

14. Ibid., pp. 7–8.

15. *Barbados House of Assembly Debates,* First Session 1986–91, March 16, 1987, pp. 788–789.

16. Ibid., p. 795.

17. See National Investment Bank of Jamaica, *Annual Report 1990,* chairman's statement, p. 4.

18. Ibid., p. 10.

5

STABILIZATION POLICY

Fiscal disequilibrium is a major cause of balance of payments deficits in small countries. Nevertheless, it is not the only cause; in Caribbean economies, monetary disequilibrium and disequilibrium in the tradeable goods sector are also important factors, and these also have a bearing on IMF stabilization policies. Monetary disequilibrium arises from excessive total domestic credit expansion, which increases the nominal money supply. If the demand for money is stable, citizens attempt to off-load these excess balances by purchasing imports, thereby running down foreign reserve holdings.

Disequilibrium in the tradeable goods sector is the result of "policy imposed" distortions in the product markets of developing countries (Balassa 1982: 1027). This phenomenon is reflected in high levels of protectionism, which give rise to inefficiencies in resource allocation and a bias against exports and in favor of import substitution. According to Balassa (1982), high levels of protectionism result in a loss of economies of scale and a low level of capacity utilization, in producing for limited domestic markets. Further, the high production costs of tradeable goods, particularly high wage rates, reduce international competitiveness and slow down the rate of growth of exports. Caribbean economies are not highly competitive with the rest of the world. However, the literature on their foreign trade problems is extensive, and I have only indicated one source of these problems here.

During the 1970s Caribbean governments made little effort to correct the distortions in the tradeable goods sectors of their economies. Their response to recession was adoption of expansionary monetary and fiscal policies, which accelerated their foreign reserves depletion. Some governments blamed the performance of the economies on "structural factors" and "external forces." Although these influences do play a role in generating balance of payments disequilibrium, my view is that policy-induced distortions in money and in product and factor markets were stronger forces, causing persistent balance of payments deficits, particularly in Jamaica and Guyana, as well as Barbados in the late 1980s and early 1990s.

Balance of payments disequilibrium caused by the above constellation of factors explains why the IMF had to intervene in the economic affairs of certain Caribbean countries in the late 1970s and 1980s. The principal objective of this chapter is an interpretation of IMF stabilization programs in the Caribbean. A general discussion of the theoretical underpinnings of the IMF policy packages will be followed by an outline of the salient characteristics of these programs in Barbados, Trinidad and Tobago, Guyana, and Jamaica. The literature on Jamaica is extensive, and the analysis avoids duplication of this work, leaning instead on the well documented work of Boyd (1988), but the reader should consult articles by Adlith Brown (1981); Norman Girvan, Richard Bernal, and Wesley Hughes (1980); Jennifer Sharpley (1984), and Colin Bullock (1986). The section on Guyana draws on the work of Elmer Harris (1988) and Donna Danns (1990), and the material on Barbados is drawn from the Central Bank of Barbados *Economic Review* for December 1982 and from Blackman (1989). For the Trinidad and Tobago case, I examine closely the 1988 and 1990 letters of intent. The effectiveness of these programs in meeting certain proximate targets, as well as the overall balance of payments goal, is then discussed.

Because of the multi-faceted nature of stabilization policy, this chapter has to be highly selective. Although my work so far has been concerned primarily with public finance, stabilization policy is a mixture of fiscal, monetary, income, and exchange rate policies. The primary focus, therefore, will be a discussion of the performance criteria laid down by the IMF. To the extent that the devaluation instrument played a pivotal role in these programs, the analysis interprets the effectiveness of devaluation in the Caribbean context.

IMF STABILIZATION PROGRAMS: A GENERAL DISCUSSION

My analysis subscribes to the view of Wilfred David (1985) that the IMF adopts an eclectic theoretical approach to its stabilization programs, based on the monetary approach to the balance of payments (the Polak 1957 version), Keynesian expenditure theory, and neoclassical free market theory. The monetary approach predominantly informs the IMF's demand management policies, especially its credit policies, while neoclassical theory determines its policy of market adjustment through implementation of appropriate prices.

The model of Jacques Polak (1957) provided the theoretical foundation of IMF demand management policies. This early attempt to formalize a relationship between domestic credit and balance of payments was further developed by Polak and Boissonneault (1959–60) and Polak and Victor Argy (1971). This approach stimulated further model building by other IMF economists, including Aghevli and Khan (1980) and Khan (1976). The fundamental conclusion of the monetary approach is that there is a correspondence between domestic credit expansion and foreign reserve losses. The original Polak model derived this relation, but the model was under-specified. It included an import function according to which imports were related to income by the marginal propensity to import. Income was equal to the product of the velocity of circulation of money and the money supply. The latter was determined by net foreign assets and the net domestic assets of the banking system. The original model is not very clear about the underlying assumptions influencing the process of money market adjustment; the role of fiscal variables, including the impact of the fiscal deficit on the monetary base; or the role of the price level. However, by incorporating structural variables such as imports and exports, Polak succeeded in formalizing the relationship between credit expansion, trade expansion, and foreign reserve changes. Aghevli and Khan (1980) retained the monetary approach and remedied some of the deficiencies of the original Polak model. This was done by tighter specifications of money demand, inflation, and expenditure functions, thereby incorporating the version of the monetary approach developed by Harry Johnson (1972), while retaining elements of the early Polak approach. Aghevli and Khan (1980: 702) reached the conclusion that the actual discretionary policies followed by government authorities in some developing countries resulted in a generally higher inflation rate and worse balance of payments, but brought a better growth performance than if the governments had allowed the domestic credit component of the money stock to grow by a constant percentage per annum.

The monetary approach to the balance of payments, as shown in Chapter 2 of this book, focuses on proximate causation. This is why the IMF has been criticized as adopting too narrow an approach to the diagnosis of the balance of payments problem. Some writers, including Wilfred David (1985), have argued that the IMF demand management approach is a broader paradigm which embraces both Keynesian and monetarist doctrines. This view can be supported, because the IMF approach is concerned ultimately with reducing total absorption. To the extent that credit facilitates the expansion of absorption, the IMF policy paradigm advocates control of credit at its source.

The other arm of IMF stabilization policy focuses heavily on neoclassical intra-market price adjustment. This involves the correction of overvalued exchange rates by means of devaluation, liberalization or increases of real interest rates, removal of subsidies, price controls, and trade restrictions. The IMF recommendation of wage restraint may be considered from two theoretical perspectives. Firstly, high wage rates are a factor in raising a nation's export prices, because wages may exceed productivity. Secondly, high wages augment levels of domestic absorption, thereby affecting adversely the balance of payments. The policy of appropriate prices can be described as economic liberalization and is in keeping with the IMF mandate to stimulate free trade throughout the world.

According to Colin Bullock (1986: 132), failure to introduce appropriate prices could result in a number of adverse consequences. The negative consequences of an overvalued exchange rate include excess demand for foreign exchange and reserve losses; foreign exchange rationing, which may lead to high bureaucratic costs and corruption; foreign currency speculation; and parallel market development. Negative real interest rates lead to a diversion of funds into less efficient uses, credit rationing, and disincentive to save in domestic currency, with its implications for capital flight. Wage rates which are too high raise domestic costs, augment government deficits, and reduce international competitiveness. Subsidies and price controls generally inhibit market efficiency. David (1985) provides an interesting discussion of the effects of interventionist policy measures in developing countries.

The considerations above add up to a valid interpretation of the IMF point of view on the process of economic adjustment in developing countries. The analysis by the IMF economists proceeds from the assumption of disequilibrium in the money, factor, and product markets of these economies. These economists particularly emphasize exchange rate disequilibrium as a cause of payments imbalances. Nevertheless, the IMF policy of deep exchange rate devaluation can be hazardous in open developing countries. Very often the balance of payments effects of price correction, particularly exchange rate devaluation, cannot be predicted with a high degree of certainty. This approach is likely to be less manageable than demand management policy, whereby credit targets can be administered and monetary performance monitored more accurately.

Modifying Cheryl Payer (1974: 33), I now outline the main components of a typical IMF stabilization program:

1. Abolition or liberalization of foreign exchange and import controls
2. Exchange rate devaluation
3. Domestic demand management policies, including:
   a. control of central bank credit to government and commercial bank credit
   b. control of the government deficit
   c. increases in indirect taxation
4. Deregulation, including removal of price controls, abolition of subsidies, and in some cases privatization
5. Wage restraint, including wage cuts in the public service
6. Settlement of arrears of foreign payment
7. Limitation of short-term and medium-term foreign borrowing.

The literature on the criticisms of this program is quite extensive, and only some of the main criticisms can be mentioned here. Firstly, the IMF programs have been criticized as being anti-developmental, since they focus on the balance of payments and ignore structural problems in the economy. Secondly, the IMF has been accused of emphasizing too heavily the internal monetary causes of balance of payments deficits, and relegating the importance of external factors. Thirdly, IMF programs have the reputation of being too harsh, since they ignore the high costs of adjustment, particularly the worsening of the income distribution which follows devaluation. Fourthly, the devaluation instrument has been heavily criticized as being an ineffective tool of balance of payments adjustment. I shall return to these issues in the section of this chapter that evaluates stabilization policy in the Caribbean. The next section describes the main features of the IMF programs in Barbados, Guyana, Jamaica, and Trinidad and Tobago.

COUNTRY PROGRAMS

Barbados

On October 4, 1982, the IMF approved a stand-by arrangement for Barbados authorizing the purchase of SDR 31.87 million, or the equivalent of 125 percent of the Barbados quota of SDR 25.5 million. The performance criteria were defined with respect to limits on the net domestic assets of the banking system, limits on banking system credit to the government, and limits on short-term and medium-term borrowing. During the 18-month program Barbados passed all the performance criteria.[1] Courtney Blackman (1989: 62), who was governor of the Central Bank of Barbados at that time, maintains that "an exchange rate devaluation was discussed but not seriously contemplated." The Barbadian dollar had been tied to the U.S. dollar at a rate of US$1.00 = Bds$2.00 on July 5, 1975. The rate has not been devalued subsequently, and it played a role in stabilizing the rate of inflation in the Barbadian economy during the 1980s.

Barbados adopted an IMF-style fiscal and monetary program in the first half of 1991, before signing a second agreement with the IMF later that year. This program comprised increases in interest rates, massive layoffs in the public sector, and reductions in public expenditure. Barbados's problems were linked to heavy public spending in 1990, at a time when the economy was contracting. The economy had recorded a 3.5 percent decline in real GDP in 1990.

On September 17, 1991, the Barbados government announced an austerity stabilization package, which formed the basis of a letter of intent submitted later to the IMF. The program with the IMF involved four components: reduction in public expenditures, increases in public revenues, rebuilding of the reserves, and resuscitation of the productive sectors. The IMF program for rebuilding the reserves was intended to guarantee US$28.4 million on a stand-by basis and US$29.7 million from the IMF's Compensatory and

Contingency Financing Facility. The program placed most emphasis on the first two components, but it was not clear how the productive sectors would be resuscitated.

The first aspect of the expenditure reduction measures, which encountered the most opposition, was an 8 percent cut in the emoluments of permanent and temporary employees in the public service. The government maintained that a voluntary pay cut was an alternative to devaluing the Barbadian dollar. This line of reasoning was invalid, however, since a devaluation impacts on the whole economy in terms of increasing the price of imports, raising the nominal value of tax revenues, and generally affecting standards of living. The second major component of expenditure reduction was severance of over 2,000 public workers in the second half of 1991.

The expenditure reduction measures were accompanied by increased taxation, composed of a 4 percent surtax, called the "stabilization tax" on incomes above Bds$15,000 and 1.5 percent on incomes below Bds$15,000. Heavy consumption taxes and increased levies were included in the package. The program also reduced import duty concessions, as well as stamp duty concessions to manufacturers, by Bds$16 million.

The 1991 IMF program announced by the Barbados government was criticized heavily at all levels of Barbadian society. The unions protested the 8 percent pay cut in the public service. In everyday discussions, the government was blamed for the crisis, with critics identifying heavy election spending in 1990 as the major cause. The manufacturers protested against the removal of import duty concessions. They argued that this policy would destroy the manufacturing sector, since the manufacturing enterprises were too small to compete in export markets without concessions. Overall, this economic dislocation was regarded by many analysts as the worst crisis of the Barbadian economy since World War II. The main dimensions of the problem were severe economic recession, fiscal disequilibrium, depletion of the foreign reserves of the central bank, and balance of payments disequilibrium. The crisis continued into 1992, and its major manifestations were massive unemployment and business closures.

Guyana

This section relies heavily on the work of Danns (1990) and Harris (1988). Negative foreign reserves and a weak economy forced Guyana into the hands of the IMF after 1977. I have already outlined some of the main causes of economic deterioration in Guyana in Chapter 2, including the role played by the fiscal deficit and the burden of the state enterprises in the Guyana economy.

According to Danns (1990), the 1978 stand-by agreement was intended to last for one year and was designed to achieve major increases in public savings. The agreement also required a more equitable distribution of credit between the private and public sectors. The performance criteria set limits on the net domestic assets of the Bank of Guyana and net bank credit to the public sector, limits on external payments arrears and on external loans contracted. Guyana observed all the performance criteria under this arrangement.[2] The 1978 agreement was followed by extended fund facilities in 1979 and 1980. The 1979 program proposed policy changes aimed at constraining public consumption and shifting the emphasis toward capital formation. The 1979 and 1980 programs were abandoned because the targets set by the IMF had not been met.[3] Primarily because of overdue financial obligations to the IMF, Guyana was declared ineligible for IMF financing on May 15, 1985 (Danns 1990: 150). By June 1990 the total overdue obligations of Guyana to the Fund were SDR 107.1. Guyana's eligibility to use the resources of the IMF was restored with effect from June 20, 1990, as a result of bridging finance supplied by other countries. Guyana entered a new program with the Fund in July 31, 1990 (Danns 1990: 150).

The stabilization policies in Guyana were accompanied by deep devaluations of the Guyana dollar. Between 1978 and 1981 the Guyana dollar was pegged to the U.S. dollar at the rate of US$1.00 = G$2.55. In 1981 the authorities fixed the rate of exchange of the Guyana dollar to the movement in the composite rate of a basket of currencies comprising U.S. dollars, pounds sterling, deutsche marks, yens, and Trinidad and Tobago dollars. In reality, however, the exchange rate continued to move in sympathy with the U.S. dollar. Guyana experienced frequent devaluations during the 1980s, leading to a flourishing parallel black market as U.S. dollars became increasingly scarce. The Guyana dollar was devalued in 1987 to G$10.00 = US$1.00, and again in 1989 to G$33.00 = US$1.00. By February 1991 the Guyana dollar had again been devalued, moving to G$101.75 = US$1.00.[4]

Jamaica

Jamaica's involvement with the IMF is a heavily researched topic. In this section I refer briefly to the major policy programs. Boyd (1988) and Bullock (1986) give extensive treatment of Jamaica's stabilization programs during the 1980s. The main policy agreements summarized by Boyd (1988: 25–66) for the period 1977–1984 were as follows:

1. *August 1977.* A two-year stand-by agreement, suspended soon after Jamaica failed the first quarterly test.
2. *May 1978.* A three-year extended fund facility, pursued for one year.
3. *June 1979.* Renegotiation of the 1978 extended fund facility. In December 1979 Jamaica failed to meet three performance tests, and the agreement was terminated.
4. *April 1981.* An agreement with the Fund for SDR 537 million, to cover fiscal 1981/82, 1982/83, and 1983/84.
5. *January 1984.* A stand-by program for one year, providing funds totalling SDR 64.0 million.

In 1987 Jamaica also finalized a US$150 million stand-by agreement with the Fund and fulfilled a precondition for rescheduling other debts. A new stand-by agreement was also negotiated in 1990, by which Jamaica would obtain credit amounting to US$108 million over a 15-month period. Jamaica failed many of the performance tests related to the above agreements, which concentrated on the restriction of bank credit. Frequent devaluations were also employed (Boyd 1988: 45–47). Exchange rate policy in Jamaica included a variety of regimes ranging from dual exchange rate systems, monthly devaluations, parallel market rates, and foreign exchange auctioning.[5]

Trinidad and Tobago

The continued decline in foreign exchange reserves in the late 1980s forced the government of Trinidad and Tobago to enter a 14-month stand-by arrangement with the IMF in the amount of SDR 99 million in early 1989.[6] According to the Trinidad and Tobago government's 1990 budget speech, this arrangement was required as a precondition for applications to reschedule the country's external debt to creditor international commercial banks and to Paris Club official creditors. The 1989 program aimed at reducing domestic and external imbalances and promoting economic growth. The aims of the program included a reduction of the public sector deficit from 7 percent of GDP in 1988 to 4 percent of GDP in 1989 and 1 percent of GDP in 1991.[7] Quarterly limits for the central government's borrowing requirement were also established. The balance of payments policy envisaged a reduction in the current account deficit as a percentage of GDP by development of non-oil exports, liberalization of trade and exchange systems, and limitations on accumulation of debt. Exchange rate flexibility was also advocated, to reduce the ratio of the current account of the balance of payments to GDP. The policy measures also included limitations on central bank advances to commercial banks. The program also emphasized that prices should reflect the interplay of market forces. The policy limited price controls to a selected number of essential goods and services. Finally, the program was preceded by a devaluation of the Trinidad and Tobago dollar on August 17, 1988, from TT$3.60 = US$1.00 to TT$4.25 = US$1.00. Our analysis examines the effectiveness of this program in the next section, on policy evaluation.

The government of Trinidad and Tobago also requested a new 12-month stand-by arrangement in the amount of SDR 85 million (50 percent of quota) on March 14, 1990.[8] The letter of intent stated the success of the 1989 program as justification for a new policy package. The 1990 letter of intent focused on the projected growth of the economy, which was heavily dependent on an increase in gross investment, from 19.5 percent of GDP in 1989 to nearly 23 percent of GDP in 1990. This investment program emphasized development of infrastructure, to stimulate expansion of output in agriculture, tourism, and non-oil manufacturing. The projected investment effort also required an increase in the national savings rate, from 15.5 percent of GDP in 1989 to 17 percent of GDP in 1990. This fiscal program was intended to raise public savings by about 1 percent of GDP. The new program also projected a decline in the public sector deficit, from 4.8 percent of GDP in 1989 to 4 percent of GDP in 1990, partly as a result of a projected decline in expenditure associated with employment reduction measures in the state enterprises. Additionally, the 10 percent salary cut was implemented in the public sector in 1989, and transfers to public utilities, state enterprises, and statutory boards were budgeted to be reduced by 0.5 percent of GDP. It should be noted that state enterprises were reduced by 1,100 employees in Trinidad and Tobago in 1989, as it was estimated that there would be a further reduction of 3,200 employees in 1990.[9]

The 1990 program established quarterly ceilings on the net domestic assets of the central bank. Total credit from the financial system was projected to expand by about 4 percent in 1990. It is still too early to examine the effectiveness of the 1990 demand management program. It should be noted, however, that the Trinidad and Tobago government was already pursuing stabilization policies before it entered the agreement with the IMF. The achievements of some of the policy targets discussed in the next section is attributable, not only to the IMF measures, but also to the cumulative effects of the demand management policies pursued after 1984.

EFFECTIVENESS OF IMF STABILIZATION POLICY

To what extent did the stabilization policies achieve their proximate objectives, for example, reduction in the fiscal deficit, domestic credit containment, and wage control? More importantly, to what degree did the stabilization measures improve the balance of payments positions of these countries? In this section two indicators will be used: the ratio of the fiscal deficit to GDP and the current account deficit on the balance of payments as a percent of GDP. Some of the constraints on the use of devaluation as a policy instrument will also be discussed.

The Barbadian case in 1982 is the least complicated of the four countries studied. It appears that the IMF's monetary diagnosis of the balance of payments problem was correct, and that the credit control measures were successful in stemming the outflow of foreign exchange. Partly because the balance of payments problem was not very severe, it was not necessary to request further support from the Fund. In terms of policy effectiveness, the ratio of the fiscal deficit to GDP fell, from 8.1 percent in 1981 to 6.0 percent in 1982 and 3.4 percent in 1983. The ratio of the current account deficit to GDP also was down, from 14.7 percent in 1981 to 4.8 percent in 1982, rising to 5.3 percent in 1983. The IMF program forced the Barbadian government to observe fiscal discipline up to 1985. In 1986 a new tax regime was introduced which led to significant revenue losses and was a factor in the high fiscal deficits in the last half of the 1980s. The effectiveness of the 1991 program in Barbados cannot be evaluated at this time.

The success of the IMF program in Trinidad and Tobago can be gauged from an examination of the 1990 letter of intent. All the performance criteria and targets of the 1989 program had been observed, and net official international reserves had risen by US$64 million, although no change had been projected under the program.[10] By year end 1989, gross official reserves were equivalent to 2.3 months of imports, nearly twice as much as at the end of 1988. The trade and exchange system had been significantly liberalized. However, the ratio of the current account balance of payments deficit to GDP had risen slightly, from 2.5 percent in 1988 to 3.0 percent in 1989, far below the 13.4 percent in 1986 and 5.2 percent in 1987.[11] The 1989 program also resulted in a reduction of the public sector deficit to 4.8 percent of GDP in 1989, compared with the projected target of 5.5 percent. Domestic financial savings rose in 1989 as a result of higher interest rates, while private sector credit contracted.

In the cases of Barbados and Trinidad and Tobago, my analysis considers the effects of stabilization policy over a very short time. These two cases are therefore not comparable with the cases of Guyana and Jamaica, where adjustment took place over a period of more than ten years. Guyana and Jamaica show some similarities, in that they experienced deep and frequent devaluations, which led to the growth of significant parallel currency markets. In the case of Jamaica, the parallel market had negative features, including leakage of foreign exchange from the banking system into the street market and retention of exports proceeds overseas.[12] The parallel market had a negative impact on the balance of payment of both countries.

Blackman (1989) regards Guyana as a sad case, arguing that Guyana was the best placed of the Caribbean Common Market (CARICOM) non-oil exporters to withstand the 1974 oil shock. Guyana possessed four strong foreign exchange earners: bauxite, sugar, rice, and timber. As Blackman points out, it was the Guyana government's ideologically motivated policy of public spending, supported by central bank credit creation, that wiped out the foreign reserves. This has already been mentioned in Chapter 2. The thesis advanced here is that the IMF policy programs, including devaluation, were unable to offset heavy money creation and the fall in productivity resulting from the miniaturization of the Guyanese private sector. The lack of fiscal restraint, migration of human capital, leakages of foreign exchange were major constraints on the IMF programs in Guyana during the 1980s. The IMF failed in Guyana, not because its policies were not well implemented, but because too much harm was already done to the economy as a result of inappropriate domestic policies. In the words of Blackman (1989: 66), the Guyanese economy became the "disequilibrium system par excellence" in the Caribbean.

The IMF stabilization programs in Jamaica achieved certain proximate objectives in the 1980s, but in 1989 the pace of recovery was affected by the damage that had been inflicted by Hurricane Gilbert in September 1988. This event placed the balance of payments under severe pressure. Nevertheless, in the 1980s Jamaica succeeded in reducing the fiscal deficit as a ratio of GDP (see Chapter 2 for details) and lowering the growth of credit to the public sector, particularly after 1986.

Despite heavy demand management in Jamaica, the ultimate objective of balance of payments equilibrium was not achieved, even though the services balance improved and the current account of the balance of payment was held within manageable limits.

Table 5.1 enables us to gauge the performance of the external sector. The analysis shows continued negative foreign reserves with the exception of the year 1988. During the latter year the current account improved significantly because of inflows of re-insurance claims. In 1989 a surge in imports following the hurricane worsened the trade balance, and negative reserve levels were again recorded. The ratio of exports to GDP showed little tendency to grow

Table 5.1
External Sector Indicators: Jamaica, 1985–1989

Indicator	1985	1986	1987	1988	1989
Reserve movements, in millions of J$*	−72.6	−24.0	−208.2	143.2	−170.4
Current balance as percent of GDP	−6.5	−0.6	−2.2	1.1	−2.5
Export/GDP (percent)	11.7	10.2	10.4	10.6	10.2
Imports/GDP (percent)	23.5	16.8	18.0	18.2	19.3
Trade balance in millions of J$*	−575.0	−379.5	−525.5	−606.0	−856.0
Services balance in millions of J$*	38.3	198.1	205.5	424.1	328.7

Note: *Increases (+)/Decreases (−) J$21.00 = US$1.00

Source: Jamaican Planning Institute, *Economic and Social Survey of Jamaica,* 1989.

between 1986 and 1989, fluctuating just over 10 percent. Jamaica's failure of the IMF test in 1989 led to a suspension of the capital inflows attendant on the stand-by agreement.[13]

The low ratio of exports to GDP and the failure of the IMF programs to achieve overall balance of payments equilibrium in Jamaica bring into question the efficacy of devaluation as an instrument of adjustment. Earlier work by Michael Witter (1983) suggests that devaluation in Jamaica failed to increase exports and eliminate the balance of payments deficit. In small countries devaluation fails to expand merchandise exports significantly because of supply-side inelasticities. Futhermore, even though the purpose of devaluation is to improve export competitiveness, the high prices of imports following the devaluation also increase the costs of producing certain exports. Devaluation achieved the objective of reducing real wages in both Jamaica and Guyana. However, the real wage declines did not significantly slow down the growth of imports. The IMF should reconsider its use of devaluation as a device for improving a country's balance of payments. Devalualtion in Jamaica may in fact have been counterproductive.

The experiences of Guyana and Jamaica strengthen the view that, of all the policies adopted, devaluation was the most hazardous. It could not correct economic distortions created by bad management, and it led to a fight of human and financial capital. Further, devaluation may not be the appropriate tool for increasing export competitiveness in import dependent economies. Sensible wage and income policies, vigorous export marketing, reductions in trade protectionism, and appropriate export tax incentives may be more effective in improving a country's export promotion efforts. Caribbean governments have not been able to restrain the rate of growth of wages without being told to do so by the IMF. Strong trade union pressure and political competition for votes are two factors which in the pre-IMF era maintained upward pressure on wage costs. Also, Caribbean tariff structures were characterized by high levels of protectionism, which inhibit the development of export-oriented production. The experiences of these countries show that it takes years to deregulate open economies that have structural rigidities. The process is usually painful and is accompanied by significant declines in standards of living occasioned by a sharp deterioration in real wages.

Structural adjustment has become the major preoccupation of Caribbean policy makers in the 1990s. Structural adjustment involves tax reform, public enterprise reform and privatization, interest rate liberalization, trade liberalization, agricultural sector reforms, promotion of exports of manufactured goods, productivity incentives, and exchange rate adjustments. The purpose of these policy measures is to achieve a level of economic development which is sustainable over the medium term. The success of structural adjustment will depend on the impact of short term stabilization policies. Further discussion of some of these structural adjustment issues is outside the scope of this book.

CONCLUSIONS

The Caribbean is characterized by severe fiscal imbalances, money market disequilibrium, and policy-induced distortions in the tradeable goods sector. Stabilization policies were adopted to reduce the imbalances. The adjustment programs called for deep devaluations of the exchange rate, on the theory that overvalued exchange rates discourage exports and encourage imports.

IMF stabilization policies are based on a mixture of the monetary approach to the balance of payments and neoclassical free market theory. However, to the extent that the ultimate aim of demand management policies is expenditure reduction, one can argue that the policies are also Keynesian in orientation.

IMF policies achieved a high degree of success in Barbados in 1982 and apparently in Trinidad and Tobago in 1989. Barbados achieved the proximate objectives of the program, and balance of payments equilibrium was restored. It is more difficult to judge the degree of success of the 1990 program in Trinidad and Tobago, but the proximate objectives of the 1989 program were met and the balance of payments showed signs of improvement.

IMF policies over many years failed to restore balance of payments equilibrium in Guyana and in Jamaica. The structures of these economies remained weak, and the growth of parallel currency markets reflected the severe shortages of foreign exchange. The use of the devaluation tool was excessive, and perhaps counterproductive, in these economies.

NOTES

1. For details of the performance criteria, see Central Bank of Barbados, *Economic Review*, vol. 9 no. 3, December 1982, p.17.

2. Details of performance criteria are given by Harris (1988: 179).

3. Ibid., p. 185.

4. Central Bank of Barbados *Annual Statistical Digest*, p. 222.

5. For a listing of these systems and an explanation of their operation, the reader is referred to the Bank of Jamaica document "Deregulation of the Foreign Exchange System" presented at the Seminar on Deregulation and the Jamaica Economy, Bank of Jamaica, Thursday, February 28, 1991.

6. See Trinidad and Tobago, *Letter of Intent*, November 16, 1988, p. 5, paragraph 7.

7. Ibid., p. 6.

8. Trinidad and Tobago, *Letter of Intent*, March 4, 1990, p. 4, paragraph 9.

9. Ibid., p. 8.

10. Ibid., p. 2.

11. Central Bank of Trinidad and Tobago, *Annual Economic Survey*, 1989.

12. For an analysis of the Jamaican parallel market, see Witter and Kirton, (1990), who maintain that between 1978 and 1987, the black market rate in Jamaica varied from 8.2 percent to 65.2 percent above the official exchange rate. For a discussion

of the parallel black market in Guyana, see Thomas (1989). In September 1991 Jamaica liberalized its foreign exchange system, making it possible for Jamaicans to hold foreign exchange accounts at home and overseas, while the Jamaica government has no special status in buying foreign exchange but has to access funds in the marketplace like anyone else.

13. See Planning Institute of Jamaica, *Economic and Social Survey of Jamaica,* 1989, p. 2.1.

6

EXTERNAL DEBT

The fiscal disequilibrium scenarios discussed in previous chapters, especially the increase in the size of government, partly explain the Caribbean external debt burden. Extensive research has been done on this topic, especially for Jamaica. The researchers have concentrated on the structural causes and evolution of the debt. The diverse aspects of the Caribbean external debt cannot be investigated thoroughly in the space of this chapter; however, the topic is important enough to make it necessary here to acquaint the reader with some broad details of the debt burden. My analysis is limited to an examination of the magnitude and composition of the debt, especially in the second half of the 1980s. For more extensive analyses of the evolution of the Caribbean debt problems after 1970, the reader should consult Owen Jefferson (1986), Girvan (1986), Girvan et al. (1991), Bernal (1985 and 1988), Pantin (1989), Daniel Boamah (1988, 1989, and 1990), Danns (1988), Compton Bourne and Oumade Singh (1988) and Kari Polanyi-Levitt (1991). The last-mentioned work is a comprehensive and well written survey of the Jamaican debt problem.

THE DEBT PROBLEM OF JAMAICA

Jefferson (1986) reported that the total external debt of Jamaica increased from US$1,734.0 million in 1980 to US$3,355.0 million in 1985, an increase of 93.5 percent. During the same period the debt service ratio, on an accrual basis, rose from 24.0 percent in 1980 to 61.3 percent in 1985. The actual debt service ratio was 40.9 percent in 1985. Following the practice of the Bank of Jamaica, it is necessary to distinguish between debt service on an accrual basis and actual amounts paid to creditors. According to Jefferson (1986), the use of accruals is important in countries where rescheduling arrangements are operational. The debt service ratio on an accruals basis is perhaps a more realistic gauge of a country's external debt burden.

The analysis in Tables 6.1, 6.2, and 6.3 looks at the Jamaican debt up to 1989, when the debt reached US$4,035.0 million, a rate of growth of 20.3 percent over 1985. The evidence suggests that the growth rate of the Jamaican debt slowed considerably between 1987 and 1989 (Table 6.1) compared with the high rates recorded by Jefferson during the early 1980s.

Perhaps more significant, however, is the decline of the Jamaican debt service ratio, both on an accrual basis and in terms of actual payments. The

Table 6.1
Jamaican External Debt by Borrower, 1986–1989
(in millions US $)

Borrower	1986	1987	1988	1989
Government	2,106.0	2,581.3	2,703.0	2,745.4
Government guaranteed	414.0	457.7	451.7	430.0
Bank of Jamaica	1,004.0	974.4	847.1	859.6
Total	3,524.0	4,013.4	4,001.8	4,035.0

Source: Planning Institute of Jamaica, *Economic and Social Survey of Jamaica,* 1989.

Table 6.2
Jamaican External Debt by Creditor, 1987–1989
(in millions US $)

Creditor	1987 $	1987 %	1988 $	1988 %	1989 $	1989 %
Commercial banks	393.1	9.8	385.2	9.6	373.1	9.3
Bilateral	1,685.9	42.0	1,765.5	44.1	1,857.2	46.0
Multilateral	1,733.9	43.2	1,606.2	40.2	1,540.7	38.2
Other	200.4	5.0	244.8	6.1	263.9	6.5
Total	4,013.3	100.0	4,001.7	100.0	4,034.9	100.0

Source: Planning Institute of Jamaica, *Economic and Social Survey of Jamaica,* 1989.

Table 6.3
Debt Service: Jamaica, 1987–1989

(in millions US $)

	1987	1988	1989
Total debt service (accrued)	1,036.92	894.85	844.85
Total debt service (actual)	774.54	816.33	759.41
Debt service ratio (accrued, in percent)	63.66	44.13	40.54
Debt service ratio (actual in percent)	47.54	40.26	36.44

Note: The debt service ratio is the ratio of debt service to exports of goods and services.

Source: Bank of Jamaica, *Annual Report,* 1989.

accruals ratio fell to 40.54 percent in 1989 (Table 6.3). According to the Bank of Jamaica, the reduction in the accrued debt service ratio was partly a function of improved export performance. Furthermore, the increase in aggregate debt was in the form of official bilateral credits, which are skewed toward the long-term end of the maturity structure and were not yet due for payment. Slight reductions in interest rates were also a contributory factor, although a gradual upturn in interest rates was evident around late 1989. The steady decline in the actual debt service ratio between 1987 and 1989 was also the result of debt rescheduling on eligible maturities due to OECD, non-OECD, and other creditors. Under the terms of the October 1989 Paris Club Accord, US$135.5 million was rescheduled.[1]

The composition of the Jamaican external debt by borrower is shown in Table 6.1. The analysis reveals that government liabilities represent the largest part of the debt, with a share of 68 percent in 1989. Most of the government debt is in the form of bilateral obligations, which amounted to 46 percent by 1989 (Table 6.2).

Jamaica also implemented a program of debt conversion in 1987, to reduce the level of its external debt. In a typical debt equity swap, the debtor government offers to exchange its debt for domestic currency to be used to purchase local equity. A potential investor buys the debt from a creditor for hard currency at the prevailing secondary discount rate. The investor sells the debt at near its face value to the central bank of the debtor country in local currency and then purchases local assets or investments (Boamah 1989: 301). In Jamaica the assets that may be transferred include local currency; local debt instruments; capital assets; and, where the government is the borrower, shares in public sector entities.[2] Jamaica's debt conversion program was designed to stimulate and encourage equity investments in Jamaican enterprises by foreign investors and to reduce the national debt burden. The Bank of Jamaica was also concerned that proceeds of a debt conversion should not be used to fund capital imports. Investors were therefore required to fund a proportion of a proposed investment with freely convertible foreign currency, or "fresh money."[3] This program has been reasonably successful. By December 1990 the total value of conversions from the inception of the program was US$55.67 million. This was accompanied by fresh money injections of US$17.94 million.[4]

Although the debt conversion option offers some hope for reducing a portion of Jamaica's external debt, some authors have identified inflationary consequences stemming from debt conversion. The argument is that heavy debt conversions lead to increases in the domestic money supply, which in turn raises the domestic price level. This argument is not particularly strong for a small open economy like Jamaica, where debt conversions are not very large. Foreign inflows from debt conversions can help to stimulate the economy, and the effect is similar to a net increase in export earnings. Care must be taken, however, that the additional fresh money does not find its way into the parallel market, where it will be exchanged at a rate higher than the official rate.

Debt conversion can also aid Jamaica's privatization program. The Jamaica government has shown a willingness to sell public enterprises to both local and foreign private sector interests. Govindan Nair and Mark Frazier (1987: 15) have suggested that one way of mitigating the risk of foreign domination is to allow both resident and non-resident nationals to participate as investors in debt conversion schemes. This approach could be directed at encouraging the repatriation of previous flight capital. Such schemes depend very much on the popularity of the political managers, which can affect the willingness of non-residents to participate in debt conversions.

THE INCREASING DEBT BURDEN OF BARBADOS

The fiscal policies pursued by the Barbadian government in the 1980s led to a sharp increase in the public debt. External debt service rose from US$93.5 million in 1986 to US$151.4 million in 1990. The debt service ratio also increased, from 17.4 percent in 1986 to 26.4 percent in 1990 (Table 6.4). Debt service became a problem for the Barbadian government, because it meant that foreign exchange had to be surrendered, thereby worsening the balance of payments problem. The fall in reserves of US$50.0 million in 1990 can also be explained by this heavy debt service, which accumulated as a result of heavy borrowing from the Japanese market and the Euro-dollar market in 1985 and 1986. The amounts borrowed were US$47.2 million from Japan and US$32.25 from the Euro-dollar market, to finance the fiscal deficits.

Table 6.4
External Debt: Barbados, 1986–1990
(in millions US $)

	1986	1987	1988	1989	1990
External Debt	531.1	590.8	576.7	549.3	539.7
Central government	276.7	353.5	349.8	408.5	418.0
Government					
guaranteed	89.4	74.2	59.8	45.3	33.7
Central bank	65.5	37.5	24.3	15.5	14.8
Private	99.5	125.6	97.8	80.0	73.2
Debt Service	93.5	134.4	125.9	105.3	151.4
Amortization	49.8	87.4	76.2	62.3	107.8
Interest	43.7	47.0	49.7	43.0	43.6
Debt service					
ratio*, in percent	17.4	27.4	21.5	16.0	26.4

*Debt Service as a ratio of exports of goods and services.

Source: Central Bank of Barbados, *Annual Report,* 1990.

Toward the end of 1990 the Barbadian government attempted to rescue the debt situation by borrowing 30.0 million pounds, or the equivalent of US$60.0 million, from Barclays Bank de Zoete Wedd in London. It was stated that this loan was to assist in financing the government's capital works program. Some concern was expressed by critics that the rate of interest, 13.5 percent, on this loan, over a 25-year moratorium period, was exorbitant. The high level of Barbadian debt service and the sharp fall in reserves led some observers to predict correctly that Barbados would become a candidate for IMF support in 1991.

The Barbadian data on the external debt are shown in Table 6.4. The central government debt shows an increasing trend, rising from US$276.7 in 1986 to US$418.0 in 1990. The rate of increase of the central government debt is faster than that of the total external debt; this is due to a decline in the other components of the debt. Interest paid on the external debt peaked in 1988 and then declined. The debt service ratio reached 26.4 percent in 1990, which can be considered high for a small country like Barbados.

THE EXTERNAL DEBT OF TRINIDAD AND TOBAGO

Ramsaran's (1988) work on the external debt of Trinidad and Tobago reports that between 1980 and 1985 the debt service ratio for that country was low, averaging about 5.2 percent. At that time, Trinidad and Tobago did not appear to have a serious debt problem. The situation changed between

Table 6.5
External Debt: Trinidad and Tobago, 1987–1990

(in millions US $)

Borrower	1987 $	1987 %	1988 $	1988 %	1989 $	1989 %	1990 $	1990 %
Central government	1,458.4	63.6	1,490.7	62.0	1,451.4	60.5	1,528.7	61.0
Government guaranteed	590.0	25.7	536.4	22.3	384.0	16.0	281.2	11.2
Other	244.4	10.7	250.4	10.4	304.6	12.7	297.2	11.9
Central government	-	-	125.1	5.2	258.9	10.8	400.2	16.0
Total	2,292.8	100.0	2,402.6	100.0	2,398.9	100.0	2,507.3	100.0
Debt service Ratio in percent	-	-	-	22.3	-	19.8	-	19.1
Debt deferred	-	-	87.1	-	243.8	-	275.3	-

Note: The debt service ratio is the ratio of debt service to exports of goods and services.

Source: Central Bank of Trinidad and Tobago, *Annual Economic Survey,* 1989, 1990.

Table 6.6
Creditor Composition of External Debt: Trinidad and Tobago, 1989–1990
(in millions US $)

Creditor	1989		1990	
	$	%	$	%
Commercial banks	829.7	34.6	821.5	32.8
Bilateral	392.8	16.4	501.1	20.0
Multilateral	310.3	12.9	468.1	18.7
Bonds	540.3	22.5	445.0	17.7
Other	326.9	13.6	271.6	10.8
Total	2,400.9	100.0	2,507.3	100.0

Source: Central Bank of Trinidad and Tobago, *Annual Economic Survey,*
    1989, 1990.

1985 and 1990, as balance of payments problems became a pressing concern.
As shown in Table 6.5, the debt service ratio was 22.3 percent in 1988, falling to 19.1 percent in 1990. Rising levels of debt forced Trinidad and Tobago
into a debt rescheduling program after 1987.

The analysis in Table 6.5 indicates a rising debt burden between 1987 and
1990. Of the US$1,528.7 million in external debt, 61 percent was central
government debt. As shown in Table 6.6, 32.8 percent of the total debt was
owed to commercial banks. In 1989 Trinidad and Tobago concluded negotiations with commercial and bilateral creditors to reschedule part of its principal payments. Table 6.5 shows that the principal payments deferred were
US$87.1 million in 1988, US$243.8 million in 1989, and US$275.3 million
in 1990. Trinidad and Tobago's rescheduling program represents an effort
to cope with a debt problem arising from balance of payments disequilibrium,
characterized by negative foreign reserve levels in 1988.

THE DEBT ARREARS PROBLEM OF GUYANA

The difficult economic circumstances experienced by Guyana in the 1970s
and 1980s led to an unprecedented debt arrears problem. Danns (1988: 82)
shows that Guyana's external debt rose from US$962.5 million in 1983 to
US$1,477.4 million in 1986. The external debt was also estimated at
US$1,970.5 million in 1989.[5] Arrears also totaled US$940.7 million by 1987.
Guyana became an insolvent economy in the context of a debt service ratio
of 81.4 percent in 1986, which is the highest for the four countries studied.

In an attempt to cope with its insolvency, Guyana concluded negotiations
in 1990 under which US$229 million in arrears owed to the Caribbean

Development Bank (CDB), the IMF, and the World Bank were cleared under an arrangement with the Bank for International Settlements and a support group of donor countries. The arrangements were chaired by Canada under the aegis of the IMF. The agreement provided the basis for resumption of lending to Guyana by these agencies and for restructuring Guyana's debt with other creditor countries.[6] In 1990 the World Bank granted a concessionary loan of US$81.0 million to Guyana for structural adjustment. The CDB and Inter-American Development Bank also provided US$44 million and US$27.0 million, respectively, to finance the agricultural sector.[7] Emphasis is being placed on economic restructuring to increase the country's foreign exchange earning capacity.

CONCLUSIONS

A major proximate cause of the debt problems of Jamaica, Guyana, and most recently Barbados has been the increase in the size of government, characterized by high levels of public expenditure in the context of declining real sector activity. Although policies such as rescheduling and debt conversion may help to ease the burden of repayment for a short time, the ultimate solution to the debt problem resides in restructuring of the real sectors of these economies, in order to generate increased foreign exchange earnings. At the same time, policymakers must reduce the size of government by privatizing financially burdensome public enterprises.

NOTES

1. See Bank of Jamaica, *Annual Report,* 1989, p. 28.
2. Bank of Jamaica, *Programme for the Conversion of Jamaican External Debt into Equity Investment,* July 28, 1987, p. 3.
3. Ibid., p. 12.
4. Debt Capitalization Unit, *Bank of Jamaica Review,* January 14, 1991.
5. See Caribbean Development Bank, *Annual Report,* 1990.
6. Ibid., p. 30.
7. Central Bank of Barbados, *Annual Report,* 1990, p.17.

INCOME INEQUALITY AND SOCIAL SECURITY

This chapter presents a discussion of income distribution and social security in the Caribbean. No attempt is made here to gauge the extent of poverty there. Some work has been done in this area on Jamaica, including that by Michael Smith (1989), Patricia Anderson (1989), Boyd (1988), Witter (1989), and Derek Gordon (1989). The literature on other English-speaking Caribbean territories is not extensive, although Ralph Henry (1975) has attempted to establish a poverty line for Trinidad and Tobago on the basis of a least cost subsistence diet. Henry found that some 35 percent of households had incomes below the poverty line for the respective household size (see also Harewood and Henry 1978). More published literature exists on the measurement of the income distribution. This chapter therefore examines some of the causes of income inequality and summarizes the findings on the income distribution for Trinidad and Tobago, Barbados, and Jamaica. The discussion closes with a look at social security in Jamaica and Barbados.

ROOTS OF INCOME INEQUALITY IN THE CARIBBEAN

During the 1960s and early 1970s, the plantation-economy variant of structuralist theory was the principal paradigm advanced to explain dependency, underdevelopment and the genesis of income inequality in the Caribbean. According to this paradigm, the roots of Caribbean poverty and inequality were to be found in the structural evolution of Caribbean economies, from production structures based on plantation slavery to systems dominated by large multinational corporations (MNCs). The plantation-economy model discussed in this section provides a valid thesis on the roots of income inequality in the Caribbean. However, in the contemporary Caribbean, other causes of poverty and inequality arise from balance of payments difficulties and from the structural adjustment policies pursued by some countries after 1970 (see Chapters 2 and 5). Structuralist theory continued to dominate scholarly writing on inequality during the late 1970s and 1980s (Harewood and Henry 1985; Sackey 1978). The failure of adjustment policies to work in the 1980s can also be attributed to the weaknesses inherited from colonialism that remain in the structure of these economies.

The model of plantation economy, as advanced by Lloyd Best (1968), provides a descriptive conceptual framework for examining the economic relationship between the metropolitan economy and hinterland or colonial economies. This model also indicates the internal economic dynamic of the plantation system. The model falls into three phases: the pure plantation economy (1600–1838); the plantation economy modified (1838–1938); and the plantation economy further modified (1938 to present).

The period of pure plantation economy was a special case of export-led growth under capitalism. This type of economy was based on slave labor producing sugar, and operating within a mercantile international capitalist system. The dominant unit of production was the plantation, controlled by proprietory planters.

The pure plantation economy exhibited a cycle of staple production which began with a foundation period, characterized by the acquisition of capital in the form of slaves and equipment. This trade was organized by the joint stock trading companies. The hinterland colonies in the Caribbean experienced a golden age, when profits were high and slaves plentiful. However, this period was followed by maturity and decline as the soil became less productive, the cost of slave labor increased, and market demand in the metropole contracted.

The period of plantation economy modified, which began when the slaves were emancipated, was initially characterized by labor shortage. This problem was addressed by importation of indentured labor from India. During this phase a peasantry attempted to establish itself, but the plantation continued to monopolize the best land. The emergence of a peasantry sharpened the conflict between export of staples and economic activity geared toward domestic production. The modified plantation economy remained structurally dependent despite the emergence of the peasantry.

The further modified phase of the plantation economy extends into the contemporary period and is characterized by new staples, such as tourism and mining. The MNCs replicate features of the old plantation system. The control of the modern MNC over primary production is tighter than that of the old merchant companies over the planters. Dependency persists, and indigenous initiative continues to be suppressed. The conflict between production for the domestic market and staple activity is exacerbated as dependent governments in the Caribbean actively promote branch-plant-type foreign investment. A characteristic of the evolution of the above model of production has been an income distribution highly skewed in favor of the merchants, planters, foreign investors, and dependent managerial elites in banks and other financial companies.

George Beckford's (1972) thesis of persistent poverty is an elaboration of Best's (1968) plantation-economy model at the level of political economy. Beckford stresses the political, social, and other behavioral aspects of the plantation system. According to Beckford (1972: 177), the plantation system created the following social diseconomies: persistent and expanding unemployment, relatively low levels of income, a most unequal distribution of income, gross underutilization of land, and extreme underconsumption. Underconsumption was reflected in widespread protein malnutrition in the presence of abundant agricultural resources.

Beckford's thesis emphasizes that plantation agriculture imparts underdevelopment biases to the economy and generates inequalities in income and wealth. These biases result from the type of resource allocation characteristics inherent in the plantation system itself. In the first place, market relationships with the rest of the world are more important than those within the national economy. This is partly explained by monoculture, as well as imperial preference. Consequently, there are weak spread effects from agriculture to the rest of the economy. The colonial norm of terminating production at the primary stage partly explains the heavy import dependence of economies dominated by the plantation system. In the second place, the plantations' monopoly of the best agricultural land leads to inherent disparities in productivity and income levels between the plantation and peasant system. These disparities are magnified by the ability of the plantation to obtain a greater share of financial and capital resources, technology, and labor.

The plantation economy model has also provided a conceptual framework for examining the behavior of other staples, such as bauxite. Girvan's (1971a) analysis of bauxite is a generic example of the model of plantation economy further modified. Girvan showed the impact of the MNCs in the mineral export industry on the Caribbean hinterland economy. Specifically, he identified the mechanisms by which these firms contributed to economic dependence and poverty in the Caribbean. These enterprises were able to internalize their growth dynamic through strategies of vertical integration. Primarily as a result of the enclave structure of the mining industry, transformation impulses are not transmitted to the rest of the economy. Highly specific technology retards the growth of employment in the mineral export economy, and its high wage levels inflate the supply price of labor to agriculture and manufacturing. The surpluses of the corporation are not reinvested in other sectors of the economy, since these surpluses are related to the global needs of the corporation. The mineral export economies therefore exhibited "dependent growth without development," thereby reinforcing a highly unequal distribution of income and wealth.

The need for income redistribution was indicated in the plantation-economy model, because the plantation system generates inequality. Land reform was recommended as an instrument of income redistribution. Beckford (1972: 223) favored a redistribution of the best lands to the peasants; Girvan (1971c) favored an incomes policy, to cut the exorbitant incomes of merchants and salesmen. However, the income redistribution analysis of the Caribbean structuralists lacked rigor, which might be partly explained by the sparse data on income distribution during the 1960s and 1970s.

The plantation-economy structuralist model was not designed to explain the fiscal and monetary problems of these small economies during the 1980s. The demand management strategies pursued by some Caribbean governments, particularly Guyana and Jamaica (Chapter 5) were a fundamental cause of the impoverishment of large sections of the working force. Although it is quite difficult, if not impossible, to measure precisely the distributional consequences attributable to devaluation, inflation, and heavy indirect taxation, it is safe to say that the IMF stabilization policies depressed real wages in the countries studied, thereby generating poverty and inequality. Further, high levels of external debt diverted government expenditure from the social services (Chapters 3 and 6). Later in this chapter we will look more closely at the implications of the difficult economic conditions during the 1980s for the social security and income maintenance schemes.

Although it is not possible to measure income inequality in Guyana during the 1980s, because of the lack of budget data and the large size of the informal sector, it is perhaps more meaningful to comment on the poor quality of life in that country. An official report of the Caribbean Conference of Churches (CCC) on Guyana in 1990 reveals a number of indicators of a declining quality of life.[1] The sharp decline in real wages in the formal sector led to the growth of a very large informal economy and prohibitive food and transportation prices. The vast majority of Guyanese people were forced to work at several jobs simultaneously to make a living. There was an alarming deterioration of health care; education; solid waste management; and the supply of water, electricity, and telephone services. The CCC data show that life expectancy at birth in Guyana fell from 70 years in 1985 to 65.2 years in 1989. The infant mortality rate was placed at 45 per thousand births in 1989, compared with 27 for Jamaica in 1989 and an average of 15.5 for Barbados in the 1980s. The crude death rate in Guyana also rose, from 6.6 per thousand in 1985 to 7.9 per thousand in 1989. Inflation was estimated at 50 percent per annum.

Political factors are highly significant in explaining the social crisis of the Guyanese people. The politicization of management of enterprises was identified in the CCC Report (1991) as a major cause of persistent poverty and inequality in Guyanese society. Extensive political patronage, rather than managerial ability, determined the promotion of those individuals intensely loyal to the People's National Congress (PNC). Political patronage and corruption fostered economic mismanagement and contributed directly to the massive emigration of skilled and professional personnel from Guyana. These developments affected every sector of the society and led to a marked deterioration of social services, misallocation of financial resources, depletion of international reserves, and a highly unequal distribution of income. The political factors contributing to the impoverishment of the Guyanese working class are discussed more fully by Thomas (1988: 251–265).

INEQUALITY IN A PLURAL SOCIETY: HENRY'S THESIS

In a series of articles, Henry (1975, 1988, and 1989) and Harewood and Henry (1978 and 1985) advanced a strong thesis on income distribution in Trinidad and Tobago. Their analysis is based on the post-colonial evolution of the plural society, which had its origins in the development of the plantation economy. This section attempts to capsulize this thesis, to show the main characteristics of income distribution in Trinidad and Tobago.

According to Henry (1988: 471), the political economy of pluralism, which reflects the divergent participation of distinct cultural or ethnic groups, is a significant factor explaining income inequality in Trinidad and Tobago. Income inequality in the plural society depends on the political power exercised by the respective ethnic groups in mobilizing resources for their own interests. The plural society emerged in Trinidad and Tobago in the colonial period, when Indian immigrant labor was needed to work on the plantations. Portuguese and Chinese workers were also part of the inflow of immigrant labor. These groups contributed to ethnic segmentation of the plantation economy.

Henry demonstrates that the level of inequality was a function of the willingness of the one political party, the People's National Movement (PNM), which controlled the government between 1962 and 1986, to alter the asset distribution. He identified four historical periods of analysis, 1962–1969, 1970–1973, 1974–1982 and 1984–1987. In the first period, 1962–1969, the PNM government adopted an industrialization policy, which although it increased employment levels, did not advance the economic well-being of blacks at the pace they demanded. This period was characterized by some increase in inequality, as the white elite benefited from the fiscal incentives granted by the government for industrial development.

The Black Power riots of 1970 ushered in a new period of economic change. The period 1970–1973 was characterized by creation of state enterprises and development of a Peoples' Sector through promotion of the cooperative movement, and encouragement of small business (Henry 1988: 840). As a petroleum export economy, Trinidad and Tobago also benefited from the high oil prices of 1974. The third period, 1974–1982, was characterized by unprecedented economic activity, which improved the income distribution for blacks and Indians, particularly in 1975/76. The fourth period, 1984–1987, was characterized by worsening economic activity (see Chapter 2).

Against this background, Henry measured income distribution in the Trinidad and Tobago economy, as well as the changes in income distribution for the major ethnic groups. He showed that the lowest 40 percent had 12.5 percent of the income in 1957/58. This share fell to 10 percent in 1971/72 and rose to 11.4 percent in 1975/76 and 11.7 percent in 1981/82. His data also revealed that the richest 5 percent improved their share, from 22.5 percent in 1957/58 to 24.2 percent in 1971/72, but that this share had fallen to 17.6 percent by 1981/82 (Henry 1988: 475).

The ethnic income distribution in Trinidad and Tobago showed a marked improvement in favor of the Indian group. The Gini ratio for this group was 0.49 in 1971/72, and by 1981/82 it had fallen to 0.43. Income distribution also improved among blacks in the first half of the 1970s, with recorded Gini ratios of 0.48 in 1971/72 and 0.44 in 1975/76. However, the distribution for blacks worsened again in the late 1970s, with the Gini ratio rising to 0.47 in 1981/82. Overall, the income distribution improved over the 1970s, as indicated by the Gini ratio for all groups, which fell from 0.51 in 1971/72 to 0.45 in 1981–82 (Henry 1988: 476). Henry's analysis is instructive in that it evaluates the influence of structural, ethnic, and policy factors in income distribution analysis. It represents a departure from the type of income distribution studies which give Gini ratios without adequate historical and sociological analysis to explain the behavior of those ratios.

INCOME INEQUALITY IN BARBADOS

Despite the economic development of the Barbadian economy after World War II, a sizeable proportion of the labor force continued to live on a subsistence income. It is difficult to make definitive statements about the changing income distribution in Barbados, because the severe paucity of reliable budget studies does not allow a meaningful statistical investigation of income distribution over the entire period. I examined income inequality by choosing representative samples of primary and secondary data for the post-World War II period up to 1981.

The institutional structure of colonial society suggests that income inequality was functionally related to underdevelopment and to the concentration of wealth in the hands of the merchant class and the plantocracy. The problem was one of asset distribution. The existence of a merchant class comprising a few wealthy families, along with a high level of disguised unemployment, were primary determinants of income inequality in the services sector. Similarly, the size of farm holdings was inextricably linked to inequality in the distribution of income and wealth in the rural areas; because by 1971, a few large farms in the estate sector, constituting about 3 percent of total farms, owned over 77.3 percent of the total acreage.[2]

The pattern of income distribution associated with institutional inequality was shown in Kenneth Straw's (1953) study of budgetary patterns in the colonial economy. Straw's analysis reveals a highly skewed distribution. His work, based on household surveys conducted in 1951 and 1952, found that average incomes were lower in the rural areas, but that in the crop season, incomes in the richest agricultural zones were higher than in the urban areas. In the "hard times" between crop seasons, 78 percent of the households had an income of less than $20 per week, while 43 percent had less than $10 per week. In the crop season the proportions were 66 percent and 30 percent, respectively. At the lower end of the income scale, some 63 percent of households with an average of below $15 received 30 percent of the total income accruing to households in hard times. In the crop season the proportions were 49 percent and 19 percent, respectively.

Subsequently, analyses by Martin Cox (1979), Carlos Holder and Ronald Prescod (1989) reached the conclusion that there was an overall decrease in income inequality during the 1970s. Their findings, like those of Henry, were based on the use of Gini coefficient. A coefficient approaching unity or one shows a high level of inequality, whereas a coefficient approaching zero reflects an improvement in income distribution. Cox found a Gini coefficient of 0.426 for 1970 and 0.404 for 1974, indicating that the distribution of income in 1974 was nearly equal to that of 1970. Cox reported that there was increasing inequality for lower-income groups in 1974, and decreasing inequality for middle-income groups. He stated that the improvement for middle-income groups outweighed the increase in inequality in the lower ranges, making the overall inequality slightly less than in 1970. Cox's analysis suffered from the fact that the Lorenz curves intersected. Methodologically, intersecting Lorenz curves cannot show whether the overall distribution improved.

Holder and Prescod (1989: 92) using a methodology similar to that of Cox, point to the decline in overall income inequality as shown by the fall in the Gini coefficient for total income less income tax, from 0.418 in 1951 to 0.400 in 1960 and 0.286 in 1981. They argue that the progressive tax system reduced the overall level of inequality. However, their ratio of 0.286 in 1981 is unrealistically low for a developing economy.

Both studies suffered from the use of income tax data to measure income inequality, in a developing country characterized by high unemployment levels. The limitations of income tax data relate to the problem of under-reporting of income and under-enumeration of income recipients. There is also the difficulty of measuring the income of subsistence farmers. Again, not all recipients are required to file a tax form, particularly at the bottom of the income distribution. In the higher levels of the scale, income tax data may also suffer from the impact of tax evasion.

More specifically, the analysis by Cox suffered because taxable returns constituted only 36 percent of the labor force in 1970, leading to the view that a high level of income was under-reported. The Holder and Prescod approach is subject to even more severe criticism. The annual financial statement and budgetary proposals for 1980 indicated that 30,000 people in the labor force were no longer liable to pay tax, effective from that income year. Therefore, the observed fall in the Gini coefficient to 0.286 in 1981 obtained by Holder and Prescod did not take into account the 29 percent of the labor force at the very bottom. Their findings reflected an improvement in the income distribution of middle-income taxpayers who submitted tax returns, rather than the income distribution of the economy as a whole.

Further, it is reasonable to argue that the purchasing power of lower-income groups may have declined during the period 1970 to 1977, attributable, inter alia, to the impact of rising unemployment levels. The years 1973–1977 were characterized by the stagflationary conditions of the "oil crisis" in international capitalism, which slowed the rate of growth of real output. Unemployment rose from 9.7 percent of the labor force in 1970 to 15.7 percent in 1977, thereby expanding the numbers in the zero income bracket, many of whom had previously been employed in the manufacturing sector.

The analysis of income inequality during the late 1970s in Barbados is buttressed by budget data for the period April 1978 to March 1979 (Table 7.1). These data show that 28.9 percent of the households sampled received a monthly income of less than $200.00 ($50.00 per week), while 60.5 percent of households received less than $500.00. At the top of the scale, 3.1 percent of households received a monthly income of over $2,000 per month. If this

Table 7.1
Distribution of Monthly Household Disposable Income: Barbados, 1978/79

Monthly Income Groups (Bds$)	Number of Households	Number of Households as Percentage of Total
Up to 99	184	17.0
100–199	129	11.9
200–299	99	9.2
300–499	241	22.4
500–699	183	17.0
700–999	153	14.2
1000–1999	56	5.2
2000–2499	20	1.9
2500 and over	13	1.2
TOTAL	1078	100.0

This table was compiled from household budget data to determine weights for a new price index.

Source: Barbados Statistical Service, 1980.

sample is an indication of the larger population, it means that the income distribution was highly unequal in Barbados during the 1970s. Using the same data, Andrew Downes (1987) found a Gini coefficient of 0.4638 for disposable income. However, his comparison between Straw's findings for the colonial period and the 1978 survey is less convincing.

The inequality problem is not only a problem of nominal income distribution, but also a problem of the asset distribution. Downes's statistical analysis of the income distribution data appears to be correct; however, I have conceptual difficulties with his conclusion, made on the basis of the Gini coefficient, that income inequality increased between 1951/52 and 1978/79. Even though a rise in inequality is possible, Downes compared an economy at two levels of development, which had undergone structural changes as well as changes in asset distribution. Besides, as Downes readily admits, the increase in income inequality might be a product of differential statistical procedures, rather than the realization of socioeconomic change. Generally speaking, long-term comparisons of inequality require data on the wealth or asset distribution which may not be readily available. Also, in the post-independence economy, the majority of people had greater access to secondary education, low-cost housing, better health care, transfer payments, and social services such as family planning, national insurance, and social security. These public goods, favorably influenced income distribution. Although the net budget incidence of these policies may be difficult to measure, the Gini ratio may not be very useful in making definitive statements on the change in income distribution over such a long period.

Representative data were available to examine the sectoral distribution of wage income during the 1970s. Table 7.2 shows the contribution of each sector to total wage incomes. The largest-factor incomes were recorded in the service sector, composed of wholesale and retail trade, as well as financial services, tourism, and other personal, community, and government services. The entire services sector contributed 60 percent to wage incomes, thereby reflecting the economy's dependence on services.

It is more meaningful, nevertheless, to analyse the distribution of wage incomes in relation to employment by sector, in order to gauge whether the share of wages in each sector was higher or lower than the related share of numbers employed. Firstly, the manufacturing sector which included sugar manufacturing, contributed 15 percent to employment but only 9.2 percent to wage incomes. Agriculture's proportion of the labor force was 9.8 percent, but this sector contributed 13.2 percent of wage incomes, which implies a better share of the income cake than the manufacturing sector. The government sector's share of wages was 21.4 percent, which was high relative to the number of persons employed (10.6 percent). This is explained by the fact that the government sector comprises a larger proportion of higher paid officials and professionals than either the manufacturing or the agricultural sector. The services sector's share of wage income was 13.5 percent.

Table 7.2
Sectoral Distribution of Wage Incomes: Barbados, 1975

Sector	Wage Incomes (millions of Bds $)	No. Employed as percent of Labor Force	Sector Share of Wage Incomes (percent)	Per Capita Wage Incomes (Bds $)
Agriculture	61.1	9.8	13.2	3,125
Mining and quarrying	1.4	0.4	0.3	4,666
Manufacturing	42.9	15.2	9.2	2,648
Construction	43.4	8.2	9.4	3,807
Wholesale and retail trade	116.8	22.9	25.2	6,790
Transport and public utilities	36.3	6.8	7.8	4,538
Government services	98.0	10.6	21.4	8,909
Other services	62.6	26.1	13.5	2,722
TOTAL	462.6	100.0	100.0	

Note: Bds$2.00 = US$1.00

Sources: U.N. Yearbook of National Accounts Statistics 1979; Barbados Development Plan, 1969–72.

This was low compared to that sector's share of employment, of 26.1 percent, because of the seasonal fluctuation of wage incomes in tourism and the low share of wages in the financial sector relative to that sector's contribution to profits, rents, and dividends. For example, in 1975 finance and business services contributed Bds$93.9 million to domestic factor incomes, of which $39.4 million, or 42 percent was in the form of wages. The services sector also comprises a large element of low-wage employment, such as domestic service, self-employed artisans, and casual labor. Per capita incomes are highest in the government sector, followed by wholesale and retail trade, and lowest in the manufacturing sector.

The theoretical implications of the analysis are a redistribution of income from agriculture during the colonial period to the trade and government sectors in the 1970s. Furthermore, given the low level of per capita income of Bds$220 per month in the manufacturing sector and Bds$226 per month in the "other services" sector, the investigations imply that a large part of the labor force living near the poverty line was to be found in these sectors.

I was unable to buttress the analysis with economy-wide data for the 1980s.

The Barbadian data illustrate some of the difficulties of measuring the true income distribution in an open developing economy. The nominal income distribution can worsen, and real wages fall, during the capitalist development process. This is so because divergences are likely to develop between private profitability and social costs under capitalism, as well as terms-of-trade deterioration. Therefore, the task of the state is to ensure that the welfare of poorer sections of the community is maintained, by guaranteeing access to low-cost housing, adequate sanitation, free education, and health and community services, which would compensate for any decline in real wages. Measures such as Gini coefficients should be interpreted with great caution in developing countries. Such coefficients are useful when data are accurate and available for all income groups, but very often these measures do not capture the high degree of inequality at the bottom end of the income scale, since subsistence incomes in both the rural and urban sectors are usually under-reported. A "social indicator" or "quality of life" approach would supplement the money income distribution approach to the inequality problem; however, a discussion of these other approaches is outside the scope of this book.

INCOME DISTRIBUTION IN JAMAICA

Studies on income inequality in Jamaica show a highly skewed income distribution.[3] Charles McClure (1977) found that the top 10 percent of households in 1972 had 50 percent of the total income. More recent analysis by Michael Wasylenko (1986) shows that in 1983 the top 20 percent of Jamaican households had 56 percent of the income, while the bottom 20 percent had less than 3 percent. In urban areas, Wasylenko found that the top two deciles had 67 percent of total income, while in rural areas, households in the top two deciles had 39 percent of total income. However the Gini coefficient in the urban areas was 0.471, compared with 0.526 for rural areas.

The data in Table 7.3 also reveal that income inequality increased in Jamaica between 1975 and 1984. The bottom 20 percent of households had 2.6 percent of income in 1983, compared with 4.1 percent in 1975. The Gini coefficient also recorded an increase, from 0.4452 in 1975 to 0.526 in 1983. However, these Gini coefficients may not be strictly comparable, since they were generated by different data sources. The deterioration in income distribution is largely a result of severe stabilization measures, which forced many people into the informal sector of the economy. According to Boyd (1988: 101), "higglering and hustling" became the pursuit of many households in Jamaica. The growth of the informal sector was a result of the decline of real incomes stemming from currency devaluation. (See Chapter 5).

Table 7.3
Distribution of Income: Jamaica, 1975 and 1983

Decile Income Range	Percent of Income	
	1975	1983
1	1.3	0.81
2	2.8	1.80
3	3.9	2.72
4	5.1	3.98
5	6.3	5.42
6	7.9	7.15
7	9.9	9.65
8	12.5	12.95
9	16.9	17.74
10	33.3	37.78
Gini Coefficient	0.4452	0.526

Sources: Derick Boyd, *Economic Management, Income Distribution and Poverty in Jamaica* (New York: Praeger, 1988), p. 100; M. Wasylenko, "The Distribution of Tax Burden in Jamaica: Pre-1985 Reform," Staff Paper No. 30, Jamaican Tax Examination Project, Syracuse University and Government of Jamaica, 1986, p. 54.

SOCIAL SECURITY AND WELFARE

The undertaking of social security and welfare schemes in the Caribbean represents a policy response to the problems of inequality and poverty in the region. Social security has a number of functions in any modern economy. Firstly, it provides insurance against the risk of an uncertain lifetime. Poor people find more difficulty in setting aside funds for old age because of the low level of incomes in their working life. In old age, these individuals are more likely to be destitute. Secondly, social security is a redistributive mechanism. Following Robin Boadway and David Wildasin (1984: 462), social security redistributes income in two ways. Intragenerational redistribution, or redistribution among the members of any given generation, results from the benefit structure of the program relative to contributions. Social security also redistributes income across generations. Intergenerational redistribution takes the form of pensions for the aged. Thirdly, social security is a form of savings mobilization. Wendell Samuel (1990) has shown the significance of social security as a savings mechanism in some economies in the eastern Caribbean. Social security funds are an important source for financing the fiscal deficits of Barbados and other small economies.

Jamaica

This section outlines the main characteristics of the social security and welfare programs in Jamaica. The National Insurance Scheme (NIS) and the Public Assistance Programme are the two pillars of the Jamaican social security program. The NIS program is obligatory to the labor force as a whole but is avoided by self employed persons and workers in the informal sector of the economy (Boyd 1988: 128). The NIS covers men aged 18 to 70 years and women aged 18 to 65 years who are employed in Jamaica. The NIS is financed by payroll taxation and provides contributors with protection against loss of income arising from old age, disablement, or injury. There is no unemployment benefit.

Table 7.4 shows the distribution of the major benefits of the NIS. Old age pensioners are the main beneficiaries of the scheme, receiving 60.6 percent of the benefits, followed by widows/widowers, receiving 12.8 percent. Incapacity benefits, as well as payments such as maternity and funeral grants, constitute a small proportion of the expenditure of the NIS. Contributions to the fund in 1989 were J$98.1 million, and the total NIS fund that year was about J$1,200 million.[4]

Table 7.4
Distribution of Major Benefits of NIS: Jamaica, 1989

| | Expenditure | |
General Benefits	J$ millions	percent
Old age pensions	67.5	60.6
Invalidity pensions	6.5	5.8
Widows'/widowers' pensions	14.2	12.8
Sugar workers' pensions	2.3	2.1
Funeral grants	3.9	3.5
Other	0.3	0.3
Employment Injury Benefits		
Disability	1.8	1.5
Temporary incapacity	1.2	1.1
Employment injury or death	0.04	0.03
Miscellaneous	0.09	0.08
All other	0.3	0.3
Administrative Expenses	13.2	11.9
TOTAL	111.3	100.0

Note: J$21.00 = US$1.00 at December 1991

Source: Planning Institute of Jamaica, *Economic and Financial Survey of Jamaica*, 1989.

The Jamaican government's Public Assistance Programme provides aid to persons who are not covered under the NIS, to those with little or no income, and to the incapacitated. The program comprises the Food Aid Programme, poor relief, and various schemes for the aged and the handicapped.

The Food Aid Programme was introduced in 1984 to cushion the effects of the Jamaican government's structural adjustment policies, after the removal of subsidies on basic food items such as cornmeal, flour, and rice. The Food Aid Programme is financed by an annual budgetary allocation form the government's consolidated fund, and through monetization of foodstuffs from agencies such as the World Food Programme.[5]

The first aspect of the Food Aid Programme is the provision of food stamps. At the end of 1989, food stamps were being received by 438,778 persons, or 18 percent of the population.[6] Polanyi-Levitt (1991) has criticized the food stamp program as a poor substitute for direct subsidization of imported food staples. She argues that the acceptability of food stamps as cash means that they can be used to purchase other commodities which the consumer may desire. Polanyi-Levitt is also concerned that the program may not have raised the level of nutrition significantly during the 1980s.[7]

The School Feeding or Nutrition Programme provided meals for 225,000 students in 1989, under the sponsorship of the World Food Programme and USAID.[8] In April 1990 the government announced an increase in the school feeding program, to provide a nutri-bun and milk to 150,000 school children and a cooked lunch to a further 130,000, especially in primary schools (Polanyi-Levitt 1991: 47).

The Poor Relief Programme deals with the destitute. The "indoor program" of institutional care provides for persons in parish infirmaries; while the "outdoor program" gives financial and food assistance to persons registered as paupers.

Barbados

The Barbados National Insurance Scheme (NIS) covers working people who are 16–64 years of age. The maximum insurable earnings are Bds$3,100 per month. All employed persons, regardless of age, are covered for the employment injury benefit, and employers are responsible for paying this contribution. The scheme pays sickness, maternity, funeral, and invalidity benefits; old age contributory grants or pensions, non-contributory old age pensions; and employment injury and unemployment benefit.[9] Welfare benefits are provided by the Welfare Department and the National Assistance Board. The discussion is mainly concerned with the Barbados NIS.

The NIS is financed by payroll taxation, shown in Table 7.5. National insurance contributions, non-contributory pensions, and unemployment benefits are equally shared between employees and employers. The severance

Table 7.5
Contribution Rates for NIS: Barbados, 1991
(in percent)

Payroll Tax	Employee	Employer	Total
National insurance	3.0	3.0	6.0
Non-contributory	2.0	2.0	4.0
Employment injury	–	0.25	0.25
Unemployment benefit	2.75	2.75	5.5
Severance fund	–	1.0	1.0
Health service levy	1.5	1.0	2.5
Training fund	0.5	0.5	1.0
Transport levy	1.75	0.25	2.0
Employment levy	0.5	0.5	1.0
TOTAL	12.0	11.25	23.25

Source: National Insurance Office, Barbados, 1991.

fund contribution is paid completely by employers. The National Insurance Board collects the health, training, transport, and employment levies on behalf of the Barbados government. These levies are not a constituent part of the NIS, but are paid into the government's consolidated fund. Table 7.5 shows that payroll taxes paid to the National Insurance Board by employees constituted 12 percent of insurable earnings at the end of 1991.

The incidence of these payroll taxes is regressive on lower-income groups, because the rate of tax does not increase beyond Bds$3,100 per month. Also, in 1991 lower-income groups earning between Bds$15,000 and Bds$30,000 per annum paid an overall marginal income tax rate of over 50 percent, including national insurance contributions, stabilization tax and levies, and individual income tax. A marginal tax rate of 50 percent on incomes is considered high for lower-income groups in Barbados.

Table 7.6 shows the revenue and expenditure of the Barbados NIS. In 1989 the benefit category constituted 53.8 percent of expenditure, and non-contributory old age pensions registered 33.4 percent. The high level of benefits in 1989 can be explained by rising unemployment payments as a result of the contraction of the economy. An unemployment benefit is payable for each day of unemployment, excluding Sundays, as long as unemployment continues, subject to a maximum of 26 weeks in any continuous period of unemployment. The unemployment benefit scheme is a major addition to the benefits provided under the NIS; however, its viability is threatened by prolonged periods of recession in the Barbadian economy.

Table 7.6
Revenue and Expenditure of NIS: Barbados, 1988–1989
(in millions Bds $)

	1988	1989
Current revenue	177.5	175.9
Contributions	122.1	137.9
Interest and other revenue	55.4	38.0
Current expenditures	130.2	140.5
Benefits	61.2	75.9
Non-contributory old age pension	49.0	471.0
Expenses	20.0	17.5
Capital expenditures	0.2	0.6

Note: Bds$2.00 = US$1.00

Source: Central Bank of Barbados, *Annual Statistical Digest*, 1990.

CONCLUSIONS

The structuralist plantation-economy theory provides a valid explanation of the roots of poverty and inequality in the Caribbean. However, in the 1980s demand management policies were a fundamental cause of the deterioration of the income distribution in Jamaica and Guyana. My analysis commented briefly on the quality of life in the latter country. The information is not robust enough to make firm judgments about the movement of income distribution in Barbados, although estimates of Gini coefficients have been made for various years by some researchers.

In Trinidad and Tobago, ethnic factors play an important role in income distribution. Henry's (1975, 1988, and 1989) work is valuable in that it recognizes the interplay of political, ethnic, and structural variables in explaining income inequality in Trinidad and Tobago.

Wasylenko (1986) expresses concern about Jamaica's highly skewed income distribution. He notes that estimates of income distribution reported in the World Bank's *World Development Report* in 1983 have relatively few countries with income distribution as highly skewed as Jamaica.

The income distribution studies all imply that direct redistribution policies should be a priority in these countries. I have already described in Chapter 3 the attempts by some Caribbean governments to use expenditure policy to alter income distribution through provision of better health care and education. This chapter outlined the social security and welfare programs adopted in Jamaica and Barbados to deal with the problem of income inequality.

NOTES

1. Caribbean Conference of Churches, *Official Report of a Goodwill and Fact-Finding Mission to Guyana, September 30 to October 5, 1990*.

2. Barbados, *Agricultural Census, 1971*.

3. World Bank, *World Development Report* (Oxford: Oxford University Press, 1983, pp. 200–201, as cited in Wasylenko (1986: 56).

4. Planning Institute of Jamaica, *Economic and Social Survey of Jamaica, 1989*, pp. 23.1 and 23.2.

5. Ibid., p. 23.3.

6. Ibid.

7. For a more detailed analysis of the impact of Jamaica's food assistance programs, see Witter (1989).

8. Planning Institute of Jamaica, *Economic and Social Survey of Jamaica, 1989*, p. 23.3.

9. Barbados National Insurance Office, *Memorandum on Benefits Payable: The National Insurance and Social Security Scheme*, undated, p. 3.

ASPECTS OF CARIBBEAN TAX SYSTEMS

Taxation is an extensive topic; this chapter is therefore highly selective. The first section presents a general discussion of the principles of taxation. This is necessary to provide a conceptual background for the issues raised in this chapter, as well as in the following chapter, on tax reform. The changes in the structure of taxation in the Caribbean are then examined, with particular emphasis on the movement toward consumption-based tax systems. The work is also concerned with the role of taxation as an instrument of stabilization policy. As I indicated in Chapter 2, balance of payments adjustment was an overriding concern in the Caribbean in the 1980s. Taxation was one of the principal tools of demand management. The other sections of the chapter look at the buoyancy and incidence of the tax systems. The final discussion deals with the issue of tax incentives for foreign investment.

ROLE OF THE TAX SYSTEM: A GENERAL DISCUSSION

Taxation constitutes an involuntary saving by taxpayers which is diverted to the government for use in resource allocation. This section considers the principles or requirements for a good tax structure, the purposes of taxation, and the potential impact of taxation on an economy.

The first principle of taxation is that the tax burden should be equitable; that is, no one should pay more than a fair share of taxes. According to this principle, a person is asked to contribute to the general revenue according to ability to pay or according to benefits received. Under the benefit principle, taxes are the prices citizens pay for the goods and services they buy through their government. Such prices are assessed on each citizen according to the benefits directly or indirectly received. The benefit principle therefore facilitates the earmarking of revenue. The benefit principle can be applied to certain forms of taxation where the beneficiaries are easily identifiable. These forms of taxation include fuel levies, highway tolls, and other user charges. However, the benefit principle has limitations as a general principle of taxation, because most citizens do not reveal their true preferences for public goods (Davis and Meyer 1983).

The other aspect of the equity principle is the ability to pay principle. Under this criterion a tax is not linked directly to the benefit received. The government fixes a revenue target, and the citizens are asked to contribute according to their ability to pay. In many systems such revenues are paid into a single consolidated fund. Under this principle, income or wealth is usually regarded as an index of a person's fiscal capacity. The ability to pay criterion can be divided into two further principles, those of horizontal and vertical equity. The principle of horizontal equity means that people in equal positions, or enjoying equal levels of welfare, should be treated equally, and they should contribute the same amount of tax. The vertical equity principle asserts that people in unequal positions should be treated unequally. This principle is sometimes interpreted as requiring progressive taxation. The main problems in applying the equity principles relate to the difficulty of defining equals. This calls for an interpersonal comparison of welfare levels, which is difficult in practice. In levying taxes, the equity principle is one of the most important considerations facing the governments of small developing countries, because most of the people are poor (see Goode 1984).

The tax system should have efficiency and growth objectives. The government should be able to collect enough revenue to carry out its welfare and development programs, without significantly disturbing the efficiency of the market system. Excess-burden analysis deals with the efficiency costs of taxation. An excess burden is said to result when a tax causes a distortion in resource allocation, or expenditure patterns leading to a fall in welfare. The principle of efficiency often conflicts with the equity criterion. For example, a neutral tax, like a general retail sales tax, may be preferable on efficiency grounds, but may be regressive in its incidence. Certain types of non-neutral tariffs in open economies may lead to consumer excess burden, but should be used judiciously to discourage the consumption of certain imports.

There are other requirements for a good tax structure. Taxation should be efficiently administered, and the taxation procedure should be understandable to the taxpayers. Further, the taxes should have low compliance costs. These are the costs people bear in paying taxes, such as legal costs and the time sacrificed in filling out tax returns.

Taxation also has a distributive purpose. All governments must be conscious of the unequal distribution of real income. Taxation can aid income redistribution by facilitating certain transfers to those persons who are most disadvantaged. These transfers include pensions, social security, national insurance, and unemployment benefits. Taxation also aids in income redistribution when government spends money on education and low-cost housing, thereby making it possible for citizens to improve their standard of living.

The major contribution of Musgrave (1959) on the distributive role of the tax system was the distinction between specific tax incidence, differential tax incidence, and budget or expenditure incidence. Differential tax incidence, which refers to the distributional changes that result when one tax is substituted for another, is particularly important in assessing the impact of tax reform. In a later section of this chapter I examine a study by Wasylenko (1986) on Jamaica which used differential incidence analysis. Budget incidence examines the effects of all aspects of government activity on private real incomes. Empirical incidence studies have focused more on tax incidence than on budget incidence. The latter requires a more comprehensive approach, investigating both the resource transfer and output effects of expenditure policy (see Musgrave 1959).

The tax system also has a stabilization role. This is very important in small open economies which suffer from cyclical instability as a result of crop failures and falling export prices. These factors reduce government revenues, and policymakers are forced to impose new taxes or increase tax rates. My discussion in a later section looks at the importance of taxation as a stabilization device in the Caribbean during the 1980s.

A widely debated issue in public finance is whether the tax system should be an income-based system or a consumption-based system. In the past an income-based tax system was considered superior to a consumption-based system because it was believed that progressivity guaranteed equity. Some modern theorists have argued that, to the extent that income taxes are progressive, their relative effect in curtailing saving is likely to be greater than the relative effect of indirect taxes. Other theorists have pointed to the negative effects of progressive income tax systems on people's desire to work and invest. These analysts also believe that steeply progressive taxation fosters capital flight from open economies.

However, despite the modern preference for neutral indirect tax systems, care should be taken in the design of the tax systems of developing countries. Often an equitable distribution of the tax burden is sacrificed, especially in recessionary times, when the government attempts to maximize its indirect tax revenue. Lower-income groups usually bear proportionally heavier burdens of indirect taxes. Further, too heavy a level of indirect taxes that discriminate against imported goods by encouraging domestic resources may reduce efficiency in the use of those resources. That is, levels of protectionism which are too high may not necessarily accelerate the domestic production effort, because the producers are sheltered from competition, which is necessary to stimulate productivity and sustain product quality.

TAX STRUCTURE CHANGE

This section describes overall changes in the structure of taxation in Jamaica, Barbados, and Trinidad and Tobago between 1974 and 1990. Roy Gobin's (1979) analysis of tax structure development in these three countries up to the early 1970s provides a useful background for the analysis of tax structure change after 1974. In Barbados and Jamaica, indirect taxation was the principal source of revenue during the 1950s and 1960s. Indirect taxes constituted 69 percent of the total tax revenue of Jamaica between 1955 and 1957. This is not surprising during an early stage of development. During the colonial period, indirect taxes were mainly in the form of customs duties (see Howard 1979a). The narrow tax base in these staple-exporting economies reduced the yield of income taxation. By the early 1970s, the contribution of indirect taxation in Jamaica had fallen to 51 percent. The comparable figures for Barbados were 58 percent in the mid-1950s and 49 percent in the early 1970s. Trinidad and Tobago showed lower rates of indirect taxation of 37 percent in the period 1955–1958, and 27 percent between 1972 and 1974.

This downward trend in indirect taxation was associated with the increased importance of income taxation as the economies pursued industrialization strategies to raise income and employment levels. The expansion of other sectors of the economies, particularly tourism in Barbados and Jamaica, helped to broaden the income tax base. In Trinidad and Tobago the ratio of income taxation to total taxes moved from 62 percent in the 1950s, to 72 percent in the early 1970s as a result of oil revenues. The proportion of income tax to total taxation was around 47 percent in both Barbados and Jamaica in the early 1970s.

The period 1974–1984 was characterized by a reversal of the trend above, as the countries relied more heavily on consumption taxation to finance the fiscal budgets during recession. The relative increases in indirect taxation as a ratio of total taxes are shown in Table 8.1. The increases were sharpest in Jamaica and Barbados, where indirect taxes constituted over 50 percent during the 1980s.

The movement of the tax ratios (the ratios of specific taxes to GDP) also reveals the increased importance of indirect taxes after 1974. These ratios are shown in Tables 8.2 and 8.3. The high income tax/GDP ratio for Trinidad and Tobago, particularly before 1982, was determined by strong petroleum revenues. Price changes in the petroleum sector have a direct impact on fiscal revenues. Table 8.2 shows that the ratio of income tax to GDP in the non-oil sector has been much lower than the oil sector, except for the period 1983–1988, when the level of corporation taxes from the oil sector declined with falling oil prices. Overall, the analysis reveals a tendency in Trinidad and Tobago for total income tax to fall in relation to GDP over time after 1982. The Barbadian income tax/GDP ratio is second to that of Trinidad and Tobago up to 1982, but has been falling over time (see Howard 1989a: 121).

Table 8.1
Indirect Taxation as a Ratio of Total Tax Revenue: Jamaica,
Barbados, and Trinidad and Tobago, 1974–1990
(in percent)

Year	Jamaica	Barbados	Trinidad and Tobago
1974	49.4	41.1	14.4
1976	51.3	44.2	14.8
1978	63.7	43.0	16.3
1980	58.4	50.4	11.7
1982	39.5	49.7	14.4
1984	50.5	57.2	19.6
1986	56.3	61.3	24.9
1988	54.2	57.2	24.4
1989	53.4	58.4	25.5
1990	–	57.1	35.0

Sources: Central Bank of Barbados, *Annual Statistical Digest*, 1983 and 1990; Central Bank of Trinidad and Tobago, *Annual Statistical Reports*, various years; Central Bank of Trinidad and Tobago; *Annual Economic Survey*, 1990; Planning Institute of Jamaica, *Economic and Social Surveys of Jamaica*, 1981–1989.

Table 8.2
Income Tax/GDP Ratio: Barbados, Jamaica, and Trinidad and Tobago,
1974/76–1989/90
(in percent)

Period	Barbados	Jamaica	Trinidad and Tobago	
			Non-Oil Sector	Oil Sector
1974/76	12.2	8.6	3.8	15.8
1977/79	12.5	6.5	6.6	15.5
1980/82	10.5	8.8	9.1	17.8
1983/85	9.7	10.1	11.7	10.5
1986/88	7.0	11.2	10.2	9.3
1989/90	8.5	12.1	6.5	9.9

Sources: Central Bank of Barbados, *Annual Statistical Digest*, 1983 and 1990; Central Bank of Trinidad and Tobago, *Annual Statistical Reports*, various years; Central Bank of Trinidad and Tobago, *Annual Economic Survey*, 1990; Planning Institute of Jamaica, *Economic and Social Surveys of Jamaica*, 1981–1989.

Table 8.3
**Indirect Tax/GDP Ratio: Barbados, Jamaica, and Trinidad and Tobago,
1974/76-1989/90**

Period	Barbados	Jamaica	Trinidad and Tobago
1974/76	9.4	10.3	4.3
1977/79	12.2	10.9	5.1
1980/82	12.5	11.3	4.4
1983/85	13.6	11.5	5.8
1986/88	16.2	15.0	6.5
1989/90	18.4	15.2	7.7

Sources: Central Bank of Barbados, *Annual Statistical Digest*, 1983 and 1990;
Central Bank of Trinidad and Tobago, *Annual Statistical Reports*,
various years; Central Bank of Trinidad and Tobago, *Annual
Economic Survey*, 1990; Planning Institute of Jamaica, *Economic
and Social Surveys of Jamaica* 1981-1989.

The Jamaican income tax/GDP ratio recorded the lowest levels up to 1982,
but averaged 11.1 percent for the years 1983-1990. The lower ratios before
this period do not suggest a lower incidence of income taxation. Boyd (1984)
has shown that in 1984 the Jamaican income tax was burdensome because
the highest income tax rate, of 57.5 percent, was levied on a low statutory
income of J$14,000. Perhaps one reason for the low income tax/GDP ratio
in Jamaica was widespread tax evasion, informal labor activity, and unin-
corporated business activity, which are important factors in reducing the taxable base of the economy. Given these factors, Boyd suggests that the pay-
as-you-earn (PAYE) system was regressive on low incomes. The Jamaican
income tax ratio increased during the late 1980s, despite comprehensive income tax reform in 1986. The ratio was 12.1 percent in fiscal 1989/90, the
highest since 1974. (See Chapter 9 for the Jamaican income tax reforms.)
    The thesis advanced in the next section is that tax policy for stabilization
purposes was the primary determinant of tax structure change in Jamaica
and Barbados after 1974. In Trinidad and Tobago, tax reforms in 1989 and
1990 also introduced a strong element of discretionary tax policy. Indirect
tax policy in Barbados and Jamaica after 1974 was determined primarily by
external forces. The years 1974-1985 were a period of stress in the world
economy characterized by the first oil shock of 1973/74 and the world recession of 1981/82. The need to adjust to world recession led the Jamaican and
Barbadian governments to modify their tax structures, as well as adopt
changes in the mode of deficit financing (see Chapter 2). Indirect taxation
and money creation by the central banks were utilized on a larger scale,
especially in Jamaica. The Trinidad and Tobago fiscal system was much

more buoyant, because of strong tax revenues from the mining sector after the 1973 oil shock. However, the Trinidad and Tobago public sector came under considerable stress after 1981, as a result of declining oil revenues from the drop in petroleum prices.

TAX POLICY FOR STABILIZATION

An analysis of discretionary tax changes in Jamaica and Barbados, primarily between 1977 and 1985, shows the importance of taxation as a stabilization device in these countries. I have found no evidence to indicate that policymakers in Barbados and Jamaica before 1985 were concerned with the efficiency of their tax systems. In Barbados after 1977 there were attempts to ease the income tax burden for the lower-income groups. However, the annual budgets in these countries were primarily revenue-raising instruments, rather than devices to improve the efficiency of resource allocation. Further, the policy of heavy indirect taxation was designed principally to suppress aggregate demand in order to contain the current account of the balance of payments. Distortionary heavy consumption taxation and stamp duties were the main instruments of contractionary tax policy.

In Jamaica, the trend in discretionary tax financing was largely related to the institution of the IMF Extended Fund Facility in 1977. For example, in 1978 alone, indirect taxation in Jamaica increased by J$251.8 million, or 96.8 percent. A large part of this was due to increases in consumption duties, which totaled $178.9 million. The 1978 budget, which was designed when the economy was in the grip of the IMF, projected that new consumption duty rates would yield J$104.3 million (see Table 8.4). Overall consumption duties rose from 21.1 percent of indirect tax revenue in 1974 to 60.6 percent in 1978. The continued presence of the IMF in Jamaica was associated with heavy indirect taxation up to 1991.

Contractionary indirect tax policy was a principal feature of Barbadian budgetary management after 1977. The income tax reforms of 1986 (see Chapter 9) did not alter this stabilization policy. The fiscal budget of 1977 articulated the view that the consumption tax should be a primary defensive measure to protect the balance of payments. Contractionary tax policy was combined with expansionary money creation policy at that time. This was dealt with in Chapter 2, where I discussed deficit financing. The shift to indirect taxation was also part of an overall policy to reform the income tax system to reduce its disincentive effect.

After 1981 the concern with stabilization policy led to the heavy increases in stamp duties. Projected discretionary tax rate changes in Barbados are illustrated in Table 8.5. The analysis shows the loss of revenue in terms of income tax concessions. These income tax concessions totaled a high of $24 million in 1980. Increases in indirect taxes were mainly in the form of stamp and consumption duties, as well as specific levies.

Table 8.4
Projected Revenue Impact of Discretionary Tax Changes: Jamaica, 1978/79, 1983/84, and 1984/85

(in millions J$)

Taxes Adjusted	1978/79	1983/84	1984/85
Income tax adjustments	–	10.0	4.0
Consumption duty	104.3	24.0	58.0
Retail sales tax	18.6	12.0	–
Stamp duty	37.3	–	39.5
Levies	–	8.0	10.0
Other indirect taxes	17.5	–	52.6
Hotel accommodation tax: increase in rates	3.0	–	26.0
Education tax	–	–	15.0
Transfer tax (adjustments)	–	6.0	7.5
TOTAL	180.7	60.0	212.6

Note: (1) J$5.50 = US$1.00 at December 1985; J$21.00 = US$1.00 at December 1991.
(2) Dashes represent none for that year.

Sources: Economic and Social Surveys of Jamaica, 1978, 1983, 1984.

Table 8.5
Projected Revenue Impact of Discretionary Tax Changes: Barbados, 1977–1985

(in millions Bds$)

Year	Income Tax Concessions	Indirect Taxes and Levies
1977	–3.3	7.8
1978	0.6	3.1
1979	–11.4	2.4
1980	–24.0	24.1
1981	–18.7	2.8
1982	–2.0	22.6
1983	–2.7	24.9
1984	–14.6	30.2
1985	8.0	28.4

Note: Bds$2.00 = US$1.00
Source: Barbados Financial Statements and Budgetary Proposals for the years 1977–1985.

The implication of my analysis is that under recessionary conditions the governments of Jamaica and Barbados increasingly resorted to indirect taxes. In Jamaica, upward adjustments in taxes were made in 1977, in the context of declining private sector activity and a slow-down in the rate of income tax collections from companies. The resort to repeated tax rate changes reflected the lack of elasticity in the Jamaica tax system under recession, as well as austerity measures imposed by the IMF, which slowed the growth of incomes.

Barbados seems to have followed Jamaica with respect to indirect taxation. However, Barbados was slightly different in the sense that the government was more committed to reducing the incidence of income taxes through a system of rebates for lower-income groups and adjustment of the income tax bands (Chapter 9). Studies by Delisle Worrell (1975) and Sackey (1981) showed the need for some downward adjustment in income taxes to mitigate the severe impact of the inflation tax after 1973. Therefore, the distributional impact of stabilization policy may have been more severe in Jamaica, where the pay-as-you-earn (PAYE) was regressive on low incomes.

Another feature of tax policy in Barbados and Jamaica during the 1977–1985 period was the use of specific levies to finance the fiscal budget. In 1974 the Jamaican government imposed a bauxite levy of 7.5 percent of the price of aluminum. The levy, which increased the earnings of bauxite between 1974 and 1983, was intended to increase the productive capacity of the economy. A large part of the levy contributed to the consolidated fund, and part may have been used to finance public consumption (Davis et al. 1985). However, the levy may also have worsened Jamaica's international competitiveness in the bauxite trade.

In Barbados, the implementation of the transport, training, unemployment, and health levies during the 1980s introduced a measure of earmarking into the Barbadian budgetary process. These levies were in the form of payroll taxation and were paid into special funds. Although the levies were designed primarily to raise revenue, earmarking had significant advantages. Firstly, earmarking introduced greater efficiency and accountability into the use of funds. Secondly, it provided a link between the costs of taxation and the benefits of expenditures. However, despite the income tax concessions granted during the period, these levies had the effect of reducing disposable income and offsetting the beneficial impact of income tax reductions. The levies were also regressive on lower-income groups. In the late 1980's these levies were all paid into the consolidated fund, thereby removing the benefits of earmarking.

The emphasis on the stabilization role of the tax system was also seen in the imposition of other surtaxes on income. These surtaxes were levied under different names, such as the "surcharge" and 'stabilization tax" in Barbados, the "education tax" in Jamaica, and the "national recovery impost" in Trinidad and Tobago. For example, a tax surcharge varying between 5 percent and 7 percent of income was instituted in the 1988 Barbados budget and raised an additional Bds$14.5 million in revenue. These surcharges were intended to aid economic recovery by reducing disposable income.

It is possible to identify some of the reasons why governments in the region have used heavy indirect taxes and levies as a first resort in times of recession. In the first place, such taxes are easy to collect and easy to manipulate through the budget. Governments have also been influenced by the trend in tax reform worldwide, which favors taxes based on consumption rather than income. An important reason, too, is that increased PAYE income taxes can have a high political cost in terms of votes forgone, and in the Caribbean, such taxes have been a heavy burden on the middle class. However, heavy indirect taxes levied for the sole purpose of raising revenue are highly regressive and can have a stagflationary impact. Thus, the stabilization policies pursued by the Jamaican and Barbadian governments had some costs in terms of deterioration in income distribution. The overall effects of indirect tax increases are difficult to measure, although some attempts have been made to do so in Jamaica by Dillon Alleyne (1991). In the Jamaican case, frequent devaluations of the dollar also affected income distribution, while in Barbados the rate of price inflation remained low, especially in the early 1980s, despite the increase in taxes (see Howard 1989a: 129).

COMPLEXITY OF THE TAX SYSTEMS

Although income tax reform led to some simplification of PAYE taxation in the 1980's (see Chapter 9), the tax systems of these countries remained highly complicated before 1991. The indirect tax systems of Jamaica and Barbados were characterized by multiple distortionary rates of customs duties, consumption taxes, and stamp duties. John Due (1985) evaluated the Jamaican indirect tax system, and it is useful to note some of his conclusions here. His observations are relevant to Jamaica before 1991, when a value-added tax (VAT) was introduced.

According to Due (1985: 11), the highly complex indirect tax structure of Jamaica (Table 8.6) had a few advantages. First, the heavy taxes on nonessential consumption goods assisted in raising the percentage of national income saved and in minimizing imports of luxury goods. Second, the indirect taxes were highly revenue productive, because the base of the system was quite broad. Third, the system minimized reliance on customs duties and applied consumption duties to both domestic and imported goods. Due contends that this feature protected the revenue against declining imports as a result of import restrictions and lowered the degree of protection given to import substitutes. Fourth, the ad valorem rates of indirect taxes protected the revenue against inflation. Fifth, there was minimal cascading of taxes in the economy. Cascading refers to the application of one tax to the same commodity at successive stages of production and distribution. Sixth, the system achieved some equity through exemption from tax of basic goods consumed by lower-income groups, as well as imposition of higher rates on luxury goods.

Against the above advantages, Due (1985: 12) lists a number of objectionable features of the pre-1991 Jamaican indirect tax system. Most importantly, the multiple tax rate system and different forms of consumption taxes interfered with the simplicity, compliance, and administration of the system. Further, Due questions the limited taxation of services, because with the growing importance of services in the society, this caused revenue sacrifice and reduced the elasticity of the system. Due also observes that since the consumption duty was applied at the import and manufacturing levels, wholesale and retail margins were not included in the base. This meant that the consumption duty had to be levied at a higher rate to achieve a given level of revenue. This higher rate increased the final burden on consumers. The high rates also varied in a haphazard manner. Further, he argues that the consumption tax encouraged manufacturers to shift functions such as blending, packaging, and warehousing to subsidiary distributors, thereby decreasing the taxable price figure.

Table 8.6
Tax System of Jamaica, 1985/86 and 1989/90
(in percentage of tax revenue)

Tax	1985/86	1989/90
Customs duty	7.7	11.7
Excise duty	1.0	0.6
Consumption duty	21.5	22.8
Income tax	45.3	42.2
Land and property tax	0.8	1.2
Stamp duty	14.7	11.6
Motor vehicle licenses	1.8	0.6
Other licenses	0.1	0.1
Entertainment tax	0.1	0.2
Travel tax	0.6	1.0
Betting and gambling	1.0	0.6
Tax de sojour	2.2	1.2
Retail sales tax	1.5	2.1
Education tax	1.7	2.8
Telephone service tax	–	0.8
Contractor's levy	–	0.3

Note: Dashes represent none for that year

Source: Economic and Social Survey of Jamaica, 1989.

Table 8.7

Tax System of Barbados, 1986/87 and 1989/90
(in percentage of tax revenue)

Tax	1986/87	1989/90
Personal income tax	12.1	13.3
Company tax	11.2	12.1
Other taxes on income	1.9	1.6
Property taxes	6.7	5.3
Consumption tax	18.9	23.4
Excise tax	0.7	0.5
Hotel and restaurant tax	2.7	2.1
Licences and service	7.3	7.1
Stamp duties	13.4	11.4
Import duties	18.1	13.7
Levies*	6.9	9.4

*Includes training levy, transport levy, health levy, and employment levy.

Source: Central Bank of Barbados, *Annual Statistical Digest*, 1990.

Due's observations on Jamaica relating to the multiple tax rate system are applicable to Barbados. The two countries show a similar reliance on consumption taxes and stamp duties (Table 8.6. and 8.7). The reliance by Barbados on customs duties fell to 13.7 percent of tax revenue fiscal 1989/90, compared with 18.1 percent in fiscal 1986/87. Therefore, consumption, stamp, and customs duties roughly constituted similar proportions of revenue in these two countries. Excessive differentiation in Barbados also leads to distortions in consumer choices, since a single good can be subjected to customs, consumption, and stamp duties levied at different rates.

An analysis of the Trinidad and Tobago's tax system requires a division between the taxation of the oil and non-oil sectors. This system is not strictly comparable with those of Jamaica and Barbados. The large number of taxes underlines the complexity of this system. As shown in Table 8.8, taxation of the oil sector constituted 44.4 percent of total taxation in 1990. Corporation taxation of the oil sector (27.2 percent of tax revenue) is the dominant feature of the system. The oil sector is also subject to other taxes, such as royalties, unemployment levies, excise duties, and a national recovery impost, all of which constitute about 17.2 percent of tax revenue. The purchase tax was replaced by the VAT in 1990.

The implementation of the VAT in Trinidad and Tobago brought a measure of neutrality to the tax system. The VAT was also a major revenue-raising instrument in 1990, as shown in Table 8.8. It is appropriate to comment briefly on the efficacy of VAT systems in small countries undergoing stabilization policy. Firstly, the VAT can make a substantial contribution to government revenue. George Lent and others (1973) found that it contributed 10 percent to 30 percent of government revenue in some developing countries. Secondly, the VAT aids stabilization because it is a general regulator of demand. A generally recognized disadvantage of the VAT is its regressive incidence.

The application of the VAT depends on the special circumstances of the economy and the efficiency of tax administration. In some small economies characterized by inadequately trained tax personnel and poor accounting records, there is no good reason to introduce a VAT. The Trinidad and Tobago economy has achieved a level of development and inter-industry

Table 8.8
Tax System of Trinidad and Tobago, 1986 and 1990
(in percentage of total tax revenue)

Tax	1986	1990
Oil sector		
Corporation tax	26.6	27.2
Withholding tax	0.2	0.2
Royalties	8.3	9.7
Oil impost	0.4	0.3
Unemployment levy	0.7	1.1
Excise duties	1.5	5.3
National recovery impost	–	0.6
Non-oil sector		
Corporation tax	7.5	7.3
Personal income tax	25.4	11.1
Unemployment levy	1.7	0.01
National recovery impost	–	0.01
Health surcharge	2.1	1.8
Other taxes on income	1.8	1.3
Property tax	0.6	0.8
Purchase tax	7.5	1.1
Excise tax	1.4	3.7
Motor vehicles	3.1	1.4
VAT	–	17.0
Other taxes on goods and services	1.6	2.0
Import duties	10.6	8.7

Note: Dashes represent none for that year.

Source: Central Bank of Trinidad and Tobago, *Annual Economic Survey,* 1990.

linkage which makes the VAT system applicable. Further research on the operational aspects of the Barbadian indirect tax system is needed before a VAT can be implemented.

The VAT in Trinidad and Tobago is levied on the basis of the tax credit or invoice system. Under this method the firm applies the tax to total sales, and claims a tax credit on tax already paid on purchases of inputs. Due and Greaney (1991: 266) outlined a number of features of this tax after its implementation in 1990. The tax extends through the retail level of all goods and services, with the exception of zero-rated and exempted goods. Zero rating means that sellers do not apply the tax to sales of goods, but are eligible for tax credit already paid on inputs to produce these goods. An exempted good or service is not subject to tax, but sellers do not receive a tax credit on input. According to Due and Greaney (1991), zero rating is restricted to unprocessed food, prescription medicines, live animals, piped water, exports, natural gas, and crude oil. Exempted specified services are health services, most education, rental or residential property, bus and taxi services, real estate brokerage, insurance, and banking. The threshold for the registration of businesses was set at TT$120,000 annual sales in 1990.

TAX BUOYANCY

The analysis in this section draws heavily on my earlier work (Howard 1989a: 129–131). In the context of heavy discretionary tax changes in Jamaica and Barbados and the contraction of oil revenue in Trinidad and Tobago, it is appropriate to examine the buoyancy of these tax systems. The buoyancy coefficient measures the overall responsiveness of taxes to income changes and must be distinguished from the elasticity coefficient, which gives the natural growth or built-in flexibility of taxation in the absence of discretionary tax changes. A low buoyancy coefficient usually indicates that tax policy is not successful in increasing revenue yield. A low buoyancy may also indicate a low elasticity.

The Jamaican case shows that the buoyancy coefficients for income tax, indirect tax, and total taxes are just above unity (see Table 8.9). They cannot be considered high, but they indicate that during the recession, large discretionary tax changes have been the main instrument maintaining the buoyancy of the Jamaican tax system, as the authorities sought to extract revenue from a contracting revenue base.

The Barbadian case is different. Indirect taxation is more buoyant compared with Jamaica and Trinidad and Tobago, but income taxes and total taxation have buoyancy coefficients much less than unity. The analysis indicates that in spite of the changes in the tax system, Barbados may have a problem of fiscal revenue insufficiency. The authorities need to consider the revenue productivity of various taxes with a view to rationalizing the tax system. Trinidad and Tobago show moderate buoyancy coefficients for

Table 8.9
**Buoyancy Coefficients for the Tax System: Jamaica, Barbados,
and Trinidad and Tobago**

	Income Tax	Indirect Taxation	Total Taxation
Jamaica	1.14	1.12	1.17
Barbados	0.85	1.30	0.68
Trinidad and Tobago	1.16	1.11	1.30

Note: The buoyancy coefficients are derived from the regression equation $\log T_c = \log a + b \log y$, where T_c is the tax category, b is
the buoyancy coefficient, and y is the GDP. The T-statistic was
significant in all cases, and R^2 was generally robust above 95
percent.

income tax and indirect tax. The buoyancy coefficient for total taxation is
1.3, which is somewhat surprising given the slowdown in revenues after 1981.

Structural and administrative factors explain the low tax buoyancies in
these economies. In the first place, the operation of the industrialization model
by way of foreign investment has produced a "revenue deprivation effect"
on the public sector. The growth of import replacement industries as well
as enclave export industries was associated with a tax incentive strategy which
exempted a large proportion of capital imports and raw materials from customs duties. Income tax concessions were also granted to such industries.
Even though these industries contributed to output and value added, these
measures appear to have deprived the governments of revenue, leading to
low tax buoyancy. Another structural argument, which is difficult to support by concrete evidence, is that the growth of an "underground" economy in Jamaica, and to a much lesser extent in Barbados, may have reduced
significantly the revenue productivity of the tax base.

Administrative factors relate to tax evasion and tax collection lags. Boyd
(1984) has argued that tax evasion may be significant in Jamaica although
it is difficult to gauge the extent of evasion. In Barbados and Trinidad and
Tobago, a similar argument is possible. It is also well known that MNCs
reduce their tax liability through transfer pricing. Although it is not possible
to estimate the magnitude of the taxes lost through transfer pricing, they
are probably substantial in relation to the value added by these firms. The
problems of tax evasion and transfer pricing are not easy to deal with administratively, and they impact negatively on the buoyancy of the tax system.

TAX INCIDENCE: JAMAICA

This section discusses the results of previous tax incidence studies on

Jamaica. I am not aware of published work on tax incidence for other English-speaking Caribbean countries. Space does not permit a detailed examination of the methodologies and data sets used for these studies. Tax incidence analyses of Jamaica have been carried out by Robert Lovejoy (1963), Charles McLure (1977), Wasylenko (1986) and Dillon Alleyne (1991). Another study, by Bird and Miller (1986), was confined to the incidence of the tax system on lower-income groups only. This review looks at the first four, comprehensive studies.

The two issues central to all four studies are the relevant concept of income and the shifting assumptions used in analysis of the various taxes. Lovejoy (1963) defined income in terms of the user side of the budget, that is, household expenditure plus saving reported in the household survey. Wasylenko (1986) regards this approach as more representative of the household's true taxpaying capacity. Lovejoy assumed that indirect taxes were shifted forward to consumers while the personal income tax, property tax and estate tax were assumed to be unshifted. He assumed that 50 percent of the corporate income tax was shifted to consumers and 50 percent borne by the holders of capital.

Lovejoy's analysis for 1958 used nine income groups and found that the tax burden was roughly proportional for indirect taxes. The tax burden was progressive for direct taxes, ranging from 2.37 percent of income for the income group of less than 0.2 pounds weekly to 13.54 percent of income for the income group of over 30.00 pounds weekly. According to Wasylenko (1986), Lovejoy's study is inapplicable to Jamaica during the 1980s because of changes in the tax system to include consumption tax on local and imported goods, as well as stamp duties on imports. Further, Lovejoy did not take evasion of the income tax into his analysis, and therefore the burden of direct taxes was more progressive than if tax evasion were considered.

McLure (1977), utilizing the Jamaican Household Expenditure Survey of 1972, found that the burden of indirect taxes in Jamaica was regressive in the first five income categories, progressive in the next four income categories, and regressive in the highest income group. Personal income taxes were progressive, especially in the upper deciles. Wasylenko (1986: 26) has criticized McLure's work for having a built-in bias toward regressivity, because McLure's weekly income measure may have underestimated the income of lower-income groups and overestimated the income of upper-income groups. This is because households use income earned in previous weeks for consumption in the current week. Therefore, Wasylenko contends that the tax burden on the households in the lowest-income groups appeared higher than it was because of the underestimation of lower-income households. Further, the households in the higher-income groups did not have that amount of wage income in every week of the year. As a result, their tax burdens were underestimated.

Wasylenko (1986) utilized three sources of data: the Household Expenditure

Survey 1975, a random sample of 5,000 individual income tax returns for 1983, and a Revenue Board survey of allowances. He found that the tax burden on both low-income and high-income residents was relatively low. The effective rate for total taxation was progressive over the first eight income deciles (up to J$19,400 in family income) and regressive for higher levels of income. "On average, the lowest 20% of Jamaican families pay about 23% of income in taxes and the richest 20% pay about 33%, but the 20% of households in the seventh and eighth deciles pay about 37%." (Wasylenko 1986: xiv).

Indirect taxes were progressive for the first three deciles, slightly regressive for the third to seventh deciles, and then progressive for the seventh to tenth deciles. Direct taxes such as income and payroll taxes, were progressive for the first eight income deciles and became sharply regressive in the ninth and tenth deciles. Tax evasion by higher income groups caused the regressivity in the top two deciles (Wasylenko 1986: xviii).

Wasylenko's study found that indirect taxes were not as steeply regressive as the McLure study showed. In fact, the finding that the overall indirect tax system may be roughly proportional implies that indirect taxes should not be condemned as regressive in the absence of empirical verification. Further, the Wasylenko study confirmed the problem of tax evasion, which reduced the effective progressivity of the Jamaican tax system before 1985.

The most recent study of tax incidence in Jamaica is that of Alleyne (1991), carried out for fiscal 1988/89. Alleyne's methodology also relates effective tax rates to the decile expenditure or income groups. Alleyne's results have significant implications for tax policy and further reform of the Jamaican tax system. He found that payroll taxes, property taxes, and taxes on food were regressive. Personal income taxes were progressive up to the eighth decile, a result which supports a previous finding by Wasylenko (1986). Alleyne also found that education taxes, as well as customs and consumption duties, were proportional. Taxes on services were also progressive. Alleyne identifies an overall progressive tax pattern up to the eighth decile. Overall tax rates fall most heavily on the middle classes between the fifth and eighth deciles. Lower-income earners were affected most by indirect taxes. The proportionality of indirect taxes was due to the interplay of a number of taxes which affected income groups differently. For example, automobile taxes fell heaviest on income groups after the first five deciles, while as expected, consumption duties on food were highest for the first decile. Alleyne's (1991) study also underlines the importance of measuring the incidence of taxes on specific categories of goods before statements can be made on the overall incidence of the indirect tax system.

TAX INCENTIVES

This chapter would be incomplete without some comments on tax incentives in the Caribbean. Since the early 1960s, Caribbean governments have employed liberal tax incentives primarily to increase the volume of foreign investment. These incentives take the form of income tax holidays, investment tax credits, accelerated depreciation allowances, and exemptions from customs duties. The purpose of this section is not to give the details of the various tax incentive laws which have changed over time. The concern here is principally with the substantial body of criticism of tax incentives as instruments of industrial development in the Caribbean.

Much of the interest in the relationship between tax policy and investment was restimulated by work on the neoclassical theory of investment by Robert Hall and Dale Jorgenson (1967). The theoretical rationale for tax incentives is that they reduce the cost of capital services. The rental value of capital can be lowered by tax credits on new investment or by accelerated depreciation allowances. Hall and Jorgenson contended that the adoption of a 7 percent tax credit in the United States in 1962 had a substantial effect on investment. In the developing countries, the theoretical reason for tax incentives is also to reduce the cost of investment and thereby its risks. Whereas work on the U.S. economy has concentrated on domestic investment, tax incentives in the Caribbean have focused on the promotion of import substitution industrialization, as well as export promotion, through mobilization of foreign capital (see Andic 1968; Lent 1967).

Tax incentive programs in the Caribbean are subject to the general criticism that Caribbean governments overconcede to foreign investors by allowing them to recover greatly in excess of their capital invested before being subject to tax. Other criticisms focus on the tax revenue losses associated with overconceding and the expatriation of profits by foreign firms. David Lim (1983) has conducted a regression analysis to investigate the "illusory compensating effect." This is the attempt by developing countries to compensate for their lack of resources, technology, and labor skills by offering generous incentives. He shows that the effect may be illusory because the provision of incentives per se does not encourage a higher level of direct foreign investment. He assigns greater influence to non-tax factors. Lim (1983: 211) finds that the level of foreign investment was positively related to the availability of natural resources and the level of economic development. The generosity of the incentive package was found to be negatively related to economic development and the availability of natural resources. Lim concludes that tax incentives had no positive influence on foreign investment. It should be noted that Lim's cross-sectional analysis for 27 developing countries included Barbados, Guyana, Jamaica and Trinidad and Tobago. Although Lim's work can be criticized for using cross-sectional analysis of countries at varying levels of development and vastly different resource endowments, it mirrors some of the specific criticisms of early work on the subject by Caribbean writers.

Early analyses of tax incentives by Eric Armstrong (1967) and Fitzgerald

Francis (1968) attempted to estimate the tax revenue which was "forgone" as a result of incentive legislation. Armstrong showed that in Trinidad and Tobago between 1957 and 1964, customs duties forgone for pioneer industries amounted to TT$20.0 million. Francis (1968), on the basis of data provided by Armstrong, argued that the company tax forgone from incentive pioneer firms in Trinidad and Tobago was in the region of TT$25.5 million. The concept of forgone revenue ignores the fact that the revenue might not have been realized in the first place if the regular taxes were prohibitively high (Goode 1984).

In Jamaica, Paul Chen-Young (1975) asserted that there was no economic justification for concessions to most firms under the pioneer industries laws. Chen-Young estimated the cost to the Jamaican government of customs duties and income taxes forgone. Against these costs he estimated revenues collected from salaries, wages, and corporate and property taxes paid by government-subsidized firms. The resulting benefit/cost ratio was 0.27.

Despite these criticisms of the tax incentive program, some degree of direct foreign capital appears to have been necessary to finance imports and supplement domestic savings in the initial stages of development, and in certain capital-intensive sectors during later stages of development. Early work on the impact of industrial incentives in the Caribbean was not very rigorous in its analysis of the role of foreign investment in small developing countries. Previous work by Jefferson (1972) on the impact of tax incentives on capital intensity in Jamaica was empirically flawed (Howard 1991). Jefferson used the aggregate concept of capital costs per job to measure capital intensity, but this magnitude is a flow concept which varies from year to year and measures neither size or heterogeneity of the capital stock by sector. Better measures are value added per employee (v/l), share of wages in value added (w/v), the capital coefficient (k/v), and the capital labor ratio (k/l). For Barbados, high levels of labor intensity have been found in the production of wearing apparel and furniture, and highest levels of capital intensity in the production of chemicals and beverages (Howard 1991). The electronics industry is regarded as marginally labor intensive.

Recent criticism has been directed at the "free zones" or export-processing zones, created by special incentive laws. These zones were designed as enclaves for the processing of imported inputs for direct re-export to North America and to European firms operating in the zones. Thomas (1988) identifies a number of injustices in these zones, including exploitation of the work force through low wages, unsafe conditions of work, poor medical facilities, and restricted mobility. The type of industrialization created in these enclaves by the incentive legislation led to a high net transfer of resources abroad, low inter-industry linkages, and a negative foreign exchange contribution.

Although tax incentives should be designed to stimulate indigenous entrepreneurship, there are many non-fiscal variables retarding the growth of indigenous industrialization in small countries. These non-tax factors increase the dependence on foreign capital. In Barbados, the small indigenous industrial enterprises lack economies of scale and are unable to penetrate export markets. Heavy dependence on the small domestic market also limits scale economies. High domestic wage costs reduce the international competitiveness of industrial firms and slow the growth of exports. In this context, fiscal incentives can play only a very limited role in stimulating indigenous industrial development.

CONCLUSIONS

Stabilization policy was the overriding concern of Caribbean policymakers during the 1980s. The Caribbean tax systems predominately reflected the stabilization role of government. Consumption taxation became a major instrument for dampening aggregate demand and raising the level of government revenues. Even after 1985, when income tax reforms were introduced in Jamaica, Barbados, and Trinidad and Tobago, the governments continued to impose income-based levies and surtaxes in order to raise revenue. There do not appear to have been any strong government efforts to implement policies to improve the efficiency of the indirect tax systems in Jamaica and Barbados during the 1980s. In Trinidad and Tobago, the introduction of the VAT demonstrated the government's intention to improve tax efficiency.

Caribbean tax systems are not very buoyant. This is partly a result of structural factors which slow the growth of tax revenues, administrative lags in tax collection, and tax evasion. This lack of buoyancy, especially in Barbados, has led to almost annual increases in tax rates. The buoyancy coefficient of total taxation in Barbados was 0.68, which is quite low.

Recent tax incidence studies for Jamaica find an overall progressive incidence of total taxation up to the eighth decile. The analyses also point to a proportional tax incidence for indirect taxation.

Tax incentives for foreign investment in the Caribbean have been heavily criticized. Some of these criticisms are valid, but most critics have not advanced viable alternative strategies of industrialization or alternative fiscal programs. The Caribbean still needs foreign investment, but more emphasis has to be placed on joint ventures, whereby indigenous enterpreneurs can meaningfully participate in the industrialization process.

9

TAX REFORM

This chapter looks at supply-side tax policy and its nexus with tax reform in the Caribbean. In the 1980s tax reforms were implemented in some Caribbean territories to reduce the emphasis on income taxation. Grenada abolished income taxation and introduced a VAT in 1986 (see Samuel 1988). Income tax reforms were instituted in Barbados in 1986 and 1992, and in Jamaica in 1986. The government of Trinidad and Tobago commenced a comprehensive income tax reform program in 1989 and implemented a VAT in 1990. For these reasons the issue of tax reform in the Caribbean needs some attention, although all the operational details of tax reform cannot be handled in a single chapter. In 1987 a seminar on tax reform was held at the University of the West Indies, St. Augustine, Trinidad, to discuss a wide range of issues. The analysis draws on two papers of this seminar, namely those of Ved Gandhi (1987a) and myself (Howard 1987b), as well as a published article of mine (Howard 1987a). It seems evident that supply-side economics, and also the modernist emphasis on broad-based consumption taxation, have influenced Caribbean tax reforms.

SUPPLY-SIDE TAX POLICY AND TAX REFORM

This section discusses supply-side tax policy, which deals predominantly with the negative substitution effects of high income-tax rates and the need to reduce these rates drastically to increase the efficiency of the tax system and stimulate economic growth. Supply-side tax policy had some impact on the worldwide tax reform movement in the 1980s. This approach has also influenced the tendency toward more neutral tax systems and flat-rate consumption taxes, such as the VAT. However, before outlining supply-side tax policy, it is useful to look briefly at the demand-centered Keynesian analysis of income tax cuts. This discussion leans heavily on the analysis in my article on tax reform (Howard 1987a: 152–153).

The Keynesian aggregative approach to the analysis of tax cuts relies on heavy dependence on the first-order income effects of a tax change (Ture 1982). A tax reduction increases disposable income and the demand for output. These first-order effects work their way through the economy, thereby stimulating investment and employment. However, the view is valid that a tax cut by itself cannot generate increases in aggregate output. Real output expansion depends on an increase in production inputs and/or more efficient use of existing factor inputs. Real output is therefore a function of a number of factors, including managerial efficiency and scale economies at the micro level. These micro variables, which are crucially important in small systems, are sometimes not adequately dealt with in Keynesian aggregative analysis.

On the demand side, tax cuts in the Keynesian framework must be accompanied by a reduction in government expenditure, primarily to avoid crowding out private sector activity. Additionally, the money supply must increase to accommodate higher levels of spending in the private sector. An expansionary monetary policy must therefore accompany across-the-board tax cuts if output increases are to be realized.

The supply-side approach to tax cut analysis is based on the neoclassical specification of the first-order price effects of a tax change (Ture 1982). This approach is concerned with the cost of work effort vis-à-vis leisure and with the price of saving relative to current consumption. The theory posits that taxes on income reduce work effort, enterprise, and saving. Reductions in personal income taxes increase the propensity to save and invest, and they also increase work effort. Decreases in corporate taxes raise the net of tax rates of return, leading to re-investment in new enterprises.

Robert Keleher (1982) has advanced the view that it is changes in marginal tax rates, rather than changes in average tax rates, that are important to supply-side tax policy. Marginal tax rate changes are equivalent to relative price changes which affect allocation. Further, marginal tax rate changes should not be seen as revenue or income changes. Proponents of supply-side tax policy do not see tax cuts as injections of purchasing power or spending; in an open economy, it is impossible to ignore the purchasing-power effects of massive tax cuts on the balance of payments.

Most research on the impact of supply-side economics has been done in the free-market U.S. economy. According the Keleher (1982), the bulk of the evidence reveals that income tax reductions have only a limited effect on the overall supply of labor. The author is not aware of any previous empirical studies to show the extent to which tax cuts increase work effort, saving, and investment in small open economies like those of the Caribbean. Tax cuts seem to have more potency in stimulating aggregate supply, via their effects on increasing the capital stock (Keleher 1982).

It is generally recognized in the literature that the Laffer curve concept is the centerpiece of neoclassical supply-side tax policy. As tax rates increase, tax revenues expand, but after a certain point, increases in tax rates become unproductive and tax revenues decline. The precise empirical point where tax rates become unproductive will vary for different economies. There is, however, little evidence in small countries relating to the Laffer curve. Tax cuts aimed at specific sectors (e.g. investment) may be self-financing. That is, tax cuts may lead to an increase in tax revenue through expansion of profits. The Laffer effect (or self-financing tax cuts) is more likely to exist for narrowly based taxes than broadly based taxes (Keleher 1982). Further, although supply siders may argue that an across-the-board cut in tax rates would produce an increase in tax revenues, there is no real guarantee that the fiscal deficit would fall. There is the view that a tax cut would produce an increase in the deficit, at least in the short run. However, if we assume that supply-side economics relates to the long run rather than the short, the first-round increase in the deficit might not be viewed as a problem. Lester Thurow (1984) posits the alternative view of the supply siders who believe that the free market would adjust quickly in the short run and that the incentive effects would be large and positive.

Supply siders accept the monetarist view of the relationship between inflation and the money supply in closed systems. According to William Orzechowski (1982), monetary restraint is advocated to curb inflation, which erodes the incentive impact of a tax cut. This last consideration is not as important in the small open system, because the money supply is endogenously determined and inflation is largely imported. Further, the principal impact of money creation by the banking system in open economies is on the balance of payments rather than on price levels (Howard 1989a).

Supply siders have identified Third World countries which have benefited significantly from low tax regimes (Bartlett 1987). These include the so-called "four tigers" of Southeast Asia: Hong Kong, Taiwan, Singapore, and South Korea. Much of this evidence has been highly selective, and it sometimes ignores the large number of other sociopolitical, national, and international economic factors influencing economic growth in Southeast Asia. These countries provide evidence of the effects of supply-side tax policy, imposed there long before it became popularized in the United States. Hong Kong represents a model of a low-rate, neutral tax system, while countries like Taiwan and South Korea demonstrate the widespread use of tax incentives to lower effective tax rates to stimulate development. These cases are special, and the successful policies followed there may not be applicable to the Caribbean, which has different labor regimes and sociocultural systems.

Winston Griffith (1987) has discussed the view that the effective lowering of the profit tax rate through the widening and deepening of fiscal incentives was an important factor in the export-led growth of Singapore. According to Griffith, this policy cannot be considered in isolation from other variables enhancing development in Singapore which are not present in the

Caribbean. Particularly, he argues that the Singapore government was able to control the trade unions, thereby depressing wages and enhancing foreign investment and economic growth. In the Caribbean, on the other hand, there are conflicts between the distributional objectives of the trade unions and the state's objective of economic growth. This factor partly explains the lack of international competitiveness of the Caribbean traded-goods sector, even in the context of efforts to lower the effective rate of profit tax through fiscal incentives.

Although supply-side tax policy provides a broad rationale for tax reform, there are a number of complex issues in any comprehensive tax reform exercise. Gandhi (1987a) has identified the following: efficiency, equity, simplicity, and revenue maintenance. A comprehensive tax reform should be evaluated on the extent to which it achieves a balance of the above objectives.

Supply siders place great emphasis on the efficiency aspects of taxation. They consider efficiency and neutrality as the most desirable objectives of a tax-system (Gandhi 1987b). Supply siders are less concerned about the equity objective of taxation. According to the efficiency criterion discussed in Chapter 8, different taxes impose welfare costs or excess burdens on the economy by distorting resource allocation. One goal of taxation is to minimize the welfare costs, thereby increasing the efficiency of resource allocation. Neutral taxes do not interfere with relative prices and are believed to be more efficient than non-neutral taxes. Thus, a broad-based VAT is considered a neutral tax, whereas an excise tax levied on a specific commodity is considered non-neutral to the extent that it can lead to a change in the price and consumption of the taxed good relative to some other good. The efficiency criterion has also been discussed in textbooks under the caption of "optimal tax theory." My discussion cannot do justice in a few pages to the highly technical optimal tax theory; for in-depth treatments of the problems of efficiency and optimality, the reader is referred to the contributions of Boadway and Wildasin (1984), Nicholas Stern (1984), Frank Ramsey (1927), James Mirrlees (1971), and Alan Auerbach (1985).

An efficiency-oriented tax system will attempt to reduce the level of differentiation in tax rates. Extensive rate differentiation may lead to greater equity in the distribution of the tax burden, but it can be counterproductive from an efficiency point of view. However, if the tax system emphasizes efficiency, tax rates on various goods and services should be inversely related to the price elasticity of demand. This is the Ramsey rule of efficient commodity taxation. The rule can be generalized for many consumers, although Ramsey (1927) assumed a one-consumer economy (Stern 1984: 350). The Ramsey rule is inegalitarian, since necessities are insensitive to prices. Ramsey's formulation in terms of one consumer deliberately ignored distributional questions.

The equity criterion has already been discussed in Chapter 8. Horizontal and vertical equity have always been regarded as primary objectives of taxation. In this regard, income redistribution is a central issue in any tax reform analysis. Massive income tax cuts may alter the income distribution in favor of higher-income groups. However, this is an empirical issue. Income redistribution becomes a more serious problem if the tax cuts are accompanied by a reduction in the area of government expenditure related to the provision of basic social services.

Despite the importance of the equity criterion, I share the view of Gandhi (1987a) and Stern (1984) that the tax system should not be regarded as a major instrument of redistribution. Firstly, certain types of indirect taxes are known to be regressive. These include the VAT, sumptuary excises, and import duties. Commodity taxes generally fall on a broad range of goods used by the poorest sections of the community. Secondly, highly progressive direct taxation was regarded in the past as a vehicle of income distribution. As Gandhi (1987a) notes, this applies to nominal progressivity, but if one allows for tax avoidance and evasion, relief from corporation tax, and exclusions, nominal progressivity will not reflect the effective progressivity of direct taxes. Modern tax reform has therefore concentrated on lowering nominal progressive tax rates and instituting higher basic exemption levels, in an attempt to balance equity and efficiency. Given these limitations of the tax system, more emphasis will have to be placed on expenditure policy to redistribute income in poor countries.

A primary consideration in tax reform is revenue maintenance. In the context of severe fiscal disequilibrium, governments in small countries like those in the Caribbean cannot afford to lose too much revenue, particularly by way of massive income tax cuts. Caribbean governments have attempted to recoup revenue losses resulting from income tax reform by increasing distortionary indirect tax rates or, as in the cases of Jamaica and Trinidad and Tobago, levying a broad-based VAT. Tax revenue insufficiency can be a constraint on income tax reform that is designed to balance equity and efficiency.

The last consideration is simplicity. Flat-rate taxation, despite its bias against equity, is more simple to administer than a system of highly differentiated rates. Modern tax reform has emphasized simplicity, which further enhances taxpayer compliance. Joseph Pechman (1989) notes, however, that in developed countries little progress has been made in simplifying the tax laws on tax returns. In some countries the VAT has been complicated as a result of the adoption of multiple rates, zero rating, and exemptions. The next section examines actual tax reforms in the Caribbean to gauge the extent to which they were designed to achieve a balance of equity, efficiency, and simplicity.

Because of the complexity of the issues involved in tax reform it appears that the latter should be tailored to suit the specific circumstances of poor countries. It makes no sense to implement a VAT in a country which has few intersectoral linkages, or in an economy based on high levels of informal activity. A simple retail sales tax or a consumption tax levied at the import stage may be better for highly service-oriented economies or for economies with a high level of imports in their consumption mix. Given the importance of sales taxes as the main revenue raiser in Jamaica and Barbados, indirect tax reform now has to be considered. In 1985 a general consumption tax (GCT) was proposed for Jamaica by the Metropolitan Studies Program of Syracuse University (Due 1985). At the time of writing, the GCT had just been implemented. The 1985 proposal, as well as the 1991 implementation of the GCT, are discussed in later sections.

INCOME TAX REFORM IN THE CARIBBEAN

The analyses here describe the salient features of income tax reforms in the Caribbean nations of Jamaica, Barbados, and Trinidad and Tobago in the 1980s and early 1990s. This is followed in the next section by an evaluation of the tax reforms. The Jamaican comprehensive income tax reform of 1986 had a number of basic objectives. An overriding goal was to reduce tax evasion by simplifying the tax system and broadening the tax base. The Jamaican tax system before the reform was characterized by horizontal inequities, with different tax treatment of individuals at the same level, as a result of the ability of certain groups to disguise their income. The reforms were also intended to stimulate economic growth. The Jamaican policymakers held the view that high marginal tax rates discouraged private sector initiatives, investment, and work effort and slowed the rate of economic growth. The main characteristics of these reforms were the abolition of tax on statutory incomes below J$8,580 and the imposition of a flat rate of tax of 33$1/3$ percent on the part of any income that was in excess of J$8,580. A revenue loss of J$200 million for 1986 was estimated as a result of the flat rate. Further, tax credits were abolished, except for donations to charitable or educational institutions. Roy Bahl (1989) has discussed in detail the major features and implications of the Jamaican reforms. This section pays more attention to the details of the Barbadian reforms.

Barbadian income tax reform showed an evolution from gradualist tax reform (1977 to 1985) to massive tax cuts (1986). Initially, the main factors influencing tax reform between 1977 and 1985 were the inflationary impact of the oil crisis of 1973 and the intention of the Barbadian policymakers to build a service economy by reducing the incidence of personal income tax. Between 1973 and 1977 there was no significant reform of the income tax system. During the latter period the government was primarily concerned with contractionary stabilization policy to curb consumption expenditure and correct the balance of payments. It was only after 1977 that income redistribution, by way of income tax reform, came to be regarded as a fundamental aspect of the government's budgetary policy.

The most important income-tax reform in Barbados prior to 1986 was the introduction of a tax credit system in 1977. This system was abolished in

1986. The primary purpose of the tax credit system was to reduce or remove completely the incidence of income tax for the lowest-income groups. For example, assuming a tax credit of Bds$60, a taxpayer of Bds$6,000 per year or less, whose net tax due was less than Bds$60 in income year 1976, was not required to pay income tax. The tax credit system is a form of negative income tax which attempts to alleviate the tax burden for individuals at the lower end of the income-tax scale.

Other reforms in the income-tax system between 1977 and 1985 can be described as gradualist in nature. Slight adjustments were made to the top rate of income tax, and the income tax bands were widened to accommodate wage changes. In fiscal 1979/80 a maximum marginal rate of 70 percent was charged on incomes over Bds$30,000. The bands were widened in fiscal 1980/81, but high marginal rates remained on incomes over Bds$30,000, with the highest marginal rate being 70 percent. This high marginal rate meant that the philosophy of tax reform was not really concerned with the efficiency of the tax system.

An evaluation of the income tax reforms between 1977 and 1985 shows that middle- and upper-income groups did not benefit significantly from the tax adjustments (Howard 1987b), while the tax credit system eased the burden for large numbers in the lower-income groups. The Barbados 1980 fiscal budget estimated that the reforms of 1980 freed 29 percent of the labor force at the bottom of the tax scale, or 30,000 people, from the income tax net. The subtstantial tax cuts of 1986 reduced considerably the tax liability of middle- and upper-income groups.

The most outstanding and popular features of the Barbadian tax reform of 1986 were the standard deduction of Bds$15,000 and the abolition of tax for persons earning Bds$15,000 or less. This system was still operational in 1991. The standard deduction significantly lowered the effective income tax rate defined as the ratio of tax payable to gross annual income. About 88 percent of taxpayers calculated their tax payable on the basis of the standard deduction. However, since the allowance by itself did not distinguish among taxpayers on the basis of financial responsibilities, it is possible to argue that the horizontal equity of the system was reduced considerably. The increase in other allowances and itemized deductions was designed primarily to benefit the middle and upper classes. An individual could claim either the standard deduction, or the total of itemized deductions and allowances, whichever was greater.

When the effective income tax rate for a Jamaican married person in 1986, under certain assumptions, is compared with that for a Barbadian married person in the same year, assuming the basic Bds$15,000 allowance,[1] Table 9.1 shows that the effective income tax rate for the Barbadian taxpayer, 8 percent, may be seen to be much lower than that for a Jamaican, 29 percent (Howard 1987a: 155). On the basis of the 1985 tax structure, the effective income tax rate for the same Barbadian taxpayer would have been 15 percent.

Table 9.1
Effective Tax Rate for Married Person: Barbados, 1986
(Assuming Basic Bds$15,000 Allowance)

Gross annual income	Bds$25,000
Minus minimum allowance	15,000
Taxable income	10,000
Tax payable (Bds$10,000 × 20%)	2,000
Effective tax rate (Bds$2,000 ÷ $25,000)	8%
Jamaican effective tax rate	29%

Note: US$1.00 = Bds$2.00

Source: Calculated from tax tables, Barbados budgetary proposals, July 1986.
The Basic Bds$15,000 was employed. The source for the Jamaican
effective tax rate is "Personal Tax: Jamaica and the Caribbean,"
Caribbean Finance and Management, vol. 1, no. 2, Winter 1985.

Table 9.2
Maximum Effective Tax Rate for Single Person or Married Person
Filing Separately: Barbados, 1986

Gross Annual Income (Bds$)	Maximum Effective Tax Rate (%)
15,000	0.0
25,000	8.0
35,000	12.9
45,000	17.7
55,000	22.3

Source: Calculated from tax tables in budgetary proposals, July 1986,
Barbados. The basic Bds$15,000 allowance was employed.

Further analysis shows that the maximum effective income tax rate for
Barbadians, on the basis of the July 1986 tax structure, rises from a low of
zero on a gross annual income of Bds$15,000 to 22.3 percent on Bds$55,000
(Table 9.2). The difference between these rates and the Jamaican example
is even greater, and the actual effective rates for individuals claiming allowances in excess of Bds$15,000 are greater still. For example, the effective
tax rate for an individual earning a gross Bds$55,000 annually, with total
allowances of Bds$17,500, was 20.2 percent. However, the Barbadian maxi-
mum nominal marginal rate of 50 percent (Table 9.3) was much higher than
that of Jamaica, 33 1/3 percent and Trinidad and Tobago, 35 percent (Table
9.4) in 1990 (see also Howard 1987a: 155).

Table 9.3
Income Tax Structures: Barbados, 1985/86 and 1986/87–1991/92

Pre-Reform Rate Structure 1985/86		Post-Reform Rate Structure 1986/87–1991/92	
Taxable Income (Bds$)	Rate (%)	Taxable Income (Bds$)	Rate (%)
Up to 5,000	10	Up to 15,000	20
10,000	20	25,000	30
15,000	30	35,000	40
20,000	40	55,000	45
30,000	50	Over 55,000	50
Over 30,000	60		

Source: Barbados, financial and budgetary proposals for the years 1985/86 and 1986/87.

Table 9.4
Post-Reform Income Tax Structure: Trinidad and Tobago, 1989 and 1990

Chargeable Income (TT$)	1989 (%)	1990 (%)
Up to 12,000	5	5
12,001–20,000	20	15
20,001–40,000	40	30
Over 40,000	45	35

Source: Trinidad and Tobago Budget Speech 1990, December 22, 1989.

Mascoll (1991) found that the 1986 tax reforms in Barbados predominantly benefited the upper-income earners. Mascoll's analysis was based on the concept of representative taxpayers drawn from the low-income, middle-income, and high-income groups. Taxable income for representative taxpayers was based on the level of allowances claimed by the taxpayers. Mascoll then calculated effective tax rates for the representative individual from each income group. The effective tax rate was calculated as the ratio of income tax paid, including surtaxes and other income-based levies, to gross annual income. Mascoll found that for the high-income individual the effective tax rate was 28.3 percent before tax reform in 1985, but fell to 20.9 percent in 1986 and 19.2 percent in 1987. The effective tax rate for the middle income individual changed only slightly, falling from 12.9 percent in 1985 to 12.8 percent in 1987. The effective tax rate for the low-income individual decreased from 9.6 percent in 1985 to 8.8 percent in 1987. Overall, Mascoll's analysis showed that middle-income groups did not benefit significantly from income tax reform. Mascoll's work is not a comprehensive incidence study and therefore cannot be compared with the incidence analyses discussed in the previous chapter. However, it represents an attempt to gauge the benefits of tax reform. The analysis also showed that the gains of tax reform were eroded by heavy taxation of incomes after 1987. Mascoll demonstrated that by 1990 the effective tax rate for a high-income individual had risen to 26.2 percent, while effective tax rates for middle- and lower-income individuals were 17.6 percent and 13.8 percent, respectively.

In May 1992, in response to a request made by the Barbadian government, an IMF mission to Barbados submitted recommendations for reform of the direct tax system. The major elements of the original IMF proposals were as follows:

1. Reduction of the top income tax rate to 40 percent, effective from income year 1992.
2. Elimination of individual and company stabilization taxes and levies.
3. Reduction of the standard deduction for all taxpayers from Bds$15,000 to Bds$12,000.
4. Harmonization of individual PAYE and social insurance tax systems.
5. Elimination of almost all itemized deductions declared on individual income tax returns.
6. Reduction of most business incentives, and broadening of the tax base to include additional forms of income such as pensions.
7. Increase of the corporate tax rate from 35 percent to 40 percent, the level equal to the proposed maximum individual tax rate.
8. Indexation for inflation of individual income tax brackets, after implementation of the reform package.
9. Increased property tax rates up to 1 percent of land value thereby modifying the structure of property taxation to remove the distinction between improved and unimproved land.
10. Tightening up on tax compliance by modifying the rules on payment dates for the major direct taxes.

The rationale for this program reflected the need to simplify the direct tax system. The IMF's mission to Barbados noted that the substantial number of income exclusions, deductions and credits narrowed considerably the income tax base, thereby necessitating higher marginal rates of tax to generate a required level of revenue. Further, certain business incentives were regarded as inefficient and inequitable, and worked to the competitive disadvantage of new businesses. The mission hoped that its new tax program would be more cost effective, by reducing special exclusions from income.

The IMF's tax model predicted increases in property taxes and PAYE income taxes for some individuals in the middle and upper-income groups. High-income taxpayers objected to the proposed elimination of itemized deductions, especially the unlimited mortgage interest allowance. Some families may have purchased or built more expensive houses, because of the deductibility of substantial mortgage interest. This provision can be interpreted as a substantial government subsidy to high-income property owners. Generally speaking, such tax preferences reduce efficiency.

In July 1992 the Barbados government announced a tax reform program which modified slightly the original IMF proposals. The major features of the 1992 tax reform is as follows:

1. The maximum tax rate for income year 1992 was reduced to 40 percent.
2. Most itemized allowances and deductions were abolished.
3. Exemptions for pension income were withdrawn, but taxpayers over 60 years may claim a deduction of Bds$20,000.
4. A 12.5 percent withholding tax on interest was instituted, along with a 12.5 percent final tax on dividends.
5. The corporation tax rate was increased from 35 percent to 40 percent.
6. Levies and stabilization taxes were to be eliminated over a period of time.
7. A general property tax rate of 0.95 percent of land value was introduced, but a lower rate of 0.35 percent for owner-occupied homes remained for the first Bds$100,000.
8. The standard deduction was reduced from Bds$15,000 to Bds$13,000.
9. Two rates of income tax were introduced. On income between Bds$13,000 and Bds$37,000 per annum, the rate was 25 percent; and 40 percent above that level.

The 1989/90 comprehensive tax reforms in Trinidad and Tobago perhaps best capture the spirit of popular supply-side tax policy. The pre-1989 tax regime was characterized by great complexity, high rates of corporate taxation, high marginal rates of personal income tax and myriad tax allowances, exemptions, deductions, and incentives. The reforms were designed to lessen this complexity, reduce the income tax burden, and increase productivity, investment, and savings.

The Trinidad and Tobago reforms had a number of basic features: the marginal rates of personal income taxation were reduced; the number of rate brackets was lowered from eleven to four (Table 9.4); a 5 percent income tax surcharge on total individual income over TT$12,000 was eliminated; a system of personal tax credits was implemented, thereby eliminating persons from the income tax net whose total income was less than TT$12,000; and personal allowances and deductions were eliminated. Table 9.4 also shows that by 1990 the top marginal rate of income tax had fallen to 35 percent. The estimated revenue loss from income tax cuts was TT$200.0 million. Corporation taxation was reduced from 49.5 percent to 45 percent by the elimination of certain levies, namely the national recovery impost, the unemployment levy, and the business levy. The corporation tax rate was further reduced to 40 percent in 1990, with an estimated revenue loss for 1990 of

TT$30 million. In 1990 a 15 percent VAT was also introduced. The objective of the VAT in Trinidad and Tobago was similar to that in Indonesia, analyzed by Malcolm Gillis (1985). In both countries the VAT was a revenue-raising tax reform measure in the context of sluggish export earnings from the oil sector.

EVALUATION OF TAX REFORM

It is noteworthy that two important supply-side features predominate in the income tax reforms. The first is the sharp reduction of marginal income tax rates across the board. The underlying theoretical argument was that such reductions increase the efficiency of income taxation by lowering its distortionary negative substitution effects. As we have discussed earlier, such unified tax rates, or flat-rate tax regimes, tend to favor efficiency. It is arguable that the Jamaican reform was more efficiency oriented than those of Barbados in 1986, and Trinidad and Tobago. The last two countries retained a higher degree of progressivity in their income tax structures than Jamaica.

The second supply-side feature was the simplification of the income tax systems. This was particularly so in Jamaica and Trinidad and Tobago. In the Jamaican case, simplification was achieved by imposition of the flat rate of $33^1/_3$ percent, whereas in Trinidad and Tobago the simplified income tax system meant removal of tax-induced distortions such as concessions, deductions, and exemptions. In the Barbadian case, some simplification was achieved by creation of a Bds$15,000 standard deduction. However, a variety of itemized deductions and exemptions remained in the 1986–1992 Barbadian tax system. The Barbadian tax reform of 1992 considerably simplified the tax system.

A tax system comprising a standard deduction and few allowances is undoubtedly simpler to administer. Firstly, tax authorities are no longer required to scrutinize numerous receipts and invoices submitted by taxpayers in support of claims for tax deductions. Secondly, a simple system removes the incentive for tax avoidance. Thirdly, the abolition of special concessions simplifies the tax law considerably. This reduces the lag in tax collection, because highly paid professionals no longer have the incentive to exploit loopholes in the tax code.

Were Caribbean tax reforms revenue-efficient? Bahl (1989) suggests that Jamaica's reformed tax system was not significantly less revenue-income elastic than the pre-reform system. This is because the standard deduction of J$8,580 was not indexed, and therefore tax rates for all taxpayers rose with increases in income. The reformed Barbados tax system of 1992 is expected to be more revenue-efficient than the 1986 system. High revenue yields are expected from the new structure of income tax rates, the lower Bds$13,000 standard deduction and the abolition of itemized deductions.

Were Caribbean tax reforms equitable, in terms of their impact on the income distribution? It is difficult to answer this question because of the absence of comparative post-reform incidence studies. Nevertheless, there are some indications that the reforms were concerned with fairness or equity. The imposition in all the countries of a basic higher exemption level for income taxation, reveals the concern with equity. In Trinidad and Tobago, the implementation of a simplified system of tax credits for taxpayer, spouse, and child was designed to promote horizontal equity.

Were the reforms cost-effective? The tax reforms increased the cost-effectiveness of the tax systems of Jamaica and Trinidad and Tobago simply by reducing complexity. Nevertheless, in Barbados the cost of administering the 1986–1992 tax system remained high. Firstly, there were the administrative costs of collecting about six direct taxes, when two or three taxes would have served the same purpose, because all the revenue was placed in the consolidated fund. Secondly, the complex allowance system resulted in high revenue costs for the government, without necessarily guaranteeing increases in productive investment. The 1992 Barbados tax reform attempted to remedy this situation, by reducing itemized deductions.

The Caribbean tax reforms incorporated most of the features of tax reform in the developing world. These features include lowering of tax rates, broadening of tax bases, and alignment of corporate tax rates with top bracket personal income tax rates. Broadening of the income tax base allows fewer taxes, and lower tax rates, on a broader range of incomes. Base broadening increases efficiency, because the tax system does not discriminate unduly among individuals. For example, in Jamaica base broadening was accomplished by including certain fringe-benefit type allowances in the definition of taxable income. Interest income, above a threshold level, was made taxable (Bahl, 1989)

Jamaica also aligned its corporation tax rate with the top personal income tax rate of $33^1/_3$ percent. The 1992 Barbados tax reform raised the corporation tax rate from 35 percent to 40 percent to align with the maximum 40 percent rate for personal income tax. Harmonization of personal and corporate income tax rates seems to be appropriate in developing countries, to remove the incentive for high-income individuals to incorporate, in order to reduce the effective tax rate payable on their income. Under the 1986–1992 tax system, it became evident that some individuals in Barbados were incorporating under the lower 35 percent corporation tax rate, to reduce their income tax liability.

The analysis did not attempt to measure empirically the impact of Caribbean tax reform on the efficiency of resource allocation. This task is perhaps impossible in small open economies, where resource allocation, investment, and growth are influenced by all aspects of macroeconomic policy. I am not aware of any empirical studies on the excess burden of taxation in the Caribbean. In general, empirical analyses of the efficiency costs of taxation are not widespread in the literature. Further, as Charles Hulten (1984) observed, tax effects may be swamped by other factors, including budget deficits. More specifically, the tax reforms in Jamaica and Trinidad and Tobago were implemented when these countries were undergoing contractionary IMF demand management policies. In the Barbadian case, subsequent heavy distortionary consumption taxation, income-based levies, and income tax surcharges during the period 1987 to 1991 exerted negative influences on equity and efficiency.

PROPOSAL AND IMPLEMENTATION OF A GENERAL SALES TAX IN JAMAICA

This section examines the rationale for the GCT in Jamaica as originally proposed in the work of Due (1985), as well as its implementation in 1991. The proposal was for a VAT at the manufacturer and large distributor level. Due's proposal specified a structure involving a basic rate of 20 percent, with a 15 percent supplement on luxury goods and higher rates on goods such as motor vehicles. A tax credit technique was proposed to prevent cascading. Under this method the tax would apply to imports and domestic sales by manufacturers and large distributors, who would in turn receive a credit for tax paid at importation and domestic purchase of goods. A few goods would be excluded from the tax, such as medicines, farm equipment, feed, and fertilizers. The proposal also suggested initial retention of traditional rates on cigarettes, liquor, beer, and moter fuel. The GCT would be a merger of consumption duties, excise duties, and the retail sales tax on motor cars and other consumer durables. Ultimately, the GCT was meant to be extended through the wholesale and larger retail store levels, using the tax credit VAT feature (Due 1985: 55).

The main rationale for the proposed GCT was the need for simplifying the Jamaican indirect tax system and the inadequacy of other indirect tax regimes in the Jamaican context. Due (1985) argued that the merging of excises, consumption duties, and the retail sales tax into the GCT would simplify compliance, facilitate administration, and allow a more rational tax structure. He identified the weaknesses of other taxes, such as the single-stage retail sales tax and the VAT through the retail level.

Although the retail sales tax is an efficient tax, it is not suited to Jamaica. The presence of a large number of small retail vendors makes it difficult to administer such a tax. Further, there is a wide range of distribution channels in Jamaica, rather than clearly delineated wholesalers and retailers. The alternative of a VAT through the retail level was regarded as too complex for Jamaica, given the complicated distribution channel and the problem of obtaining adequate administrative staff (Due 1985: 16–19).

The virtue of the proposed GCT, which was intended to be a manufacturers' sales tax extended through the large distributor level, is that it relates to the nature of the Jamaican distributional channel. Due explained the importance of a few large distributors, who are manufacturers and primary wholesalers. They sell to secondary wholesalers and retailers. Licensing of these large distributors is easier administratively than extending the tax over a large number of small retailers. Due's paper outlined a list of commodities to be excluded from the GCT, as well as commodities for supplementary luxury rates.

A uniform GCT clearly has the advantage of greater simplicity. However, Bird (1987), on the basis of a tax incidence study by Bird and Miller (1986), suggests that a uniform GCT would not only increase taxes on low-income households, but also increase the regressivity of Jamaica's already regressive consumption tax system, because under the highly differentiated system of the 1980s, many goods consumed by low-income groups, were taxed at lower rates than the 1985 proposed GCT rate. The problem of regressivity, as well as other issues relating to exemptions, tax structure, and administration may explain why the GCT was not introduced until six years after the initial proposal in 1985.

The actual GCT introduced in October 1991 was a 10 percent tax on the value of consumption of most of the goods and services supplied in Jamaica.[2] The GCT replaced the excise duty, consumption duty, additional stamp duty, hotel accommodation tax, entertainment tax, telephone tax, and retail sales tax. The GCT therefore simplified considerably the system examined in Chapter 8. Business firms carrying out taxable activities were required to register under the new tax regime. Registered taxpayers were also required to issue tax invoices for goods sold. The opposition JLP complained that the tax was introduced in an atmosphere of uncertainty. Many firms called for a delay in the implementation of the GCT, since they did not have enough time to prepare staff to program machines and issue invoices. Dillon Alleyne (1991) suggests that, from an administrative point of view, the GCT is an advance over the old indirect tax system characterized by multiple rates, a variety of taxes, and a narrow tax base.

CONCLUSION

This chapter examined the principles which guided tax reform in the Caribbean during the second half of the 1990s. These reforms emphasized that the tax system should play a major role in stimulating investment and growth, by minimizing the negative substitution effects of high marginal income tax rates. All the reforms reduced the burden of income taxation across the board and reflected the modern trend toward tax neutrality, designed to enhance the efficiency of resource allocation. The reforms made some provision for equity by the inclusion of higher basic exemption levels. Trinidad and Tobago implemented the VAT in 1990, and Jamaica followed soon after with the introduction of the GCT in 1991. Some concern was expressed about the regressive nature of the VAT.

The 1991 IMF letter of intent for Barbados announced plans to broaden the tax base and simplify the income tax system in 1992 and 1993. A tax reform package was introduced in 1992. The Barbadian government hoped to complete a study on a general consumption tax, possibly in the form of a VAT, to replace consumption and excise taxes in the latter part of fiscal 1992/93. In the absence of post-reform incidence studies on Barbados and Trinidad and Tobago, it is not possible to pursue comparative empirical analysis on the impact of tax reform.

NOTES

1. See "Personal Income Tax: Jamaica and the Caribbean," *Caribbean Finance and Management,* vol. 1, no. 2, Winter 1985. This article calculated the income tax payable by a married person under the new income tax system, effective January 1986. It was assumed that the taxpayer earns US$12,500, lives in a rented house, pays 5 percent of his salary for pension or life insurance, and has no savings and that one child is under 12 years, the other over 12. To avoid complication, this model taxpayer is compared here with a Barbadian benefiting from the standard deduction of Bds$15,000.

2. The Jamaican GCT is a VAT utilizing the tax credit or invoice method. The tax threshold in 1991 was J$144,000, that is, firms with annual sales below this amount were not eligible to pay tax. Zero-rated goods include food items, health services, exports, utilities, and certain construction materials. Exempted services include transportation, rentals of residential property, electricity, and water supply (Alleyne 1991).

10

BUDGETING AND PLANNING

This chapter looks at government budgeting and development planning in small countries. The first three sections discuss the budgetary process and the link between traditional budgeting and planning. The empirical analysis here of these two public sector functions is confined to Barbados. I examine the budget as a tool of fiscal policy in Barbados and the orientation of the policy outlined in the development plans. Development planning can be regarded as an aspect of public finance, because planning has implications for the structure and financing of the capital budget. Most public finance books omit the planning aspects of government activity, although there are notable exceptions, such as Premchand (1983) and Goode (1984). My emphasis on planning also relates to the overall role of the state in economic development.

THE TRADITIONAL BUDGETARY PROCESS

Traditional, or incremental, budgeting is the form of budgeting practised in the English-speaking Caribbean. It is appropriate to begin with a definition of budgeting. Following Aaron Wildavsky (1979: 2), the fiscal budget can be described as "a mechanism for making choices among alternative expenditures." When the choices are coordinated to achieve certain economic objectives, a budget can also be described as a plan. This analytical definition of a fiscal budget is better than those definitions which regard the budget merely as a statement of intended revenues and expenditures. When the budget is viewed as a fiscal plan, it is easier to gauge the extent to which fiscal policy attempts to achieve trade-offs among the goals of allocation, distribution, and stabilization.

Budgeting is a political as well as an economic process. The process of traditional or incremental budgeting derives from established political power relations. The administrative agencies submit requests for funds to the executive or finance minister, whose proposals are approved or rejected by the legislature. In the Caribbean, these proposals are presented in the form of annual estimates, as well as a budget speech presented by the finance minister.

Alan Prest (1975: 33) identifies four stages in the budgetary process. These are budget formulation, budget authorization, budget implementation, and the post-mortem. Budget formulation is an executive process comprising the estimates of revenues and expenditures. The considerations raised in the formulation stage would involve estimates of the costs of existing services and of outlays on continuing and new capital projects. Estimates of revenues are also prepared, and a consolidated statement of revenues and expenditures drawn up. Premchand (1983) has indicated that one of the main constraints in the formulation process is lack of information. If statistical data are not accurate or up to date, forecasting may underestimate the level of funding required. It may also be necessary to allow for the impact of price inflation on the estimates, because cost overruns often force governments to implement supplementary budgets, months after the annual budget has gained legislative approval.

Legislative authorization is the process whereby the budget proposals are presented in parliament and debated. In Barbados this is usually a rubber-stamping exercise, but it allows opposition members to voice their criticisms of all the government's economic and social programs. Parliamentary debate is therefore not solely confined to the budget itself.

Budget implementation depends on the system of tax collection and expenditure controls. In Barbados, tax revenue is usually conservatively estimated, so that actual collections exceed budgetary projections. In some countries, significant lags in tax collection, resulting from tax evasion or inefficient administrative efforts, are constraints on the implementation process. Developing countries also need proper systems of expenditure controls. Intense competition for funds between various ministries can lead to expenditure levels which are too high relative to the country's resources and productivity levels.

The post-mortem is the compilation of the auditor's report. The government's accounting systems should be consonant with the legal provisions. According to Prest (1975: 146), in some developing countries this final stage is perhaps the most inefficient, and it may take months or even years to complete.

The type of budgeting outlined above rests on a behavioral model known as incrementalism. This theory stresses that decisions made about this year's budget are influenced by the budget of the year before. The budget examines those items for which increases or decreases over the previous year are requested. In this regard incrementalism is conservative, because there is very little examination of basic programs. Wildavsky (1979) argues that this approach is cheaper in decision-making resources. Further, incrementalism aids the process of securing agreement and reduces the burden of calculation. As Wildavsky (1979: 136) submits, "it is much easier to agree on a small addition or decrease than to compare the worth of one program to that of all others."

Wildavsky's vision seems somewhat myopic, however, and many writers have questioned this rigid adherence to incrementalism. Brown and Jackson (1982: 159) identify a number of disadvantages of incremental budgeting. The system may not be quick to change or to adapt. Piecemeal changes may therefore characterize reforms of the social services. Incrementalism can also compound errors made in the past, simply because the system is not subject to in-depth revision. In short, incrementalism is a conservative system with a low level of political opportunity costs. It favors short-term political decision making.

In the Caribbean, incrementalism has been highly criticized as inadequate in the context of developing countries. Simon Jones-Hendrickson (1985: 76–85) provides a long list of perceived deficiencies of budgeting in the Caribbean. Firstly, he maintains that the budgets show inadequate attention to allocative efficiency. My later analysis of the Barbadian case supports this view, because the fiscal budget was more concerned with stabilization. Incremental changes in tax rates and bases, without regard to efficiency, usually characterize Caribbean budgets. Secondly, expenditure decisions are made without due consideration to the financial consequences. In many cases, at the time of budget authorization, no indication is given of the manner in which the total fiscal deficit is to be financed, or of its perceived impact on the balance of payments. Thirdly, Jones-Hendrickson (1985) criticizes the line-item structure, which is not adequately linked to the development plan. Fourthly, incrementalism gives excessive centralized control to the various ministers of finance, and there is an absence of performance measurements and reviews.

RELEVANCE OF BUDGET INNOVATIONS TO SMALL COUNTRIES

The weakness of incremental budgeting has led to three groups of proposals for reform: performance budgeting, program budgeting, and zero-base budgeting. This section briefly reviews the salient characteristics of these proposals and discusses whether they are applicable to small developing systems. For a historical sketch of the development of these systems, the reader is referred to Premchand (1983: 319–347)

Performance budgeting is a system of decision making which focuses on the outputs of particular programs, as well as on performance measurement in the attainment of these output objectives. This form of budgeting is therefore concerned with efficiency in terms of cost-effectiveness. The performance budget specifies a detailed account of the work load for various departments, as well as giving productivity measurements. According to Premchand (1983), this type of budgeting, when practiced in the United States in the early 1950s, encountered serious difficulties. The measurement of productivity was elusive, and the computation of costs was complex.

Program budgeting, sometimes known as planning programming-budgeting system (PPBS), has been applied to a larger number of countries than performance budgeting. PPBS emphasizes the output side of government spending and adopts a multi-year approach rather than an annual approach. The programs are related to broad objectives through a program structure. Cost-effectiveness techniques and project analysis are used to judge the effectiveness of the various programs. The program structure requires a high degree of centralization in order to coordinate the various tasks. This system of budgeting was used in the United States during the 1960s.

PPBS has been subject to a number of criticisms which are highly relevant to developing countries. Firstly, there has been controversy about the measurement of the output of PPBS. It is difficult to define the output of certain service activities, such as health, defense, and other types of intermediate outputs used in final good production (Goode 1984: 36). Secondly, and more importantly, PPBS demands highly efficient administrative structures, which are lacking in small developing countries. The high level of statistical calculations required incur financial costs beyond the capacity of small country governments (Prest 1975: 156). Wildavsky (1979: 200), a strong critic of PPBS, describes it as a cost-ineffective system which further increases the costs of correcting error.

Zero-base budgeting (ZBB) is a form of budgeting by which each program is challenged for its existence in every budget cycle. ZBB does not accept last year's budget as the starting point for the analysis examining proposed increases or decreases. Zero-base reviews are required to support the introduction of new programs. ZBB is decision oriented, focusing on feasibility and efficiency. All programs are required to compete for scarce resources (See Wildavsky 1979; and Schick 1978).

Although there is some justification for applying ZBB at a departmental level from time to time in developing countries, it is quite difficult to comprehensively adapt this system to the decision-making process in these countries. ZBB requires numerous background studies, which can incur a heavy cost. Further, developing countries lack the range of top-level managerial manpower needed to supervise ZBB systems. Again, vote-maximizing governments cannot take the risk required to change too many programs during a short five-year term of office.

To sum up, despite the deficiencies of the incremental system, I see no reason why Caribbean governments should try to adopt wholesale the other budgetary innovations. The traditional system is perhaps best suited to deal with short-term stabilization policy, which has become a priority in the Caribbean in the last ten years. However, there is scope for introducing other types of budgeting at the departmental level in the public service. For example, zero-base reviews can be implemented in such areas as health and education, in an effort to make these areas more cost-effective. Zero-base reviews should also be implemented in parastatal institutions which are presently a burden on the public purse. Such analyses may support privatization of some low-productivity, high-cost government services.

DIVERGENCES BETWEEN PLANNING AND TRADITIONAL BUDGETING

The analysis here leans heavily on Premchand (1983) in identifying the similarities and divergences between traditional budgeting and development planning. Premchand distinguishes between substantive planning and fiscal planning. Substantive planning, or development planning, involves the mobilization of a society's resources to meet certain social and economic goals. Fiscal planning, or budgeting, is an instrument of substantive planning. Budgeting involves legislative accountability and is much more than a statement of intended revenues and expenditures. Budgeting is a tool of fiscal policy designed to keep the economy on its long-term development path.

Although budgets and plans are concerned with policy, issues of resource allocation tend to dominate the development plan, while financial issues dominate the annual budget. Budgetary estimates focus on the use of funds, while the legislative debate is designed to approve the source of funds. On the other hand, the plan's emphasis is mobilization of funds on a sectoral basis. The plan is concerned with "capital spending," or "development finance," whereas the budget attemps to estimate the level of financing required for the following fiscal year.

Premchand (1983: 194) identifies divergences between planning and budgeting at the administrative level. In some countries development plans are compiled by a planning agency and the current budget is determined by a finance agency. Different time horizons for compiling the various documents are assumed by the two agencies. These divergences are less serious in administrations where the ministry of finance also has control over economic affairs. Further, budget analysts are normally concerned with the implications of line-item proposals for various ministries, rather than with the overall sectoral impact of these proposals.

I have observed efforts by the Trinidad and Tobago government to integrate budgeting and planning. The 1990 Trinidad and Tobago budget speech included a number of long-term planning strategies which are normally found in a development plan. In fact, the budget reinforces Trinidad and Tobago's draft medium-term macro planning framework (1989–1995) and draft medium-term program (1989–1991). The 1990 budget speech outlines in some detail plans for health, education, social welfare, manufacturing, tourism, and public sector investment, specifically indicating the financial allocations for 1990 in the context of the overall planning strategy. Other Caribbean countries need to integrate the budget into the planning strategy in the manner of Trinidad and Tobago. In Barbados, the budget is a revenue-raising device, with fiscal incentives given from time to time to manufacturing, agriculture, and tourism. The Barbadian budgets of the 1990s were not integrated into the development plans.

BUDGETARY POLICY IN BARBADOS

Government saving (current account surplus) assumes greater significance as an instrument for financing capital expenditure when the public sector is unable to use deficit financing on a large scale. In the colonial period, the absence of a central bank, as well as the inadequacy of the financial market, led to heavy reliance on current surpluses. The budgetary system was designed to conserve reserves in times of a boom in sugar exports, in order to spend them in times of slump. As mentioned in Chapter 3, the currency board system was unable to exercise autonomous monetary policy, since it functioned as a money changer, exchanging sterling for domestic money. This lack of monetary control meant that the government's power to pursue deficit financing was limited by the reserves at its disposal. For the economy as a whole, spending was held in check by the level of sterling balances held by the colony. This stemmed from the fact that the currency board system could only expand currency if it were "backed" by an equivalent amount of foreign assets. To the extent that aggregate spending was constrained by the colonial monetary system, there was a strong limit to the degree of monetary and financial intervention of the government in the economy.

Colonial budgetary policy enabled the public sector to accumulate sizeable reserve balances in Barbados. These reserves were placed in three funds. The earmarked reserves were funds set aside for specific purposes, for example the Labour Welfare Fund. The Revenue Equalisation Fund was composed of payments from the surplus on current and capital accounts to meet any marked fall in revenue and to enable the colonial government to avoid any reduction of the public service in bad years. The General Revenue Balance represented the colony's accumulated surplus after the annual transfers were made in respect of capital expenditure and the Revenue Equalisation Fund. The government's total reserve balance rose from Bds$7.8 million in 1947 to Bds$32.8 million in 1965. These reserves were held in cash, loans, local securities and investments in the Commonwealth. Prior to 1960 almost 70 percent of the reserves were held in cash, representing an uneconomical use of funds. After 1960 the colonial government shifted its reserves portfolio increasingly to securities, and by 1965, 83 percent of the reserves were held in advances and securities (Howard 1979a: 58).

The balance-budget philosophy of the colonial government was functional but anti-developmental. It was functional because balance of payment deficits were non-existent in the small economy, and inflation was contained because of the constraint on spending. Balanced budgeting was anti-developmental because it rested too heavily on the cyclical movements of a single crop, and therefore straitjacketed the economy in a low-level equilibrium trap. Although the colonial government recorded some success in the area of infrastructural spending, its record in the areas of capital spending on education, health, and social security was much less forward looking.

After independence in 1966, the budgetary policy of the government evolved slowly. The early post-colonial approach to public sector financing was still influenced by the policy of generating revenue surpluses in the absence of a central bank. According to the Barbados development plan of 1965–1968, the budgetary policy of the government was guided by three normative principles: (1) the yield of taxation should be sufficient to cover recurrent expenditure and also make a contribution to financing capital expenditure; (2) the tax burden should be equitably distributed; and (3) taxation policy should contribute to economic growth. The emphasis on current account surplus was reiterated in the development plans of 1969–1972 and 1973–1977, as well as in the annual budgets prior to 1973.

A major departure from colonial budgetary policy in the late 1960s was the emphasis on income redistribution. Colonial public policy was concerned more with economic growth as it related to sugar output than with the welfare effects of direct income redistribution strategies. In keeping with the dominant philosophy of that period, it was hoped that the fruits of export-propelled growth would somehow "trickle down" to the masses. The income redistribution strategy of the 1960s and early 1970s was not conceived in terms of fundamental tax reform, but in terms of resource allocation policies which guaranteed a higher level of "social overheads." The post-colonial government adopted as an objective the provision of social goods such as health, education, and low-cost housing by increasing the aggregate tax burden. In terms of direct income redistribution, new emphasis was placed on social security through the instrument of payroll taxes. The Barbadian economy may have experienced some degree of redistribution during this period, but in the absence of firm data on the budget of consumers and relevant data on income taxation, measuring the success of this policy is difficult.

After 1973 budgetary policy was primarily concerned with stabilization (see Chapter 8) and with direct income redistribution through the budget. The stabilization emphasis was largely due to the need for fiscal discipline as a result of the sharp increases in the price of oil in 1973 and 1974. In the late 1970s "incremental redistribution" was attempted, by the modification of income-tax brackets and the provision of rebates for lower-income groups. Even though the government was still conscious of the need to generate a surplus on current account, the budget after 1973 can be regarded as a device for short-term macro-economic adjustment.

DEVELOPMENT PLANNING IN BARBADOS

Colonial Development Planning

Colonial development planning was merely a longer-term version of colonial budgeting. Primarily because of the colony's inability to pursue large-scale deficit financing, the planning of capital expenditures was also constrained by revenue surpluses and the low level of general taxation.

The Barbadian planning experience was largely conditioned by important internal and external political developments. The internal decolonization process in Barbados after World War II was determined by changes in British colonial policy and by the Third World decolonization movement. A policy of gradual decolonization aided the formulation and implementation of development plans after 1946, by giving elected members of parliament more direct control in the legislative, executive, and administrative affairs of the colony. The change in the character of the state which made this control possible was the transition from a semi-ministerial system of government in 1946, to full ministerial status in 1954 and internal self-government in 1961. Prior to 1954 real control of decision making was in the hands of the colonial governor. The attainment of political independence in 1966 gave the state new autonomy in the conduct of its external affairs, thereby facilitating the inflow of foreign capital necessary to finance the state's development plans.

Long-term plans for welfare and development in the British colonies were recognized as early as 1940 and were an integral part of the operations of the 1940 Colonial Development and Welfare Act. However, at that time there was not much insistence on the obligation of colonial governments to contribute to the cost of carrying out their own development plans. Further, the 1940 act had only allocated grants totaling 5 million Pounds to the colonial empire to cover ten years. The 1945 Colonial Development and Welfare Act increased this grant to 120 million Pounds and made greater insistence on the formulation of development plans (see Howard 1989b: 22). Development planning was based on the policy of expecting each territory to utilize its local resources. Further, each territory was asked to estimate how much it could afford to earmark for development projects from its surplus balances, loans, and general taxation.

The early plans, between 1946 and 1960, were basically descriptive documents with a listing of public sector projects. Colonial development planning in Barbados was geared toward the financing of "social overheads," especially toward the end of the 1950s, but there were no explicit policies of structural change and income distribution articulated in these plans. Apart from the emphasis on infrastructural development, the state's policy was limited to supporting private captial, particularly in agriculture. The economy remained largely underdeveloped, with a highly skewed income distribution.

Steve Emtage (1969) argued that there were two principal constraints on planning in colonial Barbados. The first was constitutional, and the other related to the question of size and economic dependence. As Emtage observed, even if one accepts the view that Barbados's colonial status imposed some limitations on the use of domestic policy instruments, this constraint cannot explain the unwillingness of the colonal government to implement strategies to bring greater equity to the socioeconomic structure. As Emtage contends, the metropolitan power was even willing to countenance some degree of direct governmental intervention. Both road transport and the distribution of natural gas were nationalized and this involved shifts in the ownership of assets and the balance of economic power. But such intervention cannot be regarded as a fundamental departure from colonial policy. The colonies remained committed to the principle of British responsible trusteeship and agrarian capitalism.

Early planning was devoted heavily to the finance of sugar monoculture and to the services which supported the sugar industry. It was hoped that such expansion of sugar would be based on a scheme of consolidation of factories, which would lead to economies of scale as well as increased opportunities for the development of by-products. Development of better irrigation facilities and improvements in the public water supply would assist in broadening the basis of agriculture. The 1946–1956 plan allocated a mere 50,000 Pounds to industrial development, to be utilize in exploring the possibilities of and developing minor industries. Similarly, tourism received 10,000 Pounds (Howard 1989b: 24).

To sum up, the development plans of the 1950s were merely extensions of colonial budgeting to include the planning of capital expenditure. Most of the plans were financed by revenue surpluses and general taxation, as well as by Colonial Development and Welfare grants. The major change in the 1955–1960 plan was the shift to loan financing of capital expenditure, particularly foreign borrowing, which became a feature of post-colonial planning. Foreign loans and Colonial Development and Welfare grants accounted for 42.2 percent of total planned expenditure. The increased reliance on external financing reflected the transition from colonial rule to internal self-government and political independence.

Post-Colonial Planning

Planning in Barbados during the post-colonial period continued to be public sector oriented. The analysis here deals with the public policy aspects of planning and, to a lesser extent, the financial implications of planning. Development planning was primarily concerned with statements of intended projects for the public sector. Additionally, the development plans provided the major policy statements on the promotion of foreign investment in the pursuit of import substitution and export promotion strategies. However, the plans did not involve comprehensive structural or indicative planning of non-public sector activities.

Another significant feature of post-colonial planning was the heavier emphasis on foreign borrowing to finance development. This borrowing was mainly from international development agencies, such as the World Bank and Inter-American Development Bank. Financing from revenue surpluses gradually became less important, particularly after 1973 when the government was able to pursue deficit financing by borrowing from the central bank. My discussion now looks at the public policy foundations of post-colonial planning.

The 1960–1965 plan outlined the strategy of settler-type investment along import-replacement lines, and proposed comprehensive legislation to promote such investment. A high level of protectionism was enshrined in the Industrial Incentives Act of 1963, which granted to eligible manufacturers a ten-year exemption from customs duties on imports used in production. The plan's promotion of foreign capital was partly based on the inability of the local capitalist class to promote industrialization. It argued that to develop industry, it would be necessary to rely on foreign investors, who possessed the capital and knowledge of markets for their products. The Barbados Development Board was the chief instrument of industrial planning during this period.

The initial difficulties of industrialization in a small developing economy quickly became apparent. Subsequent plans posited that the basic reason for the continuing unemployment was that manpower resources had outpaced resources of land and capital. At the same time, however, the increased levels of capital allocated to the sugar industry, as well as export industries, had reduced employment possibilities. Further, the policy initiatives in manufacturing and tourism did not bring about a corresponding reduction in unemployment. The perceived limitations of the strategy of import replacement prompted the state to adopt a strategy of export-promotion industrialization. It was recognized that because the domestic market was small in size and purchasing power, the possibilities of import substitution on a large scale were limited, and heavy reliance had to be placed on industries producing for the export market.

Despite this adherence to the foreign investment model, planning during the late 1960s showed a departure from previous plans in terms of limited direct participation of the state in agro-industry, agricultural marketing, and the hotel industry, that is, in areas normally considered the preserve of the private sector. The establishment of the Pine Hill Dairy in 1966, as well as the Agricultural Development Corporation in 1965 was intended to provide institutional support for agricultural diversification. The Barbados government was a major shareholder in the dairy, the duty of which was to provide a variety of milk products for local consumption. The Agricultural Development Corporation was designed to stimulate and encourage the development of agriculture in the private sector and to manage government-owned estates and agricultural projects on a commercial basis.

The new role of the state as a limited entrepreneur was seen in the construction of the Hilton Hotel, which was estimated to cost $7.63 million and was intended to provide direct employment for between 225 and 250 people. Direct government participation was limited to two-thirds of gross operating profits, while the remaining one-third accrued to Hilton Hotels International for management services. However, as we have seen, this limited form of state ownership was not accompanied by broad localization or nationalization policies, as was the case in other Caribbean countries, like Guyana and Trinidad.

During the 1970–1985 period the Barbadian planners attempted to specify the nature of the development problem and modify the planning strategy in light of the initial postwar experience of foreign investment. The development plans during this phase acknowledged the importance of greater national participation in the economy. Greater emphasis was also placed on provision of public goods and infrastructure by way of project planning.

Local entrepreneurship had to be stimulated. For the first time, the heavy dependence on foreign capital became a measure of concern. According to the 1969–1972 plan, foreign capital had financed about 30 percent of gross fixed capital formation in the period 1956–1959, compared with 70 percent in the period 1960–1964. Since much of this capital was in the form of equity, the magnitude of future outflows of factor incomes was important. As the plan stated, efforts to diversify the structure of production had been accompanied by an almost total reliance on foreign capital, with the result that one form of structural dependence was in danger of being substituted for another. Despite more than a decade of factory industrialization, the structural rigidity, persistent structural unemployment, and growing balance of trade deficit remained major problems. It was necessary to utilize domestic resources more effectively and increase the participation of nationals in key sectors of the economy. This new emphasis on local capital was expecially important in the context of the tourist industry. While the participation of foreign capital had been responsible for the rapid expansion of accommodation, and while the continued inflow of such capital was welcome, the government considered that there should have been increased local investment in the tourist sector of the economy. It was hoped that local entrepreneurship and national productivity would be stimulated through the Barbados Hotel School and the Barbados Institute of Management and Productivity (BIMAP). The latter institution was proposed in 1969 and established in 1972. Further, the national orientation of the 1969–1972 plan was reflected in the stated goals of the Barbados Development Bank. This bank was founded specifically to mobilize domestic resources to finance local entrepreneurs. Shares of the bank were available for public subscription, to facilitate and encourage saving and investment.

The national participation objective was also a theme of the 1973–1977 plan, which expressed the hope that greater self-sufficiency in economic performance would be achieved. But there was some ambivalence about adoption of policies to increase self-reliance. The policy makers were concerned about the extent to which an economy historically dependent on external sources could quickly shift to indigenous sources without endangering existing standards of living. In fact, the official attitude toward self-reliance was nebulous and unsatisfactory. The 1973–1977 plan called the development of a greater degree of self-sufficiency in the economy a process of seeking adjustment of social, political and economic values at some satisfaction point between autarky and dependency.

Apart from paying lip service to self-sufficiency, Barbadian planners after 1970 made a new and definite commitment to export promotion industrialization as a major plank of the development strategy. It was proposed that during the 1970s, "enclave" industries would provide the major impetus in the export strategy. An Export Promotion Agency was to be instituted in 1974 to undertake market research. The agency would play a major role in providing information on export credit finance and insurance. Enclave industrialization did provide new jobs, particularly for women, but most of the jobs had a low skill content, with the exception of certain areas of electronics requiring engineering skills.

However, the most important feature of development planning after 1973 was heavy public sector spending financed largely by foreign borrowing. The 1973–1977 plan projected that Bds$91.7 million, or 52.2 percent of capital expenditure over the planning period, would be financed by foreign borrowing. Further, the massive public investment program of 1979–1983 was supported by substantial foreign financing, totaling Bds$239.1 million, or 42.6 percent of capital expenditure, a commitment that was quite large compared with that of previous years. Policy makers between 1973 and 1990 were convinced that the weakness of the manufacturing and tourism sectors, consequent upon the impact of the 1973 oil price hike, required heavy investment by the state in the economy to maintain levels of employment. This strong public sector philosophy, supported by considerable deficit financing, represented a change from the colonial period.

Deficiencies of Post-Colonial Planning

Although the essence of development planning is good public policy, we can identify some of the technical deficiencies of the planning process after 1960. Development planning in Barbados during this era was strongly politically oriented and was characterized by a tendency to concentrate on socially desirable projects which had a strong appeal to the electorate. Although the implementation of projects consequent on this emphasis was an important means of providing employment and public goods, the policy makers tended to pay less attention to "structural planning." Thus the postwar plans did not create the sectoral linkage effects which are fundamental for the development process. Although this deficiency was excusable in the rudimentary stages of planning in the 1950s, the later plans should be faulted for not paying attention to the linkage aspects of development.

A more serious defect of postwar planning, however, was that most of the plans minimized the importance of technical manpower planning. One of the most binding constraints on development was the shortage of skilled manpower. This constraint was critical in the construction industry during the 1980s. Manpower planning ought to be an integral part of development planning and should take account of labor force mobility, migration, transport problems, attitudes about various types of work, relative wage rates, and factors affecting productivity. There is no evidence that manpower requirements were well projected in order to identify critical shortages of skills in the various sectors of the economy.

Another limitation of the postwar plans is that forecasting techniques were usually rudimentary or non-existent. For example, in the plans of the 1980s there was no analysis of the impact of the large capital works programs on the monetary base or the balance of payments. This arose from the fact that the plans were not seriously concerned with forecasting the demand for imports or with maintaining consistency among the propensity to import, export growth, and domestic output. There is no evidence of attempts to incorporate input-output analysis in the plans, even on a preliminary basis. Although quantitative planning has limitations when applied to small, open economies, there is still a need to develop such techniques, not as substitutes for qualitative analysis, but as aids in decision making.

The introduction of an energy plan was a commendable feature of the 1979–1983 plan. However, planning for the development of energy resources should not merely be a statement of policy. The planner must analyse the relationship between energy and development by calculating energy intensity ratios (ratios of energy consumption to output) in various sectors. This approach to the analysis of energy efficiency should be combined with regression analysis to forecast the demand for electricity and gasoline. Such forecasting enables the planner to measure more precisely the impact of tourism, manufacturing, and the household sector on the balance of payments. In sum, more time should be devoted to planning development, rather than simply to writing a development plan.

However well it is done, planning in small economies is a difficult and frustrating exercise. Demas (1965) identified four fundamental limitations to overall planning in West Indian economies. These were high levels of openness, the relatively small role played by the public sector, dependence on foreign capital, and the dominance of multinational corporations. Only three of these limitations are now important, since the public sector is now much larger than it was in the 1960s and cannot be considered a constraint on planning. The high level of openness means that the difficulty of predicting foreign sales is a primary constraint on planning. Openness also implies that significant cost overruns will be encountered in the planning of projects, as a result of unforeseen increases in import prices, particularly the price of petroleum.

Foreign investment and the presence of MNCs also pose problems for plan implementation and projections. Care has to be taken in projecting the level of outflows of profits and dividends from these economies. Further, domestic tax revenues are likely to be overestimated because of the difficulty of calculating the tax loss arising from transfer pricing employed by multinational firms. These difficulties partly explain why many plans have been abandoned in developing countries.

CONCLUSIONS

Budgeting and planning are two important aspects of public sector activity in small countries. Incremental budgeting is a relic of the British colonial system in Barbados. Despite the deficiencies of this form of budgeting, it has played a major role in economic stabilization and income tax adjustments and reform. The Barbadian tax reform of 1986 was presented in the budget for that year. The Barbadian government has devoted a great deal of time to writing development plans, which are really statements of development policy rather than analytical devices for estimating the costs and impact of development projects. The plans are not concerned with structural input-output analyses. The analysis in this chapter points the way for further research on the tax and expenditure aspects of budgeting.

11

FISCAL ANALYSIS OF THE OECS COUNTRIES

This chapter summarizes fiscal trends in the OECS countries: Antigua and Barbuda, Grenada, St. Lucia, Dominica, St. Kitts and Nevis, Montserrat, and St. Vincent and the Grenadines. No attempt is made to describe the fiscal performance of each country in detail. The first reason for devoting a chapter to the OECS sub-region is that the data on each economy are not extensive enough to allow an analysis of the type that I have made for the larger countries. The second reason is that these countries share a similar currency, the Eastern Caribbean dollar (EC$), which is regulated by the Eastern Caribbean Central Bank. In monetary and fiscal policy, this monetary arrangement has different implications from the monetary arrangements of the larger West Indian countries.

The first section of the chapter reviews Samuel's (1989) work on public finance in the OECS during the late 1970s and first half of the 1980s. Samuel (1988, 1989, 1990) provides the most recent in-depth analyses of public finance in these territories. Other published work includes Francis (1977), Jones-Hendrickson (1981, 1985), Karl Theodore (1987), Laurel Bain (1987), and Arnold McIntyre (1986). My analysis also looks at fiscal indicators after 1985.

SAMUEL'S FISCAL SURVEY OF THE OECS TERRITORIES

Samuel's (1989) fiscal survey of the OECS countries deals with a number of issues, including tax structure change, government expenditure, the fiscal deficit, and the emergence of national insurance schemes. His analysis is concerned with the period 1970–1985. He also cautions readers about the varied quality of data, which reduces the reliability of statistical estimation.

According to Samuel, the tax system in these territories showed a shift from direct to indirect taxation. This was due to the imposition of heavy consumption taxes. This form of taxation became important because of the arrangement between members of CARICOM whereby import duties on regional goods were eliminated. The OECS countries then had to rely on consumption duties to compensate for the decline in import duties. In my previous analysis of the larger CARICOM countries, this was also one of the reasons for increased consumption taxation.

At the same time, tax reforms were introduced which reduced the importance of income taxation. Antigua abolished personal income taxes in 1976, while individual and corporate income taxes were abolished in St. Kitts and Nevis in 1981. Grenada also abolished income taxes in 1986. Samuel (1989: 14) attributes these reforms to Keynesian and supply-side influences. In the case of Antigua, one objective of reform was to stimulate aggregate spending power and the overall level of economic activity, while in Grenada, emphasis was placed on stimulating productivity and growth in the private sector.

These trends in income tax reform in some OECS countries were fundamentally different from those in Barbados, Jamaica, and Trinidad and Tobago. Whereas the income tax was abolished in some OECS territories, the rationale being its low yield, because of the relatively higher significance of the income tax as a source of revenue, governments in the larger territories instituted reforms in income-tax rates and bases.

Another feature of the OECS tax system, as shown by Samuel, is its low tax buoyancy. Samuel calculated a buoyancy coefficient of 1.16 for the region as a whole, ranging from 0.83 in Antigua and Barbuda to 1.42 in Grenada. These findings, as well as my previous analysis, indicate that the entire English-speaking Caribbean region is characterized by low tax buoyancy.

Samuel (1989: 17) opined that "there was no comprehensive program which guided government expenditure policies in the sub-region." His analysis seems to suggest that the expenditure process was haphazard, depending on the demands of various ministries. He argued that there was little evidence to suggest that, with the exception of the socialist interlude in Grenada, the governments were pursuing an expanded role in social investment and "in areas traditionally reserved for the private sector." Samuel is not happy with the operation of the World Bank/IMF public sector investment program (PSIP) in these countries. This program, in his view, is based on the notion that the state's role is to facilitate private sector business rather than to undertake investment in areas traditionally reserved for the private sector. Samuel points to the privatizations in Grenada and policies of privatization in Antigua and Barbuda, and St. Vincent and the Grenadines. He believes that the governments of these countries should expand their activities in "the pursuit of policies which would put these countries on the path of transition to self-sufficiency" (Samuel 1989: 18).

Samuel's analysis is closely reminiscent of the structuralist thesis of the

Caribbean economists of the 1960s. This school of thought believed that the governments of the regions should increase the public sector's involvement in the productive sectors of the economy, rather than allow these sectors to be owned and operated by the private sector. As I have shown, the increased involvement of the state sharply increased fiscal disequilibrium in the larger Caribbean countries. Efforts should now be made to develop the private sectors of Caribbean economies. The governments in the region have not displayed any ability to perform well in competitive markets.

Samuel's work demonstrates that the fiscal deficits in the OECS region, with the exception of Grenada, have been held in check by regulations governing money creation by the Eastern Caribbean Central Bank (ECCB). Credit allocations to each government by the ECCB are determined by the ratio of that government's recurrent revenue to total revenues for all members (Liburd and Tempro 1989: 137). According to Samuel, the ECCB was permitted to advance to a member country up to 5 percent of the average annual recurrent revenue of the countries combined, over the three years prior to the writing of his analysis. The restrictions on money creation meant that the OECS countries could not rely on the central bank to finance fiscal deficits. These were mainly financed by external borrowing and grants, which totaled EC$374.0 million in 1986. The overall fiscal deficit was EC$370.6 million for these territories (Samuel 1989: 20). Even though foreign financing was the principal instrument of deficit financing, the debt service ratios of these countries were relatively low, with the exception of Grenada. In 1985 the highest debt service ratios (see Samuel 1989: 24) were recorded for Grenada (20.4 percent), Antigua (7.6 percent), and Dominica (11.2 percent). Samuel's survey points the way for further research on the OECS. In the next section I look at some fiscal indicators for these countries after 1985.

FISCAL ANALYSIS AFTER 1985

This section utilizes three fiscal indicators for the OECS countries. These are (1) the ratio of the current account deficit or surplus to GDP, (2) the ratio of government expenditure to GDP, and (3) indirect taxation as a percentage of GDP. The current account balance provides a measure of government saving or dissaving, while the ratio of total expenditure to GDP is an indicator of the size of government.

Table 11.1 shows that Grenada and Antigua and Barbuda incurred current account deficits in 1989. The maintenance of public sector savings shown for most of these countries is due to high rates of economic growth in the late 1980s, even though their real GDP growth slowed, from 7 percent in 1988 to 4.7 percent in 1989. Public sector savings as a ratio of GDP were highest in St. Lucia and Dominica. In the case of Dominica, this growth after 1987 was in response to an IMF structural adjustment program which emphasized fiscal restraint. The higher level of public sector savings was used to finance Dominica's public investment program. Grenada's heavy current account deficit, of 10.8 percent of GDP in 1989, followed a surplus of 2.8 percent in 1988. This was a result of large debt repayment and higher public sector wages and salaries. In the countries where the savings performance deteriorated, a common feature was a higher rate of increase in personal emoluments. This factor is examined further below, when we duscuss the size of government in the OECS.[1]

Size of government is also shown in Table 11.1. Grenada, St. Lucia and Dominica recorded ratios of total government expenditure to GDP that were well over 40 percent. The public sector wages bill in these three countries was over 50 percent of current expenditure, with Dominica recording the highest ratio, of 59.1 percent. These figures indicate that the public sectors are too large, exerting pressure on these governments to increase current revenues. The analysis also indicates the need to broaden private sector economic activity to relieve the financial burden on the public sector.

Table 11.1 reveals extremely high ratios of indirect taxation to total tax revenue, ranging from 67.2 percent for Montserrat to 86.4 percent for Antigua and Barbuda. In perdominately service and agrarian economies, it is easier to collect revenue from indirect taxes. Accordingly, these countries have been either increasing indirect tax rates or introducing new indirect taxes. In Grenada, the introduction of the VAT was at first accompanied by administrative difficulties related to tax collection. From late 1989, in order to increase tax yield, the VAT was levied on services and local manufacturers.

Table 11.1
Fiscal Indicators for OECS Countries, 1989

	Current Account Surplus/Deficit as % of GDP	Government Expenditure as % of GDP	Indirect Tax as % of Tax Revenue
Antigua and Barbuda	−0.4	30.4	86.4
Dominica	6.5	45.4	73.6
Grenada	−10.8	54.7	86.3
Montserrat	n.a.	n.a.	67.2
St. Kitts and Nevis	3.0	34.4	76.9
St. Lucia	12.0	49.8	70.4
St. Vincent and the Grenadines	3.4	33.7	72.8

Note: n.a. denotes not available

Source: Eastern Caribbean Central Bank, *Annual Report*, 1990.

The VAT was also shifted from retailers and collected at the port. The VAT yielded substantial revenue in 1989, amounting to 45 percent of total tax revenue. For an analysis of the early problems associated with the VAT, the reader should consult Samuel (1988).

SUMMARY

The main fiscal characteristics of the OECS countries are as follows:

1. Heavy dependence on external financing of their fiscal deficits.
2. Positive levels of government savings in most of the countries.
3. A high ratio of government expenditure to GDP in a few countries, particularly Grenada, which had a ratio of 54.7 percent. This finding for Grenada indicates that the size of the public sector is too large.
4. A very heavy dependence on indirect taxation, especially in Grenada and Antigua and Barbuda.

NOTE

1. See Eastern Caribbean Central Bank, *Annual Report*, 1990.

12

LESSONS FROM THE CARIBBEAN FISCAL EXPERIENCE

The analysis in this book indicates the need to reduce the size of government in small developing countries. In each economic crisis, measures have been taken to trim the size of the public sector, through privatization, wage cuts, or severance of workers. The unwieldy public bureaucracies in some Caribbean countries had been allowed to expand, partly from ideological and political factors.

The Caribbean experience demonstrates the dangers of excessive money creation, in the form of central bank lending to governments. In the OECS countries, this mechanism was strictly controlled, and the pressure on the balance of payments was less severe. "Printing money" in the larger countries stemmed from the tendency of the governments to increase spending to maintain their political power under recessionary conditions. The consequence of such spending was usually a depletion of foreign exchange reserves, followed by defensive stabilization policies. In 1990 the Barbadian government persistently ignored calls from economists and opposition groups to reduce the high levels of government expenditure and central bank money creation. In the cases of Guyana, Jamaica, and Barbados, the central banks seemed unable to resist their governments' demands for credit.

My analysis also indicated that governments in small countries need to make early fiscal adjustments when the first signs of foreign exchange depletion appear. Both Jamaica in the late 1970s and Barbados in 1991 went to the IMF only after their foreign reserves had fallen to critically low levels. Jamaica's experience also warns small countries that balance of payments crises become chronic if not dealt with early. After 14 years of IMF involvement, Jamaica remains a disequilibrium system with an impoverished working class. The main lesson for small countries is to pursue prudent management of the fiscal deficit to avoid depletion of foreign reserves.

The Caribbean experience also suggests that governments in developing countries need to restore confidence in the market mechanism. The legacy of colonialism has caused an aversion to foreign investment in some countries, and a distrust of the market mechanism. In the period 1970–1980 these factors increased the regulatory role of Caribbean governments, which imposed heavy price controls, subsidies, and trade restrictions, especially prior to the IMF interventions.

Privatization is one means of reducing the size of government. Guyana, Jamaica, and Trinidad and Tobago developed major public enterprise systems in the 1960s and 1970s, and Grenada adopted a socialist regime in the early 1980s. These nations went too far with state ownership, as the state began to intrude in competitive areas of economic activity. Privatization increases the role of the private sector in competitive markets.

Nevertheless, governments in small countries must avoid a distress approach to privatization, which seeks to divest state assets to raise money to liquidate current debt, often as part of structural adjustment measures recommended by the IMF, the World Bank, and similar institutions. This approach is short term and does not realize development goals. Although privatization provides a rationale for increased managerial, allocative and productive efficiency, it should be a selective process based on criteria which relate to economic development. A proposed privatization program should be subject to social cost/benefit criteria identifying the effects of privatization on employment, prices, taxes, output, and productivity. Small-country governments must be cautious of the ideology of privatization which seems to be intrinsic to the actions of large lending agencies.

Another major area of interest in the Caribbean is tax reform, which focused during the 1980s on reducing income taxation to increase the efficiency of the tax system. More recently, flat-rate indirect taxes have been introduced in some countries to improve the efficiency and simplicity of indirect taxation. It is difficult to evaluate quantitatively the efficiency effects of tax reform, particularly under conditions of structural adjustment. However, it is safe to say that any perceived beneficial effects of income tax reform were constrained by severe fiscal disequilibrium and policies which reduced personal incomes in the larger territories. Foreign reserves depletion is also a severe constraint on the productivity effects of income tax reform in small countries.

Indirect taxation became the most important revenue-raising instrument in all the territories. John Due and Francis Greaney (1991: 267) advance reasons why the introduction of the VAT was successful in Trinidad and Tobago. Firstly, they identify the high degree of planning in the development of the tax, as well as the use of quantitative analysis of the proposed changes. Secondly, Due and Greaney suggest that the high level of cooperation between business and government in the implementation of the VAT was facilitated by a tax performance committee which studied and reviewed the VAT proposals. Thirdly, an extensive publicity program helped to acquaint taxpayers with the characteristics of the VAT. Fourthly, the implementation of the tax was managed by competent and manageable persons. The introduction of the VAT in Trinidad and Tobago, therefore, provides a number of lessons to small countries contemplating this type of taxation. Whereas the Grenada VAT was implemented hurriedly, the Trinidad and Tobago experience shows the importance of planning the implementation schedule, employing consultants, and developing computer systems to facilitate the operation of the VAT (See Due and Greaney, 1991: appendix, 267–268).

The most important aspect of tax reform in the Caribbean was the implementation of more neutral tax systems, which do not discriminate unduly among taxpayers. Jamaica was a leader in this approach. Over the years the tax systems in the Caribbean had become unfair, highly complex, and contained a large number of concessions and preferences. Neutral tax systems are more cost-effective, because the costs of administering two or three taxes are lower than the costs of collecting a plethora of taxes, with myriad tax rates. Further, the elimination of complex allowances and tax breaks reduces the revenue costs of government.

Finally, this book points the way for further comparative fiscal research on small countries. Such empirical research, oriented toward an analysis of the institutional and political problems of these fiscal systems, would enhance our understanding of public sector decision making. More research needs to be done on public utilities pricing, tax administration, tax reform, and tax incidence. The specific problems of public enterprises need more in-depth investigation. This book has not dealt with protectionism and other fiscal aspects of economic integration. Research in the above areas can yield valuable information for policy makers, teachers, and students in the Caribbean.

BIBLIOGRAPHY

Aghevli, Bijan and Moshin S. Khan (1977). "Inflationary Finance and the Dynamics of Inflation: Indonesia, 1951–1972." *American Economic Review*, June.

Aghevli, Bijan and Moshin S. Khan (1978). "Government Deficits and the Inflationary Process in Developing Countries." IMF *Staff Papers*, vol. 25, no. 3, September.

Aghevli, Bijan and Moshin S. Khan (1980). "Credit Policy and the Balance of Payments in Developing Countries." In Warren Coats and Deena Khatkhate (eds.), *Money and Monetary Policy in Less Developed Countries*. New York: Pergamon.

Ahiram, E. (1966). "Income Distribution in Jamaica, 1958." *Social and Economic Studies*, vol. 13, no. 3.

Alleyne, Dillon (1991). "An Analysis of the Structure and Burden of the Post Reform Tax System of Jamaica, Fiscal Year 1988/89." Mimeo, Consortium Graduate School Faculty of Social Sciences, University of the West Indies, Kingston, Jamaica.

Anderson, Patricia (1989). "Levels of Poverty and Household Food Consumption in Jamaica in 1989." Kingston, Jamaica: Institute of Social and Economic Research, University of the West Indies.

Andic, Fuat M. (1968). "Fiscal Incentives: A Brief Survey." *Social and Economic Studies*, vol. 17, no. 1, March.

Armstrong, Eric (1967). *Import Substitution in Jamaica and Trinidad and Tobago: Part A: Incentive Legislation in Trinidad and Tobago*. Kingston, Jamaica: Institute of Social and Economic Research, University of the West Indies.

Auerbach, Alan J. 1985). "The Theory of Excess Burden and Optimal

Taxation." In Alan J. Auerbach and Martin Feldstein (eds.), *Handbook of Public Economics,* vol. I. Amsterdam: North Holland.

Bahl, Roy (1989). "The Political Economy of the Jamaican Tax Reform, in Malcolm Gills (ed.), *Tax Reform in Developing Countries,* Durham, North Carolina: Due University Press.

Bain, Laurel T. (1987). "Post War Taxation Policies in the Organization of Eastern Caribbean Members States with Special Reference to the 1970s and 1980s." *Bulletin of Eastern Caribbean Affairs,* vol. 13, no. 2, May/June.

Balassa, Bela (1982). "Disequilibrium Analysis in Developing Economies: An Overview." *World Development,* vol. 10, no. 12, December.

Baptiste, Patrick (1977). "Public Finance in Trinidad and Tobago." *Social and Economic Studies,* vol. 26, no. 4.

Bartlett, Bruce (1987). "The Case for Tax Cuts." *Economic Impact,* no. 57.

Baumol, William (1967). "Macroeconomics of Unbalanced Growth." *American Economic Review,* vol. 57, no. 3, June.

Beckford, George (1972). *Persistent Poverty.* New York: Oxford University Press.

Bennett, Karl (1983). "Exchange Rate Policy and External Imbalances: The Jamaican Experience." *Social and Economic Studies,* vol. 32. no. 4, December.

Berg, Elliot (1987). "The Role of Divestiture in Economic Growth." In Steve Hanke (ed.), *Privatization and Development.* San Francisco: Institute for Contemporary Studies.

Bernal, Richard (1985). "The Vicious Circle of Foreign Indebtedness: The Case of Jamaica:" In Antonio Jorge, Jorge Salazar-Carrillo and Frank Diaz-Pou (eds.), *External Debt and Development Strategy in Latin America.* New York: Pergamon.

Bernal, Richard (1988). "Resolving the International Debt Crisis." In Omar Davies (ed.) *The Debt Problems in Jamaica.* Mona, Kingston, Jamaica: University of the West Indies.

Bernal, Richard, Mark Figuero and Michael Witter (1984). "Caribbean Economic Thought: The Critical Tradition." *Social and Economic Studies,* vol. 33, no. 2.

Best, Lloyd (1968). "A Model of Pure Plantation Economy." *Social and Economic Studies,* vol. 17, no. 3, September.

Bird, Richard M. (1987). "A New Look at Indirect Taxation in Developing Countries." *World Development,* vol. 15, no. 9.

Bird, Richard M. and B. D. Miller (1986). "The Incidence of Indirect Taxes on Low-Income Households in Jamaica." Jamaica Tax Structure Examination Project, Staff Paper no. 26, Metropolitan Studies Program, Maxwell School, Syracuse University, Syracuse, N.Y.

Blackman, Courtney (1979). "The Economic Development of Small Countries: A Managerial Approach." In Basil Ince (ed.), *Contemporary*

International Relations in the Caribbean. Trinidad: University of the West Indies.

Blackman, Courtney (1989). "The Exchange Rate in the Balance of Payments Adjustment Process." *Money Affairs,* vol. 11, no. 1, January-June.

Boadway, Robin and David E. Wildasin (1984). *Public Sector Economics.* Boston: Little, Brown.

Boamah, Daniel (1988). "Some Macro Implications of External Debt for Barbados." *Social and Economic Studies,* vol. 37, no. 4.

Boamah, Daniel (1989). "The Debt Crisis and its Implications for the Caribbean." Central Bank of Barbados, *Working Papers 1989.*

Boamah, Daniel (1990). "Debt Equity Conversions and Other Swaps: Experience and Prospects for the Caribbean." Central Bank of Barbados, *Working Papers 1990.*

Bourne, Compton (1974). "The Political Economy of Endigenous Commercial Banking in Guyana." *Social and Economic Studies,* vol. 23, no. 1, March.

Bourne, Compton and R. Oumade Singh (1988). "External Debt and Adjustment in Caribbean Countries." *Social and Economic Studies,* vol. 37, no. 4.

Boyd, Derick A. C. (1984). "Jamaica: Pay as You Earn Taxation." *Bulletin for International Fiscal Documentation,* vol. 38. no. 12.

Boyd, Derick A.C. (1988). *Economic Management, Income Distribution and Poverty in Jamaica.* New York: Praeger.

Brown, Adlith (1981). "Economic Policy and the IMF in Jamaica." *Social and Economic Studies,* vol. 30, no. 4.

Brown, C. V., and P. M. Jackson (1982). *Public Sector Economics.* Oxford: Martin Robertson.

Buchanan, James M. and Gordon Tullock (1962). *The Calculus of Consent.* Ann Arbor, Mich.: Univesity of Michigan Press.

Bullock, Colin (1986). "IMF Conditionality and Jamaica's Economic Policy in the 1980s." *Social and Economic Studies,* vol. 35, no. 4.

Caribbean Conference of Churches (1991). "Official Report of a Goodwill and Fact-Finding Mission to Guyana," September 30 – October 5, 1990.

Chenery, Hollis (1979). *Structural Change and Development Policy.* London: Oxford University Press.

Chen-Young, Paul (1975). "A Study of Tax Incentives in Jamaica." In Richard Bird and Oliver Oldman (eds.), *Readings in Taxation in Developing Countries.* Baltimore: Johns Hopkins University Press.

Codrington, Harold E. (1989). "Country Size and Taxation in Developing Countries." *Journal of Development Studies,* vol. 25, no. 4, July.

Cox, Martin (1979). "The Distribution of Income in Barbados." Mimeo, Cave Hill, Barbados: Institute of Social and Economic Research.

Danns, Donna (1988). "Guyana's Debt Problem." *Social and Economic Studies,* vol. 37, no. 4.

Danns, Donna (1990). *The History of the Bank of Guyana, 1965-1990.* Guyana: Bank of Guyana.

David, Wilfred L. (1985). *The IMF Policy Paradigm: The Macroeconomics of Stabilization, Structural Adjustment and Economic Development.* New York: Praeger.

David, Carlton, Wesley Hughes and Omar Davies (1985). "Financing Impact of Jamaica's Bauxite Production Levy: 1974-1984." *Caribbean Finance and Management,* vol. 1, no. 1, Summer.

Davis, J. Ronnie and Charles W. Meyer (1983). *Principles of Public Finance.* New Jersey: Prentice-Hall.

Demas, William (1965). *The Economics of Development in Small Countries with Special Reference to the Caribbean.* Montreal: McGill University.

Downes, Andrew S. (1985). "Inflation in Barbados: An Econometric Investigation." *Economic Development and Cultural Change,* vol. 33. no. 3.

Downes, Andrew S. (1987). "The Distribution of Household Income in Barbados."*Social and Economic Studies,* vol. 36, no. 4, December.

Downs, Anthony (1957). *An Economic Theory of Democracy.* New York: Harper and Row.

Druker, Peter F. (1973). *Management: Tasks, Responsibilites, Practices.* New York: Harper and Row.

Due, John F. (1985). "Reform of the Indirect Tax Structure of Jamaica." Staff Paper no. 6, Jamaica Tax Structure Project, Metropolitan Studies Program, Maxwell School, Syracuse University, N.Y.

Due, John F., and Francis Greaney (1991). "Trinidad and Tobago: The Development of a Value Added Tax." *Bulletin for International fiscal Documentation,* June.

Emtage, Steve (1969). "Growth, Development and Planning in a Small Dependent Economy: The Case of Barbados." Master's thesis, Sussex University.

Farrell, Terrence W. (1984). "Inflation and Anti-Inflation Policy in Trinidad and Tobago: An Empirical Analysis." *Monetaria,* Center for Latin American Monetaria Studies, vol. 7, no. 4.

Farrell, Terrence W. (1981). "The Government Budget and the Money Supply in Open Petroleum Economies: Trinidad and Tobago, 1973-1980." Mimeo, Central Bank of Trinidad and Tobago.

Francis, Fitzgerald A. (1968). *A Review and Analysis of the System of Incentives for Industrial Development in Trinidad and Tobago.* Port-of-Spain: Government Printery.

Francis, Fitzgerald A. (1977). "Government Finance in the Associated States." *Social and Economic Studies,* vol. 14.

Frenkel, Jacob A. and Harry G. Johnson (eds.) (1976). *The Monetary Approach to the Balance of Payments.* London: Allen and Unwin.

Gandhi, Ved P. (1987a). "Tax Reform: Some Considerations and Limits (Lessons from Experiences of Developing Countries)." Paper presented at Seminar on Fiscal Reform, University of the West Indies, St. Augustine, Trinidad, November.

Gandhi, Ved P. (1987b). "Tax Structure for Efficiency and Supply Side Economics in Developing Countries." In Ved P. Gandhi (ed.), *Supply Side Tax Policy: Its Relevance to Developing Countries.* Washington, D.C.: IMF.

Gillis, Malcolm (1985). "Micro and Macroeconomics of Tax Reform: Indonesia." *Journal of Development Economics,* Vol. 19, no. 3.

Girvan, Norman (1971a). "Making the Rules of the Game: Country-Company Agreements in the Bauxite Industry." *Social and Economic Studies,* vol. 20, no. 4, December.

Girvan, Norman (1971b). "Why We Need to Nationalize Bauxite and How." In Norman Girvan and Owen Jefferson (eds.), *Readings in the Political Economy of the Caribbean.* Kingston, Jamaica: New World Group.

Girvan, Norman (1971c). "Unemployment in Jamaica." In Norman Girvan and Owen Jefferson (eds.), *Readings in the Political Economy of the Caribbean.* Kingston, Jamaica: New World Group.

Girvan, Norman, Richard Bernal and Wesley Hughes (1980). "The IMF and the Third World: The Case of Jamaica." *Development Dialogue,* no. 2.

Girvan, Norman (1986). "Notes on Jamaica's External Debt." In Omar Davies (ed.), *The Debt Problem in Jamaica.* Mona, Jamaica: University of the West Indies.

Girvan, Norman, Mario Sevilla, Miguel Hatton and Ennio Rodriguez (1991). "The Debt Problem of Small Peripheral Economies: Case Studies from the Caribbean and Central America." *Caribbean Studies,* vol. 24, nos. 1 & 2 (January-June).

Gobin, Roy T. (1979). "A Survey and Analysis of the Tax System in the Caribbean Common Market." *Bulletin for International Fiscal Documentation,* vol. 33.

Goffman, Irving J. and Dennis J. Mahar (1971). "The Growth of Public Expenditures in Selected Developing Nations: Six Caribbean Countries." *Public Finance,* vol. 26, no. 1.

Goode, Richard (1984). *Government Finance in Developing Countries.* Washington, D.C.: Brookings Institution.

Gordon, Derek (1989). "Developing a Poverty Line for Jamaica." Working Paper no. 3, Jamaican Poverty Line Project, Planning Institute of Jamaica, November.

Griffith, Winston (1987). "Can CARICOM Countries Replicate the Singapore Experience?" *Journal of Development Studies,* vol. 24, no. 1, October.

Hall, Robert E., and Dale Jorgenson (1967). "Tax Policy and Investment Behavior." *American Economic Review,* vol. 67, no. 3, June.

Hanke, Steve (1987a). "The Necessity of Property Rights." In Steve Hanke (ed.), *Privatization and Development.* San Francisco: Institute for Contemporary Studies.

Hanke, Steve (ed.), (1987b). *Privatization and Development.* San Francisco:

Institute for Contemporary Studies.

Harewood, Jack and Ralph Henry (1978). "Problems of Defining and Measuring Poverty in the Caribbean." In Farley S. Brathwaite (ed.), *Poverty in the Caribbean. Special issue of Caribbean Issues,* vol. 4, no. 3, December.

Harewood, Jack and Ralph Henry (1985). "Inequality in Post-Colonial Society: Trinidad and Tobago 1956-1981." Institute of Social and Economic Research, University of the West Indies, St. Augustine, Trinidad. *Occasional Papers,* Human Resources no. 6.

Harris, Elmer (1988). "Stabilization in the Guyanese Economy." *Money Affairs,* vol. 1, no. 2, July-December.

Heller, Walter (1967). "Fiscal Policies for Under-Developed Countries." In Richard Bird and Oliver Oldman (eds.), *Readings in Taxation in Developing Countries.*

Heller, Peter (1980). "The Impact of Inflation on Fiscal Policy in Developing Countries." *IMF Staff Papers,* vol. 28, no. 2, June.

Hemming, Richard and Ali Mansoor (1988). "Is Privatization the Answer?" *Finance and Development,* vol. 25, no. 3.

Henry, Ralph (1975). "A Note on Income Distribution and Poverty in Trinidad and Tobago." *Central Statistical Office Research Papers,* no. 8, Trinidad and Tobago.

Henry, Ralph (1988). "The State and Income Distribution in Independent Trinidad and Tobago." In Selwyn Ryan (ed.), *Trinidad and Tobago: The Independence Experience (1962-1987),* Trinidad: University of the West Indies, St. Augustine, Institute of Social and Economic Research.

Henry, Ralph (1989). "Inequality in Plural Societies: An Exploration." *Social and Economic Studies,* vol. 38, no. 2.

Holder, Carlos and Ronald Prescod (1989). "The Distribution of Personal Income in Barbados." *Social and Economic Studies,* vol. 38, no. 1.

Hope, Ronald K. (1986). *Economic Development in the Caribean.* New York: Praeger.

Howard, Michael (1979a). "The Fiscal System of Barbados." Occasional Papers, no. 12, University of the West Indies, Institute of Social and Economic Research, Cave Hill, Barbados.

Howard, Michael (1979b). "A Preliminary Investigation of the Demand for Money in Barbados 1960-1976." *Social and Economic Studies,* vol. 28, no. 4, December.

Howard, Michael (1982). "Post-War Public Policy in Barbados 1946-1979." *Social and Economic Studies,* vol. 31, no. 3, September.

Howard, Michael (1986). "The Economic Development of Barbados 1946-1980." Ph.D. diss. University of the West Indies, Cave Hill, Barbados.

Howard, Michael (1987a). "Barbados: Income Tax Reform: An Analysis of Two Budgets in 1986." *Bulletin for International Fiscal Documentation,* vol. 41, April.

Howard, Michael (1987b). "Income Tax Reform in Barbados (1977–1987)." Paper presented at Seminar on Fiscal Reform, University of the West Indies, St. Augustine, Trinidad. November.

Howard, Michael (1989a). "Public Sector Financing in Jamaica, Barbados and Trinidad and Tobago 1974–1984." *Social and Economic Studies*, vol. 38, no. 3.

Howard, Michael (1989b). *Dependence and Development in Barbados 1945–1985*. Bridgetown, Barbados: Carib Research and Publications.

Howard, Michael (1991). "Industrialization and Trade Policy in Barbados." *Social and Economic Studies*, vol. 40, no. 1.

Hulten, Charles R. (1984). "Tax Policy and the Investment Decision." *American Economic Review*, vol. 74, no. 2, May.

International Monetary Fund (ed.) (1977). *The Monetary Approach to the Balance of Payments*. Washington, D.C.: IMF.

Jacobs, B. L. (1975). "Administrative Problems of Small Countries." In Percy Selwyn (ed.), *Development Policy in Small Countries*. London: Croom Helm.

Jefferson, Owen (1972). *The Post-War Economic Development of Jamaica*. Kingston, Jamaica: Institute of Social and Economic Research, University of the West Indies.

Jefferson, Owen (1986). "Jamaica's External Debt: Size, Growth Composition and Economic Consequences." In Omar Davies (ed.), *The Debt Problem in Jamaica*. Mona, Jamaica: Department of Economics, University of the West Indies.

Johnson, Harry G. (1972). *The Monetary Approach to Balance of Payments Theory: Further Essays in Monetary Economics*. London: Allen and Unwin.

Jones, Edwin (1981). "Role of the State in Public Enterprise." *Social and Economic Studies*, vol. 30, no. 1, March.

Jones-Hendrickson, Simon B. (1981). "The Dissociation Factor: Revenue Production in St. Kitts." In Fuat M. Andic and Simon B. Jones-Hendrickson (eds.), *Readings in Caribbean Public Sector Economics*. Kington, Jamaica: Institute of Social and Economic Research, University of the West Indies.

Jones-Hendrickson, Simon B. (1985). *Public Finance and Monetary Policy in Open Economies*. Kingston, Jamaica: Institute of Social and Economic Studies.

Keleher, Robert (1982). "Supply Side Tax Policy: Reviewing the Evidence." In Thomas J. Hailstones (ed.), *Viewpoints on Supply Side Economics*, Reston, Va.: Reston Publishing.

Kelf-Cohen, R. (1969). *Twenty Years of Nationalization: The British Experience*. London: Macmillan.

Khan, Moshin, (1976). "A Monetary Model of the Balance of Payments: The Case of Venezuela." *Journal of Monetary Economics*, vol. 2, no. 3, July.

Kennedy, Charles (1966). "Keynesian Theory in an Open Economy." *Social and Economic Studies,* vol. 15, no. 1.

Kreinin, Mordechai E. and Lawrence H. Officer (1978). *The Monetary Approach to the Balance of Payments: A Survey.* Princeton Studies in International Finance no. 43, Princeton University.

Lee, John M. (1967). *Colonial Development and Good Government.* Oxford: Clarendon.

Lent, George E. 1967). "Tax Incentives for Investment in Developing Countries." IMF *Staff Papers,* vol. 14, no. 2, July.

Lent, George E, Milka Casanegra and Michele Guerard (1973). "The Value Added Tax in Developing Countries." IMF *Staff Papers,* vol. 20, no. 2, July.

Leon, Hyginus (1988). "The Monetary Approach to the Balance of Payments - A Simple Test of Jamaican Data." *Social and Economic Studies,* vol. 37, no. 4, December.

Lewis, W. Arthur (1955). *The Theory of Economic Growth.* London: Allen and Unwin.

Liburd, Eustace E. and Elizabeth M. Tempro (1989). "An Assessment of Monetary and Credit Policies in the OECS Region, 1975-1985." In Delisle Worrell and Compton Bourne (eds.), *Economic Adjustment Policies for Small Nations: Theory and Experience in the English-Speaking Caribbean.* New York: Praeger.

Lim, David (1983). "Fiscal Incentives and Direct Foreign Investment in Less Developed Countries." *Journal of Development Studies,* vol. 19, no. 2, January.

Lonney, Robert E. (1991). "A Monetary Approach to Movements in Caribbean Balance of Payments." *Social and Economic Studies,* vol. 40, no. 1, March.

Lovejoy, Robert M. (1963). "The Burden of Jamaican Taxation, 1958." *Social and Economic Studies,* vol. 12, no. 4.

Martin, Alison and W. Arthur Lewis (1956). "Patterns of Public Revenue and Expenditure." *Manchester School of Economic and Social Studies,* September.

Mascoll, Clyde (1991). "Trends in Effective Tax Rates of Representative Individuals in Barbados During the 1980s." Central Bank of Barbados, *Economic Review,* vol. 18, no. 3.

McClean, A. Wendell A. (1982). "Some Evidence on the Demand for Money in a Small Open Economy: Barbados." *Social and Economic Studies,* vol. 31, no. 3.

McIntyre, Arnold M. (1986). *The Economics of the Organization of the Eastern Caribbean States in the 1970s.* Occasional Paper no. 18, Institute of Social and Economic Research, University of the West Indies, Cave Hill, Barbados.

McIntyre, Alister and Beverley Watson (1970). *Studies in Foreign Investment* in the Commonwealth Caribbean. Kingston, Jamaica: Institute of Social and Economic Research.

McLure, Charles (1977). "The Incidence of Jamaican Taxes, 1971–72." *Working Paper* no. 16, Institute of Social and Economic Research, University of the West Indies, Mona, Jamaica.

Mills, George E. (1981). "The Administration of Public Enterprise: Jamaica and Trinidad and Tobago." *Social and Economic Studies,* vol. 30, no. 1, March.

Mills, George E. (1989). "Privatization in Jamaica, Trinidad and Tobago." In V. V. Ramanadham (ed.), *Privatization in Developing Countries.* New York: Routledge.

Mirrless, James A. (1971). "An Exploration in the Theory of Optimum Income Taxation." *Review of Economic Studies,* vol. 38, April.

Mishan, Edward (1971). "The Post-War Literature on Externalities: An Interpretative Essay." *Journal of Economic Literature,* vol. 9, no. 1, March.

Morgan, David (1979). "Fiscal Policy in Oil Exporting Countries 1972–78." IMF *Staff Papers,* vol. 26, March.

Mueller, Dennis and P. Murrell (1986). "Interest Groups and the Size of Government." *Public Choice,* vol. 48, no. 2.

Mueller, Dennis C. (1987). "The Growth of Government: A Public Choice Perspective." IMF *Staff Papers,* vol. 34, no. 1, March.

Musgrave, Richard A. (1959). *The Theory of Public Finance.* New York: McGraw-Hill.

Musgrave, Richard A. (1969). *Fiscal Systems.* New Haven: Yale University Press.

Nair, Govindan and Mark Frazier (1987). "Debt-Equity Conversion and Privatization." *Economic Impact,* no. 60.

Niskanen, William A. (1971). *Bureaucracy and Representative Government.* Chicago: Aldine-Atherton.

North, Douglas C. and John J. Wallis (1982). "American Government Expenditures: A Historical Perspective." *American Economic Review,* vol. 72, May.

Odle, Maurice A. (1975). "Public Policy." In George L. Beckford (ed.), *Caribbean Economy.* Kingston, Jamaica: Institute of Social and Economic Research, University of the West Indies.

Odle, Maurice A. (1976). *The Evolution of Public Expenditure.* Kingston, Jamaica: Institute of Social and Economic Research, University of the West Indies.

Odle, Maurice A. (1979). "Towards Understanding the Dynamics of Nationalization in the Caribbean." In Basil Ince (ed.), *Contemporary International Relations in the Caribbean.* St. Augustine, Trinidad: Institute of International Relations, University of the West Indies.

Orzechowski, William P. (1982). "Monetary Aspects of Supply Side

Economics." In R. H. Fink (ed.), *Supply Side Economics: A Criticial Appraisal.* Maryland, University Publications of America.

Pantin, Dennis A. (1988). "Whither Point Lisas? Lessons for the Future." In S. Ryan (ed.), *Trinidad and Tobago: Independence Experience, 1962-1987.* St. Augustine, Trinidad: Institute of Social and Economic Research, University of the West Indies.

Pantin, Dennis (1989). *Into the Valley of DEBT.* Port of Spain, Trinidad and Tobago: Dennis Pantin.

Payer, Cheryl (1974). *The Debt Trap: The International Monetary Fund and the Third World.* New York: Monthly Review Press.

Peacock, Alan T. and Jack Wiseman (1961). *The Growth of Public Expenditure in the United Kingdom.* National Bureau of Economic Research, Princeton University.

Peacock, Alan T. (1979). *The Economic Analysis of Government and Related Themes.* Oxford: Martin Robertson.

Pechman, Joseph A. (1989). *Tax Reform - The Rich and the Poor.* London: Harvester Wheatsheaf.

Polak, Jacques J. (1957). "Monetary Analysis of Income Formation and Payments Problems." IMF *Staff Papers,* vol. 4, November.

Polak, Jacques J., and L. Boissonneault (1959-60). "Monetary Analysis of Income and Imports and its Statistical Applications." IMF *Staff Papers,* vol. 7.

Polak, Jacques and Victor Argy (1971). "Credit Policy and the Balance of Payments." IMF *Staff Papers,* vol. 17.

Polanyi-Levitt, Kari (1991). *The Origins and Consequences of Jamaica's Debt Crisis 1970-1990.* Kingston, Jamaica: Consortium Graduate School of Social Sciences, University of the West Indies.

Poole, Robert (1987). "The Political Obstacles to Privatization." In Steve Hanke (ed.), *Privatization and Development.* San Francisco: Institute for Contemporary Studies.

Prachouny, Martin (1975). *Small Open Economies.* Boston: Heath.

Premchand, A. (1983). *Government Budgeting and Expenditure Controls: Theory and Practice.* Washington, D.C.: IMF.

Prest, Alan R. (1975). *Public Finance in Developing Countries.* London: Weidenfeld and Nicolson.

Pyhrr, Peter (1973). *Zero Base Budgeting.* New York: Wiley.

Rampersad, Frank (1988). "The Development Experience - Reflections." In Selwyn Ryan (ed.), *Trinidad and Tobago: The Independence Experience 1962-1987.* St. Augustine, Trinidad: Institute of Social and Economic Research, University of the West Indies.

Ramsaran, Ramesh (1988). 'Observations on the Public Debt." In Compton Bourne and Ramesh Ramsaran, *Money and Finance in Trinidad and Tobago.* Kingston, Jamaica: Institute of Social and Economic Research, University of the West Indies.

Ramsey, Frank P. (1927). "A Contribution to the Theory of Taxation." *Economic Journal,* vol. 37.

Robinson, Edward A. G. (1963). "The Size of the Nation and the Cost of Administration." In Edward A. G. Robinson (ed.), *Economic Consequences of the Size of Nations.* London: Macmillan.

Robinson, Roger and Lelde Schmitz (1989). "Jamaica: Navigating through a Troubled Decade." *Finance and Development,* vol. 26, no. 4, December.

Romer, Thomas and Howard Rosenthal (1979). "Bureaucrats Versus Voters. On the Political Economy of Resource Allocation by Direct Democracy." *Quarterly Journal of Economics,* vol. 93, pp. 563–587.

Ryan, Selwyn (ed.) (1988). *Trinidad and Tobago: The Independence Experience 1962–1987.* St. Augustine, Trinidad: Institute of Social and Economic Research, University of the West Indies.

Sackey, James A. (1978). "Dependence, Inequality and Poverty in the Caribbean: Synthesis of Alternative Perspectives." In Farley S. Brathwaithe (ed.), *Poverty in the Caribbean, Special Issue of Caribbean Issues,* vol. 4, no. 3, December.

Sackey, James A. (1980). "Underdevelopment Disequilibrium and Growth in Government Expenditures: Some Empirical Generalizations." *Social and Economic Studies,* vol. 29, no.4.

Sackey, James A. (1981). "Inflation and Government Tax Revenue: The Case of Trinidad and Tobago with Comparative Reference to Barbados and Jamaica." *Social and Economic Studies,* vol. 30, no. 3, September.

Samuel, Wendell A. (1988). "Tax Reform in Grenada." *Bulletin for International Fiscal Documentation,* vol. 42, no. 3, March.

Samuel, Wendell A. (1989). "Government Finances in the OECS Countries." In Neville Duncan (ed.), *Public Finance and Fiscal Issues in Barbados and the OECS.* Cave Hill, Barbados: Faculty of Social Sciences, University of the West Indies.

Samuel, Wendell A. (1990). "Caribbean: Social Security, Saving and Investment in the OECS Countries." *Bulletin for International Fiscal Documentation,* vol. 44, no. 5, May.

Samuelson, Paul A. (1954). "Pure Theory of Public Expenditures." *Review of Economics and Statistics,* vol. 36, November.

Saunders, Muriel and Delisle Worrel (1981). "Government Expenditure in Barbados." Central Bank of Barbados, *Quarterly Report,* vol. 8, no. 2, June.

Schick, Allen (1978). "The Road from Zero Base Budgeting." *Public Administration Review,* vol. 38.

Schumacher, Ernst F. (1974). *Small is Beautiful: A Study of Economics as if People Mattered.* London: Abacus-Sphere.

Seers, Dudley (1979). "The Meaning of Development" and "Postscript: The New Meaning of Development." In David Lehmamn (ed.), *Develop-*

ment Theory. London: Frank Cass.

Sharpley, Jennifer (1984). "Jamaica: 1972-1980." In Tony Killick (ed.), *The IMF and Stabilization*. Washington D.C.: IMF.

Shultze, Charles L. (1986). *The Politics and Economics of Public Spending*. Washington: Brookings Institution.

Smith, Michael G. (1989). *Poverty in Jamaica*. Kingston, Jamaica: Institute of Social and Economic Research, University of the West Indies.

St. Cyr, Eric B. A. (1979). "A Note on the Trinidad and Tobago Inflationary Experience." *Social and Economic Studies*, vol. 28, no. 3.

Stern, Nicholas (1984). "Optimum Taxation and Tax Policy." IMF *Staff Papers*, vol. 31, no. 2, June.

Straw, Kenneth H. (1953). "A Survey of Income and Consumption Patterns in Barbados." *Social and Economic Studies*, vol. 1, no. 4.

Tanzi, Vito (1978). "Inflation, Real Tax Revenue, and the Case for Inflationary Finance: Theory with an Application to Argentina." IMF *Staff Papers*, vol. 25, no. 3, September.

Tanzi, Vito (1982). "Fiscal Disequilibrium in Developing Countries." *World Development*, vol. 10, no. 12, December.

Theodore, Karl (1987). "Fiscal Reform: An Analytical Review of the Grenada Experience." *Bulletin of Eastern Caribbean Affairs*, vol. 13, no. 2, May/June.

Thomas, Clive Y. (1974). *Dependence and Transformation*. New York: Monthly Review Press.

Thomas, Clive Y. (1988). *The Poor and the Powerless: Economic Policy and Change in the Caribbean*. New York: Monthly Review Press.

Thomas, Clive Y. (1989). "Foreign Currency Black Markets: Lessons From Guyana." *Social and Economic Studies*, vol. 38, no. 2.

Thorn, Richard S. (1967). "The Evolution of Public Finance during Economic Development." *Manchester School of Economic and Social Studies*, January.

Thurow, Lester C. (1984). *Dangerous Currents: The State of Economics*. New York: Vintage.

Ture, Norman B. (1982). "The Economic Effects of Tax Changes: Neoclassical Analysis." In Richard H. Fink (ed.), *Supply Side Economics: A Critical Appraisal*. Maryland, University Publications of America.

Turnovsky, Stephen J. (1977). *Macro Economic Analysis and Stabilization Policy*. Cambridge: Cambridge University Press.

Van de Walle, Nicolas (1989). "Privatization in Developing Countries: A Review of the Issues." *World Development*, vol. 17, no. 5.

Vernon-Wortzel, Heidi and Lawrence H. Wortzel (1989). "Privatization: Not the Only Answer." *World Development*, vol. 17, no. 5.

Wasylenko, Michael (1986). "The Distribution of Tax Burden in Jamaica: Pre-1985 Reform." Staff Paper no. 30, Jamaican Tax Examination Project, Metropolitan Studies Program, Maxwell School: Syracuse University, Syracuse, N.Y.

Wildavsky, Aaron (1979). *The Politics of the Budgetary Process.* Boston: Little, Brown.

Williamson, Jeffrey G. (1961). "Public Expenditure and Revenue: An International Comparison." *Manchester School of Economic and Social Studies,* January.

Wiltshire, Kenneth (1987). *Privatization: The British Experience.* Melbourne: Longman Cheshire.

Witter, Michael (1983). "Exchange Rate Policy in Jamaica: A Critical Assessment." *Social and Economic Studies,* vol. 32, no. 4.

Witter, Michael (1989). "Analysis of Food Assistance Programmes in Jamaica." Jamaican Poverty Line Project, Planning Institute of Jamaica. *Working Paper,* no. 1.

Witter, Michael and C. Kirton (1990). "The Informal Economy in Jamaica: some Empirical Exercises." *Working Paper,* no. 36. Mona, Jamaica: Institute of Social and Economic Research, University of the West Indies.

Worrell, Delisle (1975). "Erosion of Real Disposable Income in Barbados and the Combined Effects of High Inflation and a Progressive Tax System." Mimeo, Central Bank of Barbados.

Worrell, Delisle (1987). *Small Island Economies: Structure and Performance in the English-Speaking Caribbean Since 1970.* New York: Praeger.

INDEX

ABOUT THE AUTHOR

MICHAEL HOWARD is a senior lecturer in the Department of Economics, University of the West Indies, Cave Hill, Barbados. He has served as deputy dean of the Faculty of Social Sciences and president of the Barbados Economics Society. His main research interests are in the areas of public finance, monetary economics, and development economics. He has published *Dependence and Development in Barbados* (1989), as well as a number of articles in academic journals on fiscal and monetary issues.